HATS OFF!

Langley celebrated its 75th anniversary with three large cakes in 1994

A Celebration of 90 years of Beckenham County School through to Langley Park 1919-2009

Memories compiled and narrated by Pat Manning and Jill Jones for the Adremians, the past members and staff of the school

First published September 2008

ISBN 9780-9540202-6-2

Published by

Jenna Publishing

29 Birchwood Avenue, Beckenham, BR3 3PY

ben-ja@ntlworld.com

INSIDE COVER DESIGN

Designed by Cheryl Murdoch & Charlotte Simpson who were influenced by the work of Diane Arbus, the NY photographer 1923-1971

COVER DESIGN

Badge design from centre of Adremians' plate; school drawings by Nancie Pelling

PRINTERS

Andrew Lawrence Print

TECHNICAL SUPPORT

Daniel Day
ddpcservices@onetel.com

Every care has been taken to ensure the accuracy of the information herein and to find owners of images and text to obtain permission for their use.

Foreword from the Chair of Governors

Dear Reader

I am delighted to introduce to you this rich and fascinating history of Langley Park School for Girls and its predecessors starting as the Beckenham County School for Girls, on the occasion of its 90th birthday.

For the last decade it has been a privilege for me to be associated with this outstanding and popular school which has achieved so much, and meant so much to its pupils.

I am especially pleased to have had two daughters who attended the school and who were able to enjoy an excellent education and wealth of opportunities. Tens of hundreds did before them and will for years to come.

It is of course easy for me to sing the school's praises, but Ofsted does too. Inspectors consistently judge Langley Park School for Girls to be 'outstanding' and rate us as one of the top 20 comprehensive schools in the country. With an 'inspirational' Head Teacher in Jan Sage the school has achieved this position at the leading edge of achievement and innovation in an ever increasingly complex educational climate.

I hope you enjoy this book which I will treasure both as a memento of the school's 90th birthday and as a celebration of excellence.

In conclusion I want to say a huge thank you to all the contributors and to the indefatigable editors from the Adremians, Jill Jones and Pat Manning.

Nick Moore

The Adremian Committee

President	Jan Sage
Vice President	Elizabeth Adams
Chairman	Monica Duncan
Secretary	Jill Jones
Treasurer	Marion Spicer
Committee	Brenda Brent, Jean Parrott, Helen Riley, Frances Boyden, Fiona Bratt, Ruth Marchant.

Introduction by Pat & Jill

Nine decades, eight House changes, seven headmistresses, six summer dresses, five names for the school, four reigns, three school badges, two locations BUT just one school howbeit never quite large enough. The title of our anniversary book is the brainwave of **Janice Wright,** a salute to the school's success but also good riddance to a piece of school uniform appreciated by nobody for the first fifty years of its existence. Even the teachers were reprimanded by Miss Fox if they left school without hat and gloves.

The Adremians had the idea of a book to contain memories and pictures of the school from its beginning to the present day. What began as a small project just grew and grew. We asked for contributions and certainly were surprised at how much we received – photos and reminiscences from far and wide and from everyone from 11 to 95 years old. What became clear is that memories of our schooldays and those who taught us last throughout our lives. Things we thought long forgotten can come back unexpectedly through a phone call to a friend, a piece of music, a book or a photograph.

That's where the Adremians come into the picture – keeping people in touch with each other and supporting the school. Over the years we have presented the school with glass trophy cases, wrought iron plant stands, a handrail in the hall and recording equipment. In 2008 we are buying a sundial which will be inscribed to celebrate the anniversary in 2009. All the profits from the sale of this book will go to the school.

So – hats off to our school from everyone in these pages to everyone who was there, is there now and will be in the future.

NB Past pupils are often referred to by the names that we used at school. We have also used the following notation: Forename (Maiden name) Married name.

Acknowledgments

You will see in the following 'Contents' pages that many of the contributors are named there. In addition, it would not have been possible to produce this book without the help supplied by numerous others, so many that we apologise for help given that we have not acknowledged here. Foremost we must thank the present staff for the photographs and information so willingly handed on to us from Linda Ball, Claire Brown, Jean Carson, Jennifer Chalmers, Lynda Christian, Mandy Cornell, Brigid Doherty, John Evans and his team, Ed Fox-Joyce, John Hargreaves, Helena Jedlinska, John Leary, Terry Loader, Jane Nicholls, **Headmistress Jan Sage**, Nigel Sharma and Catherine Shelley.

The Adremians Committee has been unsparing, contacting members, proof reading, listing and naming. The cartoon drawings throughout have been drawn by **Joan (Weatherley) Lunn.** Thanks to our final proof readers Val Harrison and Sue Roberts.

Technical help has been readily available from computer expert Daniel Day, graphic designer John Mitchell, photographer and historian Cliff Watkins, local historian Ian Muir and printer Andy Short.

Finally, members themselves, including recent leavers, have been so willing to send in their contributions, confirm dates and name photographs. Among these we cannot go without thanking Janet Lambert for all her expertise and knack of finding answers to every problem that came her way.

CONTENTS

Sincere apologies to all those whom we must have omitted! Please let us know.

Our Time Line

Date	What happened
28.9.1919	The Beckenham County School opened with 153 girls, 10 teachers and Miss Fox.
28.9.1920	280 girls on the roll needed converted cycle shed and staff dressing room.
23.11.1922	**Old Girls Society** formed.
1923	Sister school at Gravesend installed an **organ**. This became the unfulfilled desire of Miss Fox for Beckenham County.
1924	Two girls reached the U6; X fund started; first Sale of Work.
2.3.1925	First Speech Day, held in Public Hall.
1927	Sir Mark Collett chose the school motto: **Ad Rem: Mox Nox.** Until then, it had been 'Speedwell.'
1928	**Hall and Dining room ready for use**; official opening 18.12.1929. **Pavilion** built on field up the road.
1929	Miss J M Earle died. Old Girls collected to fund the Maths prize in her name.
1930	School governor, Miss Marion Vian, died. **Parents Association** founded. Old Girls blazer available at Ardec, Beckenham.
1934	**House system** started, red, blue, green, yellow, orange, Wedgwood.
26.5.1936	**Grand piano** first played in public at Lower School Speech Day.
1936	School celebrated its own birthday with the **hymn board** in the hall.
1937	**Organ fund started**. The magazine devoted 9 pages to news of Old Girls but regretted that half of leavers went into employment in banks, insurance, commercial, civil service or stayed at home and urged girls to go on into the sixth. The 21st **Beckenham Guide Company** was formed with Miss O'Dell as Captain, helped later by Miss Broadhurst, Mrs Grunspan and Miss Rabson.
1938	Founder school member, **Miss Dora Matthews**, retired. School party to Rudesheim saw **Hitler** pass through by train one day before plebiscite where only 4 out of 400 residents were anti Hitler and were victimised as a result.
3.9.1939	**War declared against Germany**. School had to be fragmented since it has no air raid shelters.
5.1.1940	Small party **evacuated to Exeter** for 17 months and there was accommodation in the school trenches for 300 girls.
23.9.1940	A few days into the blitz and **two time bombs fell on the school trenches** and a week later, **incendiaries** fell on the studio and room 26 causing flooding. The school closed for one day while the staff mopped up. Attendance restricted to half days only.
Dec-43	**Miss Fox retired**. Miss Rose ran the school for two terms.
16.6.1944	**Flying bomb** attacks started on Beckenham.
Jul-44	Party evacuated to Wath on Dearne, Yorkshire met the **new Headmistress, Miss Henshaw**.
Jan-45	V2s on Midland Bank and Cyphers sports grounds caused late opening of school term as teachers stuck netting to all windows. The summer term saw the **Cricket Challenge Cup won back from Gravesend** for the first time since 1937. Miss Henshaw suffered appendicitis and was away for the Spring term. **Miss Rose** retired after 20 years. Chairman of the Governors, Mr Elgood, died.
1946	Parents Association revitalised and started Travel Fund. **Miss Henshaw led a party to Viggbyholm, Sweden.**
1947	**Seven day timetable** started. Miss Preston led a party to Meiringen, Switzerland. **Cyphers annexed for lessons. The school choir led the singing at the Empire Youth Rally.**
1948	**Lloyds Bank pavilion** annexed for lessons.
1949	The choir broadcast on Children's Hour. **Miss Grice** retired after 25 years.
May-50	Name **Adremians** coined for past members of the school from school motto.

Date	What happened
1952	The **new extension** from the dining room completed. Neither Lloyds nor Cyphers needed but loss of field replaced by use of Tablonian field for lunch break. Official recognition as Beckenham Grammar School for Girls.
1953	All the choirs came first in their classes at the Beckenham Festival.
1954	**Miss Broadhurst** retired after 26 years.
1958	**Miss Barnard** retired after 27 years.
1959	With move to Langley, the houses were renamed **Burrell, Elwill, Goodhart, Kelsey, Langley, Raymond** and later **Style**. School dedicated 29 October 1959.
1960	**Miss Fox** died, also Miss Preston.
Nov-62	School roll numbers 716.
1963	**Miss Henshaw retired succeeded by Miss Chreseson. Miss Wiseman** died and Miss King became Deputy Head.
1965	Responsibility for the school passed from Kent to Bromley.
1966	**Mrs Molnar replaced Miss Chreseson** as school Head.
26.9.1969	**Golden Jubilee service** at St George's church.
27.9.1969	Formal lunch for 300 with Philip Goodhart MP, governors, past and present staff and Old Girls from every year of the school.
1969	Wearing of a **boater became optional** and 'died' instantly closely followed by the winter hat. Head Girl Jane Dawson designed the current school **badge** using the Style arms and omitting the Kent horse. **Miss Burton** and **Dr Schofer** retired after 23 and 21 years.
9.9.1971	**Miss Henshaw** died.
1972	Performances of **Carmina Burana** by combined choirs and orchestras with LPBS.
Sep-72	Mrs Molnar started vertical registration groups using house areas, except for first years, named after Greek letters for LPSGBK; **Lambda, Pi, Sigma, Gamma, Beta, Kappa.**
1973	**Mrs Molnar left to be the Head of Mayfield School**, Putney and **Miss Grimsey took over** with a school building once more not large enough to contain the increasing numbers.
Mar-74	Margaret Robinson organised trip for **90 girls to Athens**(Glyfada).
Sep-74	School **magazine** for all discontinued on account of cost. **Mrs Elisabeth Blackburn** appointed second Deputy Head.
Mar-76	Chairman of the Governors, **Mr Atkins**, retired after 29 years.
Jan-76	**Joint VI form block** with Boys School ready.
Sep-76	**New block extension** ready with lecture theatre, drama studio, pottery room, home economics dept, open plan resources and fully carpeted sports hall. Eight science labs and language lab in main building. First 'all ability' intake.
Autumn 1977	**Miss Grimsey married** the Chairman of the Governors, **Mr G Scales**. David Blake appointed Joint Head of 6th forms.
Jul-78	Mrs Scales resigned and went on a world cruise.
Sep-78	Deputy Head, **Mrs Barnard**, (formerly Partridge) ran the school for a term until **Mrs Herzmark** was appointed for Jan 1979.
Summer 1979	First Artists and Craftsmen Exhibition by PTA.
Sep-79	Due to the closure of Springpark Lower School, entry became 7 form with 210 girls coming into the first form. The extra forms were called D and J after the school's Diamond Jubilee.
Aug-80	**Mrs Marian Freeman** replaced the retired Mrs Joy Barnard as Deputy Head.
Sep-82	School roll over 1,000. Mrs Elisabeth Blackburn left.
Sep-83	**David Blake** became Director of Studies (second deputy head).
Sep-85	Mrs Marian Freeman switched to Director of Studies and **Miss Jane Nicholls** became Deputy Head as David Blake left.
Sep 1987	Mrs Freeman left to be replaced by **Miss Sue O'Neill**.
Dec-90	First outside performance used Fairfield Hall for '**African Jigsaw.**'
Dec-92	**'Ocean World'** story of the humpback whale at Fairfield Hall.

Date	What happened
Dec-92	**Mrs Herzmark** retired to be replaced by **Miss Jan Sage** in Jan 1993.
Sep-94	**75th anniversary** of school opening in Lennard Rd celebrated at Langley with 3 cakes and blue balloons. Miss Sue O'Neill left for a Headship in Dec 1994.
Sep-96	Status as a **Technology College** to raise standards of Sc, M, ICT, Tech. Duke of Edinburgh Awards training started.
Sep-97	**Investor in People Award,** re-awarded three times.
May-98	Tree planting in memory of **Felicity Langford** died August 1997 from meningitis. Teddy bears' picnic and balloon release to raise funds for Meningitis Trust. First **Triple Science** GCSE candidates since 1990.
Oct-98	Miss Sage one of 8 head teachers to visit ICT conference in Nashville, Tennessee.
Jan-99	**Charter Mark** for Excellence celebrated by balloons and a three foot long cake.
Mar-99	Acceptance of **second phase of Technology College** status, followed twice more.
May-99	**Mad Hatter's picnic** fund raising day by Year 13 for Meningitis Trust.
Sep-99	The grant maintained school became a **Foundation** school.
Dec-99	Formal opening of first floor **business suite** and library; **new science block** opening with 11 laboratories.
Jun-00	**Investor in Careers Award** and Careers Library Accreditation. Investor in Careers reawarded **2003** and **2006.**
Jul-00	**Challon Oak Baby Grand Piano** replaced the old Bluthner. Toshiba laptops for all full-time staff.
Sep-00	New sixth form base and new school pond ready.
Jun-01	**Gold Artsmark Award** in design, music, drama and art.
Dec-01	**Susan Fey Award** for the most improved GCSE results in Science.
Feb-02	Retained Charter Mark for Excellence, re-awarded Feb **2005** and Jan **2008** but with a name change.
Jan-05	**Opening of Dalo building** (name came from French manufacturer).
Sep-05	Previous 2002 Beacon status that identified high performing schools replaced by **Leading Edge** to encourage further partnerships between schools.
Nov-05	**Mrs Molnar** died.
Apr-06	**MFL** award granted with £130,000 pa as a specialism alongside Technology.
Jan-07	**Mrs Barnard** died.
Feb-07	Head of Music, John Hargreaves, produced '**Encore**' at the Fairfield Hall.
Mar-07	Cellist Hannah Masson-Smythe won **Norman Trotman** Competition.
Apr-07	**Sports Specialist Status.**
Jun-07	**Third Artsmark Gold** (second was awarded in June 2004). **Health School status** including effective anti-bullying.
Nov-07	LPGS girls starred in '**Annie**' at the Churchill theatre; school production of Arabian Nights.
Mar-08	**Fifth Technology College Award.**
Apr-08	Drama and citizenship visit to **Cape Town** (second time, last in 2005). **Ellen Gandy** nominated for 2008 Olympic Squad after winning silver in 200m butterfly at the National Championships.
Jul-08	'**Les Miserables**' produced in the Courtyard at Langley with full orchestra. John Evans, site manager, bid farewell after 30 years.
Jan-09	**50th anniversary** of the school at Langley Park.
Sep-09	**90 years** since Beckenham County School began in Lennard Rd.
2009	Sundial presented by the Adremians; fixed to the Technology block.

Edith Margery Fox

1919- Dec 1943

and her school

Beckenham County School for Girls

ONE   AT THE BEGINNING, MISS FOX

Those of us who remember Miss Fox, our school's first Headmistress, are fast dwindling in number. To most of us she was a strict disciplinarian who would bring instant silence if she appeared in the corridor and who would somehow know if we ventured out without a school hat. However if you take time out to read the Forewords of the school magazines, a wise and cultured lady emerges, an expert Shakespearian, resilient and caring.

School with its new extensions of dining room and hall

We wondered how we came to have a close association with the Gravesend County School, and found out later that in 1918 Miss Fox had been its Headmistress and brought Miss Matthews with her to Beckenham. Born in Greenwich in 1883, Edith Margery Fox was the youngest of four sisters who all became teachers and in 1920 she was proud to bring Eleanor and Dorothy as guests to our school.

The school opened in September 1919 with 153 pupils, only 'school' was a euphemism for the building at that time. Its conversion from the military hospital that had taken over in 1914 was incomplete, with allotment holders occupying the grounds. A railway strike was planned for the first week and with most of the furniture still at the factory, the determined Miss Fox had her problems.

Mr Watts of the Boys' School helped out with equipment but the question of accommodation has never really been solved over nine decades although in 1928 the extension provided a hall in which the whole school could meet, a beautifully proportioned dining hall and a registration room for each form. At a meeting of the Old Girls in 1934, Miss Fox reminded them that the hockey pitch at the back of the school was a source of mint sauce for years as a relic of the allotments. Nevertheless, the Beckenham Journal of July 1920 described it as the 'splendid County School for Girls' and some twenty free place scholarships were announced.

The Course was planned for girls from the age of eight and the first term saw the intake of juniors and middle school with ten members of staff; Miss Earle for mathematics was the second mistress, Miss Matthews took Geography and Miss Dora Matthews taught Art. When Dora retired in 1938 after 19 years at the school, Miss Fox wrote *'I hate to think that there is no one in the school with whom I can share my memories of those early days.'* Then there were Miss Warren, Miss Partridge, Miss Newman for Classics and Miss Thomas for Science who left in two years to teach in Lahore. The final three members of staff were Miss Paget for Needlework, Miss Cooke for Housecraft and Miss Benson but six more staff were added the following term. These were Miss Bishop taking History, Miss Finken for Music, Miss Flower to teach Mathematics, Miss Oakes for French and English and Misses Johnson and Beamish.

If you are surprised that all these teachers were single ladies, let us remind you that when a teacher married she could not continue her employment in teaching.

ONE   AT THE BEGINNING, MISS FOX

Nevertheless when Miss Inge married at Easter 1925, Miss Fox with Miss Beamish and Miss Partridge represented the school at her wedding and had the first glimpse of her as Mrs Oakshott.

Staff in 1923. Back row L to R Misses ?, Gobbett, Newman, ?, ?, Oakes, Collier, Partridge. Front row, Misses Martin, Bishop, Paget, Earle, Fox, Matthews, Cooke, Johnson, Warren.

The catchment area for the school at this time was local because the housing at Eden Park and up from Elmers End to West Wickham was not built before about 1928 to 1936. See the poems below of the feelings of the girls as they saw the countryside vilified.

In Elmer's End
The country lane was white and singing birds awoke the day, the place to laugh and play was Elmer's End.
The trees stood stately to the sky, the sound of brooklets rushing by, thrush's call and cuckoo's cry, filled Elmer's End.
But now brick houses fill the lane; the birds will ne'er be heard again. The trees crash down, oak, elm and plane, in Elmer's End.
The brooks beneath the culverts lie; the trees that stood up to the sky, all broken and forlorn they die, in Elmer's End.
The departed village 1930—an ode to West Wickham
Scarcely a league from Beckenham, not very long ago,
 Stood a tiny village, delightful, quaint and slow.
With grassy slopes and bluebell woods that gave one's heart a thrill,
With winding lanes so twisted that they named it Corkscrew Hill.
The village street, the village church, the usual village inn,
The village store with wondrous stock from apples to a pin.
Then came alas, ' Development.' Gazed long upon the site.
And quoth, 'Ho, Ho' tis too near town, we'll soon have things put right.
Road makers came with drills and picks, their concrete, tools and such,
They hacked down trees and filled each ditch; lanes soon went at their touch.

ONE   AT THE BEGINNING, MISS FOX

Beautiful fields were marked in plots, houses came by the score.
Houses in rows and terraces, 'Development' said, 'More.'
So butcher, baker, tailor too, set up all down the street.
The 'General' sent their omnibus; the suburb's now complete.
The village has gone, the nightingale too, tadpole, bluebell and bramble.
Now Beckenham girls when out for a tramp avoid that place for a ramble.

In the realms of sport Miss Fox encouraged lacrosse and cricket as well as the more usual netball, hockey and tennis. The annual cricket match against Gravesend County School where the Headmistress was Miss Fox's friend, Miss Wills, was a great occasion with strawberries and cream for lunch.

Cricket team in 1925 L to R Back row Doris Peters, Nessie Aitken, Margaret Cripps, Connie Apted. Middle row Eileen Evans, Alice Willsher, Agnes Haddow (captain), Marion Brian, Claire Jeal. At front ? ?, Gwen Skinner.

Afterwards the whole school watched the match. In 1928 the KCC agreed to a pavilion being built at the school field across Kent House Rd. The cost rocketed from the original £700 divided between the KCC and the Beckenham UDC each providing £250, Penge UDC £50 and the rest by the school itself. The only fund available was the X Fund intended as a bursary to help girls stay at school to continue their education. It was collected from all kinds of activities going on at school from the sale of sweets to plays put on by the sixth form at the end of term. Eventually the X Fund was incorporated into the School Voluntary Fund. The accounts show that it held £1,209 in 1947.

Charity was important to the school and on one occasion 1,260 eggs were collected in a week to give to the Beckenham Cottage Hospital. The school supported many causes like miners in Mr Watt's village, the dispensary for sick animals, the Sydenham Hospital for sick children and many others. Miss Fox did not think these funds should be used for the new pavilion.

ONE   AT THE BEGINNING, MISS FOX

The Parent Teacher Association was formed in 1929, not to raise funds but Miss Fox announced that she would not *'be satisfied until every parent belonged to the PTA and visited her at least once a year.'*

The first of Miss Fox's girls to reach the upper sixth and go on to college were Helen Calder and Constance Turner who in 1927 graduated in French and History respectively.

One of the first girls enrolled was Alice Anstey whose daughters Annette and Jennifer Coppard both followed their mother to be pupils at the school. A retired music teacher, she was awarded the Vancouver Peace Prize at the age of 88. She appears in various of the school magazines as being in the lacrosse and netball teams, the choir and the sketch club, awarded a prize for the most improved piano player and by 1924 having gained her general school certificate with a distinction in Music and credits in Arithmetic, Botany and English.

The first marriage was between Jean Marion Chapter and Edmund Donald Johnson at the Beckenham Congregational Church in 1927.

In 1928, Marian Morris and Mary Thorp were awarded State Scholarships, followed by Nancy Wiseman the following year although she did not accept it as she could not use it at the Royal Academy of Music.

Perhaps girls of today would be surprised at the number of visits and outings that were available in Miss Fox's day. Miss Fox herself regularly gave lectures at the Beckenham Shakespeare Society such as one entitled 'The Psychology of the Shakespearian Murderer.' Then there was the triumphant visit in 1938 to the Isle of Dogs with 54 patchwork blankets and 7 cot covers made from knitted squares, 52 Christmas puddings and 278 Christmas stockings in return for the Rev Nankivell's visit the previous year. How about the Ideal Home Exhibition, The Persian Art at Burlington House, Kew Gardens, Regent's Park Zoo, Whipsnade, Rochester, Houses of Parliament, Natural History Museum, picnics on Hayes Common, the chance to line the route to see Prince George open the new Beckenham Town Hall (it rained) and a lecture given about Television in 1932 by a friend of Mr Baird?

L to R Back row: Nos 2 and 3 from L Miss Savage, Miss Loxdale. Middle row Miss Newman,??, Miss Rose, Miss Fox, Miss Grice,??, Miss Partridge. Front row 3rd from L Miss Lumb. Staff c 1928

There were many school societies and prizes were given for everything including a daffodil bulb growing competition and a geography competition for the best illustrated album about the Americas where there were four first prizes and three second prizes.

ONE   AT THE BEGINNING, MISS FOX

The one that I like most was Miss Fox's competition for the *'best washing frocks made in the holidays'*. Fifty frocks were made, most of a very high standard but I wonder whether Mum or Auntie lent a hand!

It remains only to say that Miss Fox was a hard act to follow having produced a school piece by piece over 25 years to the highest of standards. She paid many visits to the school before she died in October 1960 aged 77. As we shall see, she was followed by six worthy headmistresses each of whom added a particular talent. The school motto of Ad Rem: Mox Nox was not adopted until May 1927 but it became a timely reminder for us to make the most of our days, especially when modified to Ad Rem: Mox Fox.

Special Money Making Efforts of 1936

Making money for good causes was characteristic of Miss Fox's school. Houses competed for the Charity Cup by weekly charity collections largely for Beckenham Cottage Hospital where they supported a cot, the Children's Hospital at Lower Sydenham, PDSA, the Madagascar Mission and countless others over the years. The school had its X Fund to assist grants for travelling, the Organ Fund and the fund for the Grand Piano. It is for this last requirement that special form efforts were made during the school year 1935/36 that together raised £22 16s.

Lower III sold silkworms for 10s 2d. Upper IIIc collected and sold medicine bottles for 10s 6d. Upper IIIb made bookmarkers for the magnificent sum of £2 18s and Upper IIIa gave a performance of 'A Midsummer Night's Dream' to raise £2 0s 5d. Lower IVa made 10s from collecting farthings and Upper IVa ran a tennis tournament for £2 8s 6d while an auction sale raised 15s.

Lower Va also collected £1 worth of farthings and gave an entertainment with a parody of Macbeth for £1 13s 9d. Upper Va sold sweets for £1 12s 6d and raffled a dressed doll to make 14s. Finally Upper IVb and Lower Vb held a sale of work and jumble sale with many side shows and competitions to raise a tremendous £8 3s 3d.

The cot is mentioned way back in 1922 when the school of only about 200 girls collected £29 3s 7d to support a cot in the Beckenham Cottage Hospital. In 1926, Miss Fox and Miss Grice with some of the charity collectors were invited to tea at the hospital and were presented with two photos of the cot and a bed by Mr Dobell on behalf of the hospital staff.

Another venture in which the school participated was the donation of eggs during Hospital Egg Collection Week. In the 1930s, about 800 eggs were collected each week with the record of 1,260 in 1932/33. They were collected and taken each day to the hospital.

Miss Fox's Dating Agency

When Beccehamian Dr Ron Cox, 1935-1942, reads the Adremians newsletter with his wife Audrey Gilbert, 1936-1942, he is struck at the number of Adremians who married Beccehamians. He recalls that the lunchtime activity of the County School boys was to go down to Lennard Rd to peer through the railings until shooed away by the mistress on playground duty. There were reserved carriages for the girls between New Beckenham and Hayes but that neither stopped the girls from calling from the train windows nor prevented the boys waiting to 'suss out the market.'

ONE   AT THE BEGINNING, MISS FOX

There was a time when Audrey's father was summoned to Miss Fox's presence because his daughter had been seen brushing her hair in the street using her reflection in a shop window. She was actually on her way to meet Ron. Miss Fox should have been pleased that her 'gals' cared about how they looked.

Ron remembers the brilliant group of girls in his class at Hawes Down Junior School 1934/35 who completely outshone the boys academically and others who were sisters of his friends. He names the following and wonders what became of them all: Elisabeth Aston, Isabel Bonner, Maisie Butterfield, Molly Chubb, Gloria Dale, Margaret Donald, June Dunbar, Joyce Eales, Ella Gosney, Barbara Grierson, Jessie Harrison, Pamela Hicks, Pat Hoey, Edna Hubble, Audrey Paish, Muriel Pudney, Joyce Spackman, Heather Ware, Barbara Westall and Kathleen Westropp.

Perhaps one reason that Ron knew so many of the girls was that two members of the girls' school staff who were 'lent' to the boys' school to teach Maths and Latin taught the boys ballroom dancing in the lunch hour. The staff members were Miss Coot and Miss Jarret who apparently found discipline difficult at the girls school, especially Miss Coot until she turned out for a staff/girls lacrosse match and played the fantastic game of a county player. Legitimate activities between the two schools included drama productions like Twelfth Night with Pat King as Olivia, Audrey Handy as Maria and Mary Thomas as   Viola.

Feste and Olivia

Except for 1940, the Boys' School produced a play from 1932 onwards and girls were occasionally 'borrowed' to play female roles. This was the case not only in 1944's 'Twelfth Night', but also ' Major Barbara' in 1952 and 'L'Aiglon' in 1955. The Beckenham Journal report on the latter stated that it was the best they had ever done.
 It was the story of the son of Napoleon I, the Eaglet. Felicity Edden played his mother, Maria Louisa, Norma MacLeod was Therese de Loget and Jennifer Cryer was the Countess Napoleone Camerata.

ONE AT THE BEGINNING, MISS FOX

Our school more than eighty years ago by Olive Rippengal

As my sister, Doreen, joined the school in 1923, I am in a good position to write about its early days. My mother and I used to meet Doreen from school and, being members of Cator Park where my parents played tennis, we could walk through the park, into the allotments crossing Thayers Farm and Chaffinch Rds and up the steps opposite Clockhouse station. There were two changes in 1927 as first we lived temporarily at Grandma's until our new house at Eden Park was built and then I too joined the school in April in the first form. In the September, the first and second forms joined to form the Preparatory and the upper division had some of their lessons in the cycle shed. When in the Prep, my friend Violet Henniker and I would hold the Lower 3rd at bay at rounders. Violet was at school with her sister Cecilia but when we were in the Upper 3rd Violet contracted rapid TB and died.

At that time we had school prayers in what was then the gymnasium opposite Miss Fox's office where there were ropes for climbing but later it became the science laboratory and we lost our ropes. We would line up in the gym to go upstairs for lunch but then the extensions were built at each end of the school; a new hall was built at one end near the cycle sheds (still no ropes!) and a large dining room at the other end with a staircase leading up to the staff room.

Starting school in April 1927, the first Head Girl I remember was Marjorie Forrester. Winifred Crabbe was appointed our train prefect as we walked solemnly in twos between New Beckenham station and school. Marion Morris and others earned State Scholarships and staff came and went. We used to watch the staff go home for lunch in the summer to see who came back wearing short sleeves. We had various societies like the Classical, Literary and Debating, League of Nations and I remember speaking to the Science Club in 1931 about George Leigh Mallory's attempt on Everest in 1924. In 1934, Miss Fox announced that we would have six Houses. I was the first vice captain of Green House and its second House Captain, the other Houses being Red, Blue, Yellow and Orange and Wedgwood.

In my Upper 5th year in 1934, we had our first House General Knowledge Competition and I managed to get second prize and congratulations on my excellent description of the game of chess although it was said that girls did not play chess. Miss Fox would not let us do athletics as she thought it was bad for girls but we had house matches and gymnastic competitions. We

were not allowed to give presents to the staff so when Miss Trickey and Miss Chambers left at Christmas we gave the Trickey Trophy for General Knowledge and the Chambers Gym Cup. When Miss Fox was appointed Head of the Headmistresses' Association, Miss Rose had to do more to run the school especially when Miss Fox left suddenly to help her friend, Miss Wills of Gravesend, who died a little later. She had refused to consider taking three months leave of absence. I called to see Miss Fox in September 1939 when some sixth formers were studying for their exams but the whole school and staff could not attend until there were air raid shelters to accommodate them. I also managed to visit her in Totnes in 1959 on returning from missionary service in India. I was at the last Old Girls' Meeting at the Lennard Rd School in 1958 before the move to Langley and have done my best to attend every meeting since then.

Miss Rose

ONE   AT THE BEGINNING, MISS FOX

<u>General Knowledge Competition 1935</u>

1. For what are these scientific instruments used? Metronome, hygrometer, micrometer, lactometer, anemometer, aneroid, chronometer, stethoscope.

2. In what cities are the following? The Kremlin, Eiffel Tower, Newnham College, Scott Memorial, Unter den Linden, Bridge of Sighs, Vatican, Louvre, Doge's Palace.

3. Name the science of the study of animals, the structure of the earth, the study of birds, the study of insects and the study of fossils.

4. Name the book or poem from which these quotations come and supply the author:
a) a lone lorn creetur
b) So faithful in love and so dauntless in war
c) She weaves by night and day, A magic web with colours gay
d) Full well they laugh'd with counterfeited glee, At all his jokes, for many a joke had he.
e) His queer long coat from heel to head, Was half of yellow and half of red.
f) Her voice was ever soft, gentle and low.
g) They wept like anything to see, Such quantities of sand.
h) Even the blind men's dogs appeared to know him; and when they saw him coming on, would tug their owners into doorways and up courts.

5. What countries compete for these trophies and for which sport?
a) Calcutta Cup
b) Wightman Cup
c) The America's Cup
d) The Ashes
e) Ryder Cup

6. In what sports or games are the following terms used? Upper cut, a fault, feathering, the trudgen, woods, a chukka, in baulk.

7. Name the building in London where each of the following may be seen.
a) The picture 'The Laughing Cavalier.'
b) The Woolsack
c) The Regalia
d) Admiral Jellicoe's tomb
e) The Whispering Gallery
f) The Banqueting Hall built by Inigo Jones
g) A mural painting of the Fire of London

Answers can be found on the next . page

ONE   AT THE BEGINNING, MISS FOX

General Knowledge Competition 1935 – Answers

1. Tuning by musicians; humidity of air; measuring linear distance; milk density; wind speed; air pressure; time; heartbeat.

2. Moscow; Paris; Cambridge; Edinburgh; Berlin; Venice; Rome; Paris; Venice.

3. Zoology; geology; ornithology; entomology; palaeontology.

4. a) David Copperfield – Charles Dickens
    b) Lochinvar from Marmion – Sir Walter Scott
    c) Lady of Shalott – Alfred Lord Tennyson
    d) The Deserted Village – Oliver Goldsmith
    e) Pied Piper of Hamelin – Robert Browning
    f) King Lear – Shakespeare
    g) Alice Through the Looking Glass – Lewis Carroll
    h) A Christmas Carol – Charles Dickens

5. a) England/Scotland rugby
    b) Tennis England/USA
    c) Yachting Challenger from USA, Australia, UK, New Zealand and others
    d) England/Australia cricket
    e) USA/Europe golf

6. Boxing; tennis; rowing; swimming; bowls; polo; snooker.

7. a) Wallace Collection
    b) House of Lords
    c) Tower of London
    d) St Paul's Cathedral Crypt
    e) St Paul's Cathedral
    f) Banqueting House, Whitehall
    g) Museum of London.

*Even the PE teacher,Miss Gibb, wore a tunic in the 1920s. L to R Back row Olive Beadle,
Phyllis Roberts, Kathleen Daniels, Doreen Rippengal, Kathleen Walker, Elsie Vince, Margaret
Hedley, Anita Dodds, Hazel Chatfield, Irene Burton. Middle row Betty Beck, Stella Widgery,
Yvonne Cath, Sylvia Cole, Joy Salway, ? ?, Elizabeth Billiness, Catherine Phillips,
Front row Mary Wood, Barbara Oliver, Joyce Barlett, Miss Gibb, Rosemary Hawley, Audrey
Forrester, Connie Radford.*

ONE   AT THE BEGINNING, MISS FOX

Memories of the County School for Girls 1931-1937

Lois Baker (née Dunk) and Connie Semple share their memories of the school in the 1930s and name many of the girls with them, including Olive Rippengal, who still comes regularly to the Adremians' lunches. Connie was a war bride, going to London, Ontario in 1946 with two small children. She had four more children although one little boy died from leukaemia aged two but her marriage lasted until her husband died after 45 years. She has kept in touch with several school friends, visiting them whilst in England: Betty (Capon) Cripps at Godsmersham near Canterbury and Betty's sister Pat, also Canterbury, Cath (Bowden) Rawles from Calstock, Cornwall, Doreen (Davies) Eccleshall South Brent, Devon who wrote regularly for magazines, and Vera Rose from Bromley, Kent.

Just going through her autograph book mostly dated 1932 brings up many familiar names: Elizabeth Bone, Sheila Chandler, Evelyn Chapman, Joan Cole, Iris Dineen, Jean Eames, Doris Frost, Connie Jones, Doreen Jones, Flora McNeil, Joan Servante, Gwen Shorter, Hermione Stoyle and Margaret Wright. Iris Cane had drawn a pirate and Mary Wootton had drawn a beautiful blue 'Speedwell fairy.' Brenda Wixey had lovely blue eyes that matched the floor length dance dress that she made.

Of the teachers she remembers the Art teacher, Miss Matthews as a dear soul in spite of the fact that Connie can only recall trying unsuccessfully to do Battersea power station as a lino cut. Miss Loxdale and Miss Chambers took Gym and Games, Miss Babbs Geography, Dr Liddle and Miss Ironsides (Tinribs) Maths, Miss Grice History, Miss Broadhurst French, Miss Sale English, Miss Stephenson Science and Miss Rose Latin.

Lois adds more about their teachers, how she enjoyed Miss Stephenson's lab experiments but could not understand Physics. Miss Grice loved her subject and made her love it too. Miss Babb's lessons were fun when she used the epidiascope but that was mostly after exams. Miss Rose, also Deputy Head, taught poetry and the rumour went round that she had been engaged to the war poet Rupert Brooke such is the romantic outlook of girls the world over. As Lois could not draw, when Dora Matthews set homework to 'paint speech day' she just went home and cried. She thought that Miss Loxdale was very masculine as she rode a motor bike to school and addressed the girls as idiots, donkeys and fools as they struggled to 'cradle' the ball with those strange lacrosse sticks. For swimming, they had to walk to Beckenham Baths, undress in cubicles like horse boxes, and don itchy woollen navy blue costumes and red hats. Thankfully this was only in the first form. Lois also included Latin mistress Miss Andrews teaching a subject she enjoyed and Music mistress Miss Smith who ran the choir that took part in the South London Festival at James Allen School.

Miss Smith also did the school plays when Lois was 'Rattie' in 'The Wind in the Willows' with a beautiful long tail made by her father.

ONE   AT THE BEGINNING, MISS FOX

As the candlestick maker in Walter de la Mare's 'Crossings' Lois had to play 'Here we go round the mulberry bush' on a tin whistle. Lois wished she had done cookery and needlework, only ever doing some 'run and fell' seams and bib with a parrot in drawn thread work. French with Miss Barnard was not a problem as Lois had a bi-lingual friend in Marguerite Jaulmes, also valued by Connie!

Speech Days were always an embarrassment to Lois as her grandfather, Francis Percy Hodes was Chairman of the Penge Council and sat on the platform. Sadly the only prize that Lois remembers getting was for General Knowledge for a paper that we did twice, one sight unseen and the other after we had researched the answers.

Then what about School Rules in the 1930s? No eating in the street, hats worn at all times, all clothes marked and inspected on the first day of term. Bicycles must have straight handlebars, not racing ones and you must ride your cycle, not push it walking beside your friends.

Betty (Capon) Cripps continues: - I started school in the Upper Third where I met my friends Connie King and Iris Cane. We were issued with an incredible number of text books to be covered with brown paper. Our homework was to learn the school motto and hymn.

In the hall with its removable steps at the front was the stage and at the back all the PE apparatus was kept, the box, vaulting horse and rib stalls. We seemed only to perform Shakespeare's plays and before every performance Miss Fox would ask the ladies to remove their hats. (Today it would be to turn off their mobile phones.) The silver collection was in a metal bucket so the contributions made a noise, except for the silent silver threepenny bits.

There was one auspicious occasion when the poet **Walter de la Mare** came to the school. He had lived locally at three different addresses in Mackenzie Rd, Worbeck Rd and Thornsett Rd although he had moved away to Twickenham by the time he died in 1956. A long haired gentleman wearing a velvet jacket came on to the stage and began to speak. Sadly he spoke so quietly that only the front two rows could hear anything but like the good little girls that we were, we sat in complete silence. Who knows what words of wisdom he may have uttered!

We conducted experiments in the Chemistry laboratory that nowadays would be regarded as terribly unsafe. We lit up Bunsen burners to heat iron filings and boil chemicals with gay abandon.

Then there was the day when Miss Stephenson turned the handle of a mangle-like contrivance to remove air from a metal ball after which we all took part in a tug of war to pull it apart.

ONE   AT THE BEGINNING, MISS FOX

The Art Room was a rather romantic room placed high in the attics with a glass roof for a

good light. There was a plaster figure of Venus and a ball, a perfect sphere.

The House system started when I was at the top of the school and there was one very strange positively Victorian competition called Deportment. We used to walk round the hall and up and down the stage steps as though a book was balanced on our heads. Another was the Music competition where the whole class was meant to sing a rehearsed song but most people just mouthed the words because they were too scared to sing out loud.

King George V died during our school days and my mother took me to his Lying in State at Westminster Hall. We walked to the Town Hall to hear the Mayor proclaim the new King Edward VIII. It does not seem possible today but hardly anyone owned a wireless so a parent who had recently opened a shop brought a large wireless to school for everyone to hear the abdication speech of the King. In no time at all we were walking to the Town Hall again to hear the proclamation of King George VI. Our world was old fashioned and tranquil. Girls walked or cycled to school as only a couple of girls in my class had parents with cars. Most families had a week's holiday away in Bognor, Margate or Folkestone where the highlight of the week was the concert on the pier. As Girl Guides we often went to Guide Camp in the summer and we were scarcely aware of the black clouds of war approaching.

Betty married during the war to an old boy of the Boys' School who worked in the Colonial Service. Sadly he died when only 40 leaving Betty with three children. Fortunately her General School Certificate taken at school qualified her for Teacher Training and a career in Primary Teaching that she enjoyed immensely.

Perhaps here we should mention a project dear to Miss Fox, an organ for the hall. Plans for it to be supplied by Messrs Norman & Beard were thwarted by the uneasy political situation in 1938 and eventually in 1948, Miss Henshaw wrote to Miss Fox at Brookfield in Totnes, Devon with the proposal that the organ fund amounting to some £775 should be used to buy instruments for the orchestra. Although the two women were good friends, Miss Fox was strongly opposed to this and felt that the money should be returned to the subscribers. In October 1952, the organ fund was still in existence and it seems as though we may never know the fate of the money since all those likely to know are deceased.

ONE   AT THE BEGINNING, MISS FOX

Miss Fox's school has its 21st birthday and other tales by Pamela Daymond

Opened in September 1919, the same month in 1940 was the occasion of the school's 21st birthday. Miss Fox paid for every pupil to attend a celebratory party. She was a formidable person with her pebble spectacles but underneath she was very kind. Her tiny maid Doris became well known in the school because she helped in the kitchens. Doris used to come to the meetings of the Old Girls when she retired.

Miss Fox was very particular about school uniform and did not think that we needed any other clothes. From September 1939, we were supposed to buy the uniform from Gorringes in Buckingham Palace Rd although previously it had been supplied by Mrs Quinnell in Beckenham Rd near Mackenzie Rd. The plain gym tunic with a square neck was supposed to be four inches from the ground when kneeling. The white poplin or rather less white Viyella blouses also had square necks. A navy coat and gloves, a navy velour hat with hat band and thick taupe coloured lisle stockings completed the winter uniform.

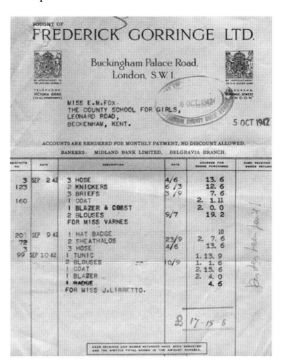

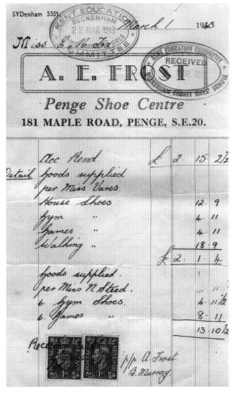

Four pairs of shoes kept in a shoe bag with your name embroidered on it were bought from Frost's in Maple Rd: brown outdoor shoes, black single buttoned strapped house shoes, black leather games shoes and black plimsolls for gym.

The summer dresses were very pretty in finely striped blue material with white Peter Pan collars and cuffs to the short sleeves. They must always be worn with Panama hats and the same long lisle stockings. Girls joining the school a year later than me were lucky because clothes rationing brought permission to wear white ankle socks instead. Previous years used to wear extra long lisle stockings for gym. After a few washings they turned pink!

Miss Fox advocated plenty of sleep and had a table of bedtimes depending on age. Ten year olds should be in bed by 6.30pm and increasing by 30 minutes each year meant that 16 year olds were in bed by 9.30pm. Art teacher Miss Dean used to ask her classes as to when they went to bed the previous evening. This was difficult for me as I had Art on Tuesday when on Monday evenings my family all went to the Penge Empire with tickets two for the price of one (4d in the gallery).

ONE AT THE BEGINNING, MISS FOX

<u>Joan (Weatherley) Lunn has an interview with Miss Fox</u>

Oh yes, I passed the scholarship
Though it gave my mother shocks
Because there was an interview
With formidable Miss Fox
Her bedtime will be 7.15
The august lady said
'Please make sure that by that time
She's well tucked up in bed.'
'Oh no, that's much too early'
Said mother greatly daring;
Bun aquiver, glasses steamed
Miss Fox was really glaring.
'Go out into the corridor
And wait until you're called.'
I quickly did as I was bid
(My mother was appalled).
'Of course she'll never go to sleep
While you are on her side.'
She lectured her so soundly
My mother nearly died.
It was a sad beginning
A really awful shame,
She was so deeply wounded
She NEVER went there again!

Joan's friend, Brenda (Wixey) Brent, 1932 to 1938, recalls what went before that terrifying interview in order to gain a 'free seat' with fees paid by the KCC. The Primary Schools would select pupils likely to pass the entrance exam and we assembled on a Saturday morning in May to do English and Arithmetic papers and to write an essay. Those with the highest marks attended an oral with Miss Fox where she asked us to read and explain certain words.

The final hurdle was the interview attended with a parent where she told us all the rules, where to buy our uniform (at Ardec's in Beckenham) and all the shoes that we needed. Every term we had to take 1/ 4d, one shilling for books and 4d for games. Among the books was a hymn book and psalter from which in music lessons we learnt to sing psalms to the Gregorian chant.

After 5 years, many of us applied for the Civil Service with results of the November examination not declared until February. To fill in the time after our school certificate, we took a Commercial course in shorthand, typing, double entry book keeping, business French and some German. Looking back I fully appreciate the excellent education we received which without the 'free seats' many of our parents would not have been able to afford.

Brenda remembered that Alice Willsher, who appears on page 4 as the wicket keeper in the 1925 cricket team, opened the Manor Rd Preparatory School in Manor Rd, Beckenham in 1938. It was highly successful and the boys and girls were well known in their brown school uniforms until the school closed in 1972.

From Centre group clockwise: Miss Barnard, Miss Colyer, Miss Partridge, Miss Bone, Miss Watts and Miss Happs

PREWAR STAFF

Kathleen Henshaw
1944-1963

As the school became Beckenham Grammar School for Girls and moved to Park Langley

Staff 1947 L to R Back row Lois Brooker, Miss Cooper, Miss Broadhurst, Miss Kingston, Miss Coote, Miss Walters, Mrs Grunspan, Miss Partridge, Miss Rabson, Miss Barbara Taylor, Miss Taylor, Miss Thompson, Miss Reynolds. Middle row Miss Barnard, Miss Atkinson, Miss Preston, Miss Henshaw, Miss Stephenson, Miss King, Miss Burton Front row Miss O'Dell, Miss Webb, Miss Kobrak, Miss Pelling, Miss Wiseman.

TWO   MISS HENSHAW 1944-1963

I had Miss Henshaw as a colleague for the rest of my time at Beckenham. She was in the class of great headmistresses. She was always ready to cooperate with us. I was indeed fortunate to have her as a colleague.   Mr L W White, Headmaster of the Boys' School (1941-1962)

She came with the Flying Bombs! A memorable occasion for us all!

In 1944 the school building in Lennard Road was war damaged; there were fewer than 200 girls in attendance, and a large party had been evacuated to Yorkshire. Miss Henshaw's difficulties were colossal, but she dealt with one problem after another with courage and inspiration; she foretold the rapidly growing numbers, and forestalled overcrowding by 'acquiring' two of the nearest Sports Pavilions. Cyphers and Lloyds were not popular, but they were necessary.

She was in the vanguard of a new interpretation of education, and she wished it to be wide and comprehensive. She introduced to her bemused and conservative staff and school a seven-day timetable. 'How mad!' we thought, but it worked. It allowed time for out-of-school visits, for House activities, and most important of all, it gave the opportunity for a wide selection of subjects by the senior girls. It gave the chance, too, in the Sixth Form of a course of general subjects – Local Survey, Science for the Arts section, and English studies for the scientists.

Very early during her years as Headmistress, Miss Henshaw appointed a speech training specialist, and our girls of all ages learned to speak easily and fearlessly in public. With her whole-hearted encouragement the Music Department developed its many talents and was able to share its gifts with the town.

In 1948 she expanded the House system and gave to our School something different from other day schools. It provided for many senior and middle school girls opportunities of organisation and responsibility, which they would otherwise never have had. The House system, together with the Parents' Association, which she resuscitated and supported untiringly, has given to Beckenham Grammar School its easy, friendly and co-operative atmosphere.

When international travel again became possible, visits abroad were encouraged and Miss Henshaw, already an experienced party leader, took one of the first groups to Sweden. The Travel Fund, to help girls financially, was born under her aegis in 1947. It began as a purely internal affair, but the Parents' Association quickly stepped in and produced money in generous amounts by annual bazaars.

Miss Henshaw's work for education went beyond the confines of the School, as the town and county were soon to appreciate her worth and demand her services in many capacities. These she gave generously and untiringly.

In spite of all these calls on her time and energies, the individual girl was always her concern. Advising, encouraging, and sometimes admonishing, she took endless trouble to help those in difficulties at home or at school, or uncertain about their future careers. Many of Miss Henshaw's former pupils have reason to look back with gratitude to her nineteen years with them.

Recollections of an Adremian:

A fourth former from a party of Beckenham Grammar School girls, evacuated to the small mining village of Wath-on-Dearne, was cycling along a footpath.

TWO   MISS HENSHAW 1944-1963

She came to a sudden stop as her way was barred by the Physics Mistress and an imposing tall companion, who nevertheless had a twinkle in her eye as she asked to borrow the girl's bicycle … and as I saw my cycle borne away, I realised that my introduction to Miss Henshaw was over. My cycle saw a great deal of the district as, with a concern for the welfare of her girls which never faltered, Miss Henshaw located us all. It was arranged for us to attend a co-ed school, although this pleasant prospect was somewhat marred by the Autumn Term beginning much earlier than was expected at home. When Miss Henshaw found that German was not taught at the school, she insisted that a tutor be found, even though the subject was required by only one girl. In later years this regard for the individual was still apparent, as the timetable would be turned inside out to accommodate normally impossible subject combinations.

Miss Henshaw's first term began, therefore, with the members of the School scattered over the country, but as we returned to Beckenham we found a new democracy growing in the School. Prefects and sub-prefects were given responsibility previously reserved for members of Staff, and as Miss Henshaw encouraged us to think more for ourselves and others, such organisations as the School Travel Fund were begun. The Sixth Form grew from seven or eight to thirty, sixty and over one hundred, as Miss Henshaw persuaded more and more of us to fit ourselves for professional training, and how delighted she was to hear of our successes! As Adremians married, she was fond of stating 'Educate a girl, and you educate a family', and commiserated with those of us who could only produce boys, who could not follow to be educated at her school in their turn!

One of the first School Journeys abroad after the war was led by Miss Henshaw in 1946 when she took a party from Form VI to Viggbyholm, near Stockholm in neutral Sweden. We shall never forget the lush cream cakes and couponless clothes unknown in wartime Britain. Nevertheless, most of us found time to glance at the passenger list on board 'The Suecia' to commit a certain lady's age and birthday to memory, especially as 'the certain lady' was masquerading under the name of Diana for the duration of the trip.

Diana, Ruth and Freda en route for Sweden 1946

Our party in Viggbyholm with our Swedish hosts. 'Tony' is sitting far right in the front

TWO   MISS HENSHAW 1944-1963

Eventually the School outgrew its building, and when Miss Henshaw at last found herself in a brand new school, isolated at the end of the administrative block, she missed the easy contact she had had with the girls when her room opened on to the busy corridor, but those of us who have known her since the beginning will always appreciate the warm-hearted friendship she has given to us all.

Although born in Wales, the youngest of a family of two boys and two girls, Kathleen was brought to London when only 6 weeks old and never strayed far from the capital. She attended London University's University College for her BSc in Chemistry & Physics, followed by a year's teacher training. She had posts at Sittingbourne, Chatham and Tulse Hill, teaching Science until she was appointed Head of Lewes Grammar School in 1938. She also became the Area Commander of the Girls Training Corps. At one time Kathleen thought of following music as a career and was delighted to come to a school not only where the former pupil Nancy Wiseman ran the music department but also where concert pianist Patricia Carroll rattled the ivories of the school piano and went on to make her name in the musical world. She was the founder President of the Beckenham Soroptimists and a keen supporter of the children of the Pestalozzi village in Sussex. She had been a keen sportswoman, in the college boat, president of the gym club and a good skater and horse rider. It would have been difficult to have found a more worthy Headmistress for the Beckenham County School in 1944.

Miss Nancie Pelling joined the staff with Miss Henshaw having been interviewed in August by Miss Rose. She became a firewatcher at the school before the term started and by January 1945 was helping to make the school windows safe from the effects of the V2s. She painted a precarious Miss Cutler fastening netting to the dining room windows and the Chemistry lab being used for dinner because the dining area was too fragile. The caretaker, Mr Nash, brought supplies of glue in a heated bucket. The girls were not allowed back to school for two weeks after the V2 fell in the Midland Bank Sports ground and on Cyphers cricket pitch at the beginning of January.

Miss Pelling taught Art but did not discover the Art room upstairs until the war ended. Instead she taught in room 7 opposite Miss Henshaw's study! However she joined the party going to Sweden in 1946 and called herself Ruth to match Miss Henshaw's Diana, Miss Cutler's Tony and Miss Trost's Freda. Mary Moore went to Sweden in 1947 and remembers bringing home items like Rice Krispies and currants unobtainable in England. She also comments on all the after-school activities run by the staff during the war, like Field Club excursions on Saturday afternoons and the German Club at the Boys' School. Miss Jackson, who soon married and became Mrs Long, fostered a life long interest in travel as her inspired geography lessons went well beyond the actual syllabus.

In praise of Miss Henshaw and her staff by Janet and Margaret Lambert

My sister Margaret and I spent 11 years between us (1946-1957) at the Lennard Road building.

TWO   MISS HENSHAW 1944-1963

This will always be school to us, and are we forever grateful, in common with fellow pupils who have remained lifelong friends, for the stability and firm platform for future life that our school provided. Routines, such as morning assembly, 7-day timetable and House system were important early lessons in discipline and setting boundaries. In fact discipline and respect were ever present, and apart from normal high-spirited behaviour from time to time, we don't remember any major problems.

We can all still name and recall most members of staff, particularly those who were constant during our years there – Miss Henshaw, Miss Preston, Miss King, Miss Stephenson, Miss Rabson, Miss Walters, Miss Barnard, Miss Burton, Miss Thompson, Miss Pelling, Miss O'Dell and Miss Wiseman. It was probably only after we left that we fully appreciated their wisdom, teaching skills and devotion to their chosen careers. I was pleased to stay in touch with Miss Rabson, Miss Stephenson and Mrs McPhail until their deaths.

Pupil numbers were fewer than present day schools and that, together with the House system, meant that we were able to mix more easily with those older and younger than us. Even so, before the building extension was completed, there was no room to accommodate us all and who can forget time spent at Cyphers as first formers, ably shepherded by Mrs McPhail, and also at Lloyds?

And what about the annual Speech Day with school governors Alderman Atkins and Mrs Helena Normanton ever present on the platform? We accepted the school uniform rule and I believe were proud to wear it, although there are memories of occasional admonishments from prefects for not wearing our berets en route to the station! However **Philippa Kyle**, when her PTA Chairman father took his place on the platform, was afraid everyone would laugh at her *mother's* choice of hat!

Staff and Prefects party 1956: L to R Back row Miss Ord, Miss Child, Miss Henson, ??, Miss O'Dell, Miss Rabson, Miss Newland, Miss Cutler, ??. Middle row ??, Mrs Kaye, Miss Thompson, Miss Cooper, ??, Miss Taylor, Miss Hatfield, Miss Swan, Miss Uglow, Miss Barnard, Miss Minty, Miss Savage, ??. Seated Miss Burton, Miss King, Miss Stephenson, Miss Preston, Miss Webb, Miss Maynard.

TWO   MISS HENSHAW 1944-1963

How fortunate we were that the school timetable catered for all abilities, and with very few exceptions, teaching in all subjects was of a high standard. Those of us with sporting interests and abilities were able to participate in a wide range of team games, and even the 300-yard walk up Lennard Road to the games field didn't dampen our enthusiasm! The active Parent Teacher Association hosted the annual Garden Party, the funds from which contributed to travel abroad, and the Fathers enjoyed challenging the 1st cricket X1 to a match each year.

Before penning this I decided to 'flip through' our school magazines, beautifully bound (albeit with paper yellowing from age!) but instead spent hours totally absorbed in nostalgia. I had forgotten the complete range of activities and interests open to us in those years – orchestras and choirs, drama, school council, road safety, field club, debating society, Christian discussion group, charities, geographical society, swimming gala, inter-form gymnastic competition, inter-House drama, singing, reading and games competitions, travel at home and abroad, Christmas carol concert at St. John's Church and the annual Gilbert and Sullivan production under the guidance of Miss Wiseman with her usual energy and vitality.

Prefects 1956 Back row - Joyce Jolliffe, Janet Lambert, Heather Thornton, Brenda Porrer, Briony Crisp, Anne Whitehead, Jane Lee, Patricia Wheeler-Holohan, Patricia Howard, Daphne Clark, Marjorie Gardner, Valerie Kyte   middle row - Edna Talbot, Jill Saunders, Jacqueline Scott (Head Girl), Sheila Andrews (Deputy Head Girl) Elizabeth Honey Front row - Kathleen Sears, Ann Jolliffe, Helen Sears, Patricia Braddick.

TWO   MISS HENSHAW 1944-1963

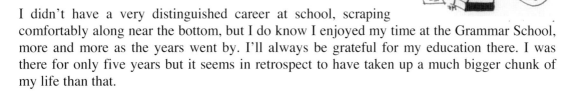

So schooldays were certainly among the happiest years of our lives and how satisfying it is that the Adremian Association continues to keep our interest alive. Janet received the Elgood Special Service Prize in 1957 and she still has her choice 'The Sports Organiser's Handbook.' Her friends would agree that Janet was a worthy winner!

My Years at the Grammar School by Jane Fabb (née Janet Webber)

I didn't have a very distinguished career at school, scraping comfortably along near the bottom, but I do know I enjoyed my time at the Grammar School, more and more as the years went by. I'll always be grateful for my education there. I was there for only five years but it seems in retrospect to have taken up a much bigger chunk of my life than that.

I went to a small private school, nearer to home and better during the air raids apparently. I remember going along to the Grammar School to sit the scholarship exam as it was called then. We were in room 23 in the Lennard Rd building and I recognised only one girl, Hazel Green, who lived near me. How I passed the exam remains a mystery. English and the intelligence test were fine but my grasp of simple maths was, and remains, nil. Later I had an interview with Miss Henshaw and heard that I was to be admitted.

Getting the uniform was not easy in 1946 and it was years before I had a blazer. Those awful navy blue knickers we used to roll up to make them as small as possible. Hilary Whybrow was the only other girl from my primary school and we stuck together until we made our own friends in the first form. Three of my cousins, Margaret, Pauline and Audrey Webber were already at the school in forms 5, 3 and 2 respectively and I used to call for Margaret and Pauline in the morning. Sometimes they were still eating toast and marmalade as we hurried to catch the train from Elmers End to New Beckenham.

Miss Kobrak was our form mistress and she told us that it was her first term too. We were in room 23, a room that I always liked, painted blue. Elise (Billy) Beeton was our sixth form prefect in whom we felt very fortunate. I had done a little French at my old school so initially I was considered very good at it. I was put into the top set but when we reached the stage where my prior knowledge ended, I sank like a stone and passed rapidly through the second set into the third. I always felt this ignominy was unfair because I'd *told* them I'd done French before.

I loved my first Christmas at school and indeed all those that followed; the tree in the hall, the carol service at Holy Trinity church and the Christmas dinner, surely the best in Britain especially as food was rationed.

1947 was a very hard winter. The first form was moved to the Cyphers pavilion where it was

freezing cold but I suppose we were used to it. We slid on the ice on the river and got water inside our Wellingtons. Our form room was upstairs where there was a bar (unstocked) in the corner. Phyllis MacDonald hid in there throughout the class and couldn't come out afterwards as the teacher remained in the room. There was a hue and cry when Phyllis was reported missing. Another time she cut off one of her long ginger plaits during needlework. I was no angel and talking in class was my besetting sin.

TWO   MISS HENSHAW 1944-1963

The day after Prince Charles was born in November 1948, Miss Grice took us for History and gave a most interesting talk on the Royal family.

The first form saw my introduction to swimming at which I was never much good but I liked it. I quite enjoyed tennis and netball but again with very little skill. I avoided sports if I could. A little non-sporty group of us would hang back in the pavilion and emerge too late to be chosen for a team. We would be told to go and practise elsewhere which suited us fine. The only time that I went willingly to the sports field was one House afternoon when a teacher was going to read out my poem. A head round the door announced that it was Yellow's turn for the pitch so I escaped willingly with the sporty girls for once, quaking with embarrassment at the thought of my poem being read.

My closest friend was Margaret Lambert but we were separated in year three when our year was divided into four smaller groups instead of three, although we probably met up in some classes as we were streamed according to the subject and our ability in it. We found ourselves back together again in the fourth and fifth forms and became part of a lovely group of classmates. One year, our form won the Gym competition, no thanks to me, and the trophy was a bust of a young boy whom we called 'Jimmy.' I can still remember the words of the songs we learned for the House Singing Competitions but, if there's something I'm equally hopeless about as Maths, it's singing. I was usually put at the back and told 'just open and shut your mouth dear.'

Janet Webber and Margaret Lambert.

 In the fifth year, I missed the performance altogether as I went to the domestic science room to iron my blouse and didn't get back in time. I have a feeling that Yellow House won! One of the school outings was to see the Lawrence Olivier film of Hamlet but a few of us didn't go as we were going with our parents. In spite of the fact that lesson ended at 3.45 in the afternoon, we were given a long, boring lesson that went on until 4.00 and I was most indignant. Hamlet became my favourite play and I fancied myself as Queen Gertrude. I finally got to play her in a mini Christmas production at my Theatre Class, tiara and all. One year I had a go at Lady Macbeth in my evening class but alas, as with Maths and Singing, an actress I am not!

The sixth form used to keep mice in the conservatory. The second form would look after cleaning and feeding them in the lunch time, which I much enjoyed. The senior science students used to dissect frogs.
They would be laid out in the science labs where everybody took a turn to eat lunch once in every seven days of the timetable. (They were called 'Lloyds dinners' because they came from a central kitchen at Lloyds Sports Ground). A deceased frog pinned out displaying its internal organs was not the best accompaniment to stew or whatever the meal of the day was.

TWO   MISS HENSHAW 1944-1963

One day when we were at Lloyds, a cricket match was being played, the visiting team including the then-famous cricketer and Brylcreem boy, Dennis Compton. Barbara Owens, aka Titch, asked him for his autograph and he said pleasantly, 'Yes, later.' However word reached Miss Henshaw and Titch bore the telling-off for all of us.

One year we had an 'election' at school to coincide with the General Election. We had great fun leading up to it and the fact that the Liberal candidate (Anne Blatchford) won by a landslide was due more to the candidate's popularity than to her politics.

I loved History and Geography but never seemed to earn good marks for them. English was fine and I enjoyed General Science but being innumerate was never able to finish an experiment with its equation. I still remember how to make coal gas: unfortunately nobody in all the years of my adult life has ever called upon me to do so. When in the fifth form, when studying for GSE O-levels, our mock exams were held at Lloyds where it was so cold that Maggie Lambert and others would rub my hands at break to try to make them warm enough to hold a pen. I was obviously not put in for the Maths exam but I had to attend one Maths lesson a week. We were given a little homework that two girls would do immediately. For the rest of the week, the rest of the class would copy it up. As the two girls did not always agree, usually half the class produced one set of answers and the other half another. We had an 'in-house' exam for which I was given 3%. This was for writing my name and the date neatly and for copying all the geometrical shapes on the paper. I have realised in recent years that I suffered from DYSCALCULIA although I would not say

I suffered from it because I've always got by with not bothering to count my change and ringing several wrong numbers before I hit on the right one.

Julius Caesar was our O-level Shakespeare and the play was shown on television. Only two girls had TV and I went to the home of Yvonne Cliff with half the class to see it. As the fifth year drew to a close I wanted to stay on at school. Miss Henshaw said I must pass two or more GCE subjects or otherwise I must go to a secretarial college. I had a knack for exams and passed them all but I had said that I would go to Bromley Tech with my friend, Anne Hornidge, to do shorthand and typing and I left the Grammar school after all. We had a wonderful time after the exams, playing tennis, sunbathing, a short German course and the film Henry V at a Penge cinema with the fifth form from the Boys' Grammar School.

On the last day, we said our goodbyes, wrote in each other's autograph books and cried all the way to New Beckenham station. I was back again for Speech Day to receive my certificate from the Bishop of Rochester and to see my classmates again. In the summer I went to the Parents Association Garden Party and have been to the Adremians reunions in the old Lennard Rd building. So much has changed that I want to put everything back where it used to be.

I have often felt that I could have made much more of my Grammar School education if I had been there in my twenties. However, life is a great teacher and I am sure it was my school background that gave me my continuing love of learning.

TWO   MISS HENSHAW 1944-1963

A Cyphers Circus Act? By Valerie (Thornton)Sheldon

I was sitting on a chair outside the Headmistress's study, the toes of my shoes just touching the wooden floor of the corridor. Was I alone? I can't really remember, although my mother must have accompanied me to get me there to the school. I was awaiting my interview to see if I was a suitable addition for the next September intake.

 The door opened and I was ushered inside to a wooden chair in front of Miss Henshaw's desk. I recall a comfortable, pink-faced, grey-clothed lady, smiling benevolently at me from behind sparkling rimless glasses, but exuding authority. I can't remember what she asked me regarding my school progress, or how I answered, but one question and answer is forever engraved on my mind courtesy of my mother's reminder many years later.   My lack of academic objectives had obviously been passed on to her via the staff at some future Parent Teacher meeting!
>'*And what would you like to do when you leave school?*' asked Miss Hens haw.
>'*I want to join the circus.*'

It must have been the answer all Grammar School headmistresses would wish to hear from a prospective new student! But she calmly went on,
>'*And what would you do in a circus*?'
>'*I would like to be an acrobat*!'

The current book which had fired my imagination was about a girl who had run away from home, and joined a circus.   I was at that stage of climbing trees, turning somersaults, and generally being a tom-boy and that was my ambition at the time!

In spite of my aspirations, I duly started at Cyphers Cricket Club later that year - the overflow classrooms for first-formers as there was no room for us at the main school in Lennard Road. I was in Miss Uglow's form, and we were in the main hall.   Two other classes were taken in the upstairs committee room and another downstairs room.   We were seated in alphabetical order, so I was near the back - a position I usually chose for the rest of my school career!   I was envious of the girls allocated the two small rooms, they had proper classrooms!   Ours was a rather large, impersonal space used by everyone who had to pass through to get from one part of the building to another.

School lunches were also provided in the same hall, and prefects would come over from the main school to help serve out the meals.   This was our major contact with other students from the school, but we were all very happy in our compact world of girls of the same age.   We had the good fortune to enjoy the outside delights around the cricket club - the grassy areas for games and general play; the shady trees in the hot summer, where we occasionally held our sewing classes - hand stitching our aprons which took a whole year to complete; open spaces for snowball fights in winter, and the streams, the Beck and the Chaffinch.

 Oh dear, those streams! I believe we were the last intake to be allowed anywhere near them - they then became out of bounds to future first years!   The water seemed to draw the girls toward them.   I think it was the Chaffinch which flowed behind Cyphers, just a very small stream with shallow grassy banks - a place for exploring, maybe there were tadpoles or frogs, or even little fishes, very good reasons for upturning stones to have a look, or poke about in the water with a tree branch or stick, stirring up the silt.   And in summer if we could take off shoes and socks to go for a paddle, before being seen by a teacher or prefect, it was a good game to play.   The big entertainment on colder days was to jump across from one bank to the other side, daring each other to take on the wider sites, and decrying those who were too timid to have a go.   There were, of course, many wet shoes, wet socks and wet feet on numerous occasions, with frantic actions to cover up discovery by the teachers! But the crowning and final act which probably put an end to, and banning of, the area was when Ann Bardwell, in her Wellington boots, took a run and flying leap across the widest part, sadly misjudging the distance, and promptly sat down in the water!

TWO   MISS HENSHAW 1944-1963

Not only were her Wellingtons filled with water, but her tunic and navy blue knickers were soaked too, and there was no way of hiding this from the staff.

Did this first year's isolated existence create firmer friendships amongst our contemporaries? Having reached the main school at Lennard Road in our second year, we retained our closeness although we dispersed into different groups and classes. I think the House System each led by a senior member of staff, produced team spirit and loyalty. I recall the fierce competitiveness of the inter-house sports events, the annual drama productions, the music competitions, and the swimming gala especially. Many activities were undertaken on the weekly House afternoons, and the opportunity to mix and interact with girls from all years helped to build confidence. Who remembers making a variety of different gifts for sale at the Annual Travel Fund Bazaar? Then came the hard work of the actual November Saturday sale, and the joy of finding a special souvenir to buy which had been donated by one of the lucky girls who had gone on a trip abroad the previous summer.

It was about this time that the seven day working week was introduced. Printed blank timetables were produced, and we each had to fill in our lessons for that term. If a Monday was Day 1, Friday was Day 5, and the Monday following the weekend became Day 6, Tuesday Day 7, then Wednesday started back at Day 1 again. This was organised to allow more periods to be allocated to each subject, and generally we all found it fairly easy to follow, although most parents became puzzled when they were shouted at for not knowing that this particular Monday was Day 7!

A strange ritual at school was the wearing of 'house shoes'. Every girl had to have a pair of black button-strapped shoes, which had to be put on every morning, leaving outdoor shoes in the cloakroom. It was deemed so important that two older girls were stationed either side of the corridor outside the cloakroom to check that everyone had changed their shoes! If you were wearing plimsolls or outdoor shoes you had to report to the teacher on duty, and I remember that some girls who did not have house shoes resorted to finding a back door into the school to avoid the inspection!

Wet lunchtimes, when we were not allowed outside, very often ended up with impromptu dance classes in the Hall, usually run by a couple of prefects who put the Edmundo Ross and Victor Sylvester records on to the gramophone, and we waltzed around in pairs, arguing over who should take the man's part!

Once we had reached the lower sixth form we were deemed ready for some social grooming, and once a week, during the winter term, after school we made our way to the Peggy Spencer School of Dancing in Penge. Here we met with our counterparts from the Boys' Grammar School, and were taught the correct steps for the waltz, quickstep and tango. Then came that moment when the reluctant boys had to ask the girls to take to the floor with them, for a stumbling, toe-crunching progression round the floor! I was lucky - my boyfriend and I already went to dancing classes, and we were both in the same group at Peggy Spencer's classes.

There were other collaborations with the Boys' School, and one which appealed to my dramatic inclinations was to take a part in their annual school play production. I was fortunate to land the part of Sabina in Thornton Wilder's "The Skin of our Teeth", and together with five other girls rehearsed regularly after school with the large cast of boys. It is a fairly incomprehensible work, and some of the more suggestive lines and language were censored and replaced with more appropriate words. In Act 2 Sabina appears in a red swimsuit, but firm instruction was sent over from the headmistress that it was not appropriate for one of her girls to appear so scantily dressed! So I had to wear a red satin dress for modesty's sake! The play was great fun to do and was received with acclaim.

TWO   MISS HENSHAW 1944-1963

Another procedure in the sixth form was the Careers' Advice afternoon, which was in the capable hands of the Deputy Head, Miss Stephenson.   It was billed as the opportunity to discuss your aims, hopes and targets, and to be advised on the possibilities of success in your chosen career. I had no idea what I wanted to do.   I had toyed with the idea of becoming a dietician, but when I saw the qualifications required I rather went off that idea.   I've no doubt one or two other ideas had been considered and rejected, so when my turn came for discussion I went armed with the sensible suggestion from my mother.   She had advised,

'If you really don't know what you want to do, you should take a good secretarial course. You then have your way into any business or profession which interests you, and once there you can always develop further qualifications.'

I was called into Miss Stephenson's little dark room behind her science lab. and I trotted out the suggested lines on secretarial courses.

'What sort of business would you like to go into?' she asked.

Again my mother's words about travelling and seeing the world came to me.

'I would like to become secretary to the Purser on a large ship,' I replied.

Miss Stephenson languidly lent back in her chair and regarded me over her spectacles.

'Are you sure you wouldn't prefer to be the Captain's wife,' she intoned.

I'm sure the sarcasm wasn't lost on me, but maybe my previous aspirations were on record, and her hopes for an academic profession for me were beyond doubt!

Sport played a big part of my school life, and I took pleasure partaking in all the different games.   Netball was enjoyed at class, house and inter-schools level; hockey and lacrosse in the winter, played on the sports field further up Lennard Road. I recall those cold, wet games afternoons, trudging up the road to change into sports gear in the unheated wooden hut, then out on to the wet, muddy grass, or on occasions out on to hard frost covered soil.   But we soon warmed up running up and down the pitch, tossing and catching the hard black rubber ball in the lacrosse nets, or dribbling the slightly larger hockey ball, trying to keep control with the curved end of the stick.   Summer saw us out on the cricket pitch - not my favourite game, so I always opted for long leg (or some other far out position with a stupid name) and spent the time making daisy chains.

Tennis was my preferred option and I enjoyed the tutelage from Miss Broomhead, who always moaned to me that I would make a very good tennis player if only I would not spend so much time on my swimming! We were so lucky to have the benefit of games, sports fields, PE and gyms, and I am sure we are healthier in our later years from good exercise during our school years. I retain fond memories of my schooldays, and am still in touch with many friends in my year. Through my contacts I hear of other contemporaries and their present circumstances, so even now after so many years have passed we are all still linked.   As mentioned earlier, are we special?   I think we are and I am thankful for circumstances which brought us all together at school.

Miss Broomhead 1953

Did I join the circus?   Of course, I didn't!   Did I marry the Purser of a large ship?   Of course, I didn't!   But I did become a Secretary, working for three very different companies over the years, which has given me so much pleasure and enjoyment.   My happy marriage to Richard, also at the Boys' School, continues in our lovely home by the sea, with visits from our two sons and our grandchildren. Working days led to travel in many parts of the world; meeting people from various different countries and cultures; working and mixing with important, famous, infamous and illustrious characters. A rich career based on a sound education and a confidence gained from the encouragement engendered by the staff and atmosphere of the Beckenham Grammar School for Girls 1950-1956.

TWO   MISS HENSHAW 1944-1963

Our school by Christine (Stenning) Dolman1947 – 1953.

On the day of the scholarship exam I can remember being taken to the Beckenham Grammar School at Lennard Road, Beckenham. This was a very large building originally built as a hospital and very different from Eden Park Lodge which had been my junior school.

On arrival we were assembled into groups and ushered into what seemed an enormous hall, given our seats. We sat waiting for the examination to start. I cannot remember being worried in fact I think I quite enjoyed the different papers. At mid morning break we left the exam room and went to the dining hall for milk. In those days milk bottles had cardboard tops with a small marked circle which one pushed in to insert one's straw. I was evidently too eager and the whole top plunged down into the bottle shooting milk everywhere much to my embarrassment. With the help of a member of staff I was cleaned up and returned to the hall with the others for the rest of the examination.

The next landmark was my interview with the head mistress, this I attended with my mother. We entered the main entrance of the building and we were taken into the head mistress's room on the left hand side of the small entrance hall. The room felt cosy and Miss Henshaw the head mistress, a rather large lady with a warm friendly smile sat behind her desk and proceeded to ask me questions. Most of these have disappeared in the mists of time, however I do remember her pointing to two colourful paintings on her wall. She asked me to choose the one I preferred and tell her why. I chose the one that was very colourful and showed a group of people sitting at a table chatting. This set my imagination going, who were they and what were they talking about and I happily chatted away.

On the first day of term my journey to school involved catching a train from Eden Park Station and getting off at New Beckenham, then walking a short way down Lennard Road to the main gates. We were assembled into groups and let into the building. My life in the big school had begun. Pupils were divided into House groups and mine was Orange group 11, and my tutor was Miss Thompson. The main house room where all four of the Orange House groups met was up a small staircase to a room at the top of the building. This I grew to love as this was also the room for Art classes and Miss Pelling.

All the new first years had their lessons in the Cyphers Club (now a ruin destroyed by fire). Being a smaller building than the main school this was a gentle start to a new school life and we were a united band not intimidated by older girls. My class was 1U (U standing for Miss Uglow our young and kind teacher) and I soon settled in and made new friends. I was made form captain, possibly because I sat in the front row near the teacher's desk. Time passed very quickly and memories fade but I soon had my favourite lessons. Geography with Miss Marshall, Needlework and Art with Miss Kobrak, Mathematics with someone whose name sadly I have forgotten but signed my early reports with the initials of M.L.D. Miss Kobrak also taught us handwriting; this was of the Marion Richardson style and very different from the one I was taught in my junior school which was copper-plate. I found the change very difficult as I was no longer able to use loops.

One of our first lessons involved drawing a plan of the class room. I was in my element with anything that meant drawing. The purpose of the lesson was to understand North, South, East and West and help us get to know the names of our class mates and where they sat. The needlework classes with Miss Kobrak stand out clearly in my memories. We chose two coloured materials which we each made into a small waist apron. We drew a design for a pocket which we then embroidered. Even today I can still see my results, a bright orange and blue apron with an embroidered picture of cotton reels and needles on the pocket. In the second year I was in Miss Broadhurst's class which was 2L. In this year we started Latin, a subject I found difficult. It was only many years later when my son studied Latin and Greek I found a real interest in the subject and was amazed how much I remembered.

TWO   MISS HENSHAW 1944-1963

The school arranged with Lloyds Bank to use their grounds for our games lessons. This so called 'privilege' came with 'showers'. The school felt as the showers were on site we should make use of them. There was nothing more embarrassing in my mind at this time then stripping while our teacher stood watching telling us to line up and run through the showers. These were all of varied temperatures ranging from freezing to very hot. We were all growing up fast and at different levels of maturity which made this exercise prove most undignified to many of us. Many years later I heard from a friend who was in a class lower than me at school that her class refused to do this unless they were allowed to wear swimsuits; this request was evidently granted.

The school ran many activities that could help develop one's interests and confidence. My sporting skills were not as good as I would have liked so I did not make the school teams. Most of my interests were centred round the art room way up at the top of the building and reached by a narrow staircase.

Miss Pelling's puppet drama group in 1951. Christine is second from the left.

4L in 1951 L to R Back row Ann Saunders, Janet Guiver, Joyce Andrews, Betty Luff, Jean John, Moira Redford, Janet Biggs, Elizabeth Shilley, Pamela Lilley, Brenda Grundy, Maureen Haggis. Middle row Christina Watkin, Janet Grimslade, Diana Hall, Ann Malton, Anne Merigan, Jill Tarryer, Miriam Sallis, Christine Stenning, Ann Spackman. Front row Beryl North, Shirley Twyford, Jennifer Roberts, Geraldine Fitz, Mary Alcock, Celia Antrobus, Pamela Goodman

TWO   MISS HENSHAW 1944-1963

During art club we made papier mache puppets for a production of Cinderella. History of Art was another area I became interested in. Many hours were also spent producing posters for the school.

Our form teacher for years 4 and 5 leading to the O level examinations was Miss Partridge who was also our Geography teacher. I have very fond memories of her guiding us through what can be regarded as quite pressurized years. Having successfully gained my O levels the next decision making stage was A levels. I did not really know what I wanted to do eventually in the way of a career so I chose my favourite subjects, Art, Maths and Geography; only three students had opted for this last subject so we were told that this subject would not be on offer. I therefore chose English instead. At this time our O level results were only given to us as pass or fail and there was no way of telling how well one had passed in a subject. One could pass with flying colours or only just scrape through.

I enjoyed my senior status at school and holding the post of Orange House Captain helped to develop my confidence particularly when organising a craft club for the younger house members. Then in conversation Miss Pelling suggested I take my A level Art exam in the lower sixth and that I might try the local Art School and follow a career linked with art. This I duly did and had an interview with Mr Cole the principal and was accepted. I will always have the fondest memories of Miss Pelling. Her advice and encouragement led me to achieve a career in teaching Art and Craft which I did for 40 years. It opened up awareness and an insight into the world around me for which I shall be forever grateful.

I loved my school days and can remember with pleasure many members of Staff who helped and encouraged me during those years. Chemistry lessons with Miss Stephenson. An inspiring teacher that we watched fascinated while she explained chemical properties – Phosphorus igniting, the magic of Mercury, Hydrogen bubbling up through water, and the strong light given off by Magnesium; Physics with Miss King and learning all about pulleys and levers stresses and strains. Mathematics with Miss Webb and being introduced to the fascinating and challenging aspects of Trigonometry and Geometry and History with Miss Hatfield who made the past come alive instead of being a lot of dates to remember.

A few words from Felicity (Edden) Boyden (1949-1957)

Taking part in the Boys' School production of L'Aiglon and receiving good 'crits'; producing 'A Midsummer Night's Dream' for Wedgwood House; being envious of Sylvia Brooks's magnificent Austin 7 that she drove daily to school when in the sixth form; enjoying all sport except lacrosse and cricket because the balls were too hard; adult world initiation reading 'The Vicar's Son' passed round surreptitiously; the strangeness going back to Lloyds' pavilion as a hockey boyfriend's supporter; recently playing golf with Nicky Meek, Pam Meek née Mitchell's daughter and feeling old when Nicky

introduced me to *her* daughter serving behind the bar.

TWO   MISS HENSHAW 1944-1963

Janet (Robinson) Barret still remembers very well her first days as a timid new girl at the Grammar School in 1949. She says, 'In those days we had our lessons in the Cyphers Sports Pavilion. I found it quite hard, no doubt like many others, coming from a primary school where I had in the last year or two been very near the top of the class, to have to adapt to being 'average'. Of course the main building was quite overpowering to us newcomers. During the first year I developed a serious knee problem, which meant very little sports, culminating in a very large operation at about the age of 27. On and off I was able to play some tennis and lacrosse, which I really enjoyed. I did not excel on the academic side, but gained a number of O levels, and went on to do a secretarial course which resulted in some very interesting jobs.

One thing I did gain from the school was a love of French and all things French. I discovered that I found both French and German fairly easy, and when asked to learn a page of prose as a punishment for blowing up and bursting a paper bag in the dining room, I chose French, read it and never did appear before the teacher in the morning as I was sure she would not remember asking me to.!

I will always be grateful to Miss Rabson, who asked in the second year if we would like a French pen friend. I was given the name of Colette Bolla, who lived in Cannes and the village of Mougins on the way to Grasse. The friendship between all our families has lasted fifty-eight years and means a great deal to us both. One reason we were linked was that we were both Girl Guides, and I still meet Colette's Captain each time I visit. I hoped to join a school trip to Limoges, but it was fully booked and my parents managed, with the help of the school to arrange a month in Strasbourg, which became a special time with a lovely family. Two years ago we, together with friends, made a sentimental trip back there and I was able to find my home and school and relive many happy memories.

In 1953, I and a few friends joined Doris Nicholl's dancing class on Saturday morning, where we were joined by boys from the Grammar School. John Barret, David Loades, Colin Berry and Alan Boyden were among those who came. John and I married in 1960 and we have all kept in touch to a greater or lesser degree. We used to meet after school, on our bicycles, at the corner of Village Way and sometimes we met in the lunch times over on the old Tabs Field.

Pauline Crichton recalls the exchange visit to Lille in April 1947

Miss Broadhurst, Miss Barnard and Miss Rabson took 19 girls from the upper school to Lille in the Easter holidays for a fortnight to stay with our different French families who were due to pay us a return visit in July.

We had a very rough crossing to Calais and reached Lille by about five o'clock but after that we saw little of each other. We were surprised to find how quickly we settled in to French customs and became familiar with the language. When we went to school with our French friends, it was odd to hear Latin spoken with a French accent and decided that to be expected at school at 9 o'clock in England was the greatest of luxuries after a week of lessons in France starting at eight!

One day we visited a village called Barque that had been almost totally destroyed in the war. Already the ancient cathedral was being restored and in the centre of the village was a flourishing community of prefabricated shops and houses. Near Dunkirk the land had been deliberately flooded by sea water and the remains of houses were caked with salt. The dead hollow trees were grey and ghostly but still the patient farmers toiled endlessly to make the land fertile again.

TWO   MISS HENSHAW 1944-1963

At Dunkirk we ran down the golden sands to paddle in the sea, thinking of that time when it had been the scene of the great evacuation in the summer of 1940.

This holiday had been a splendid opportunity to see something of life in France with all the problems facing ordinary people at that time.

The French Exchange Visit to Lille in 1948 by Ruth (Jordan) Marchant

At Easter 1948, Miss Barnard took sixteen girls by train from Victoria station on an exchange to Lycée Fénelon at Lille in Northern France and Miss Rabson also was there some of the time although not in the photograph. I only remember going to school in the morning and certainly enjoyed getting home to see the younger children playing games like snakes and ladders, shouting 'A toi, a toi.' At 4.30 we had a tartine of bread with a choice of butter or jam, not both and everyone except the baby gathered at 7.00pm for le diner. On my first weekend, the streets were crowded with religeuse of every costume attending a conference. It was astounding for me with my Protestant background. Each Saturday and Sunday morning, crowds streamed into Belgium where they had a lend-lease from USA. The franc was 7-1 so they were buying butter etc.

I relished lessons and cheerfully repeated 'C'est bien' and 'Ca va' all day. One afternoon I gave Maman six snails that I had bought from a stall. She looked startled but dipped into cookery books and conferred with her 'La bonne' so that they were served at dinner with a sauce and fancy forks. We all chattered as usual but as I ate one I could see they were new to everyone. We each went to different families and it was wonderful for me because my home had ten children aged from 17 down to a baby and also a shy English boy on an exchange visit too. No one could be tongue-tied in the warmth of this family as they tried to put me at my ease with compliments about 'mon chapeau blanc'. Maman ran a well organised home.

She put coins on the table for our single fares by 'le tramway' to our respective schools. We could choose to ride either way or to walk and my friend Odile chose to ride to school. We strolled home giggling, with 'Espion' as a password.

Trip to Lille 1948. Left to Right - Back Row - Pauline Saunders, H, H, Brenda Fox, Heather Ansell,??, H, H, Margaret Loft. 3rd row Pat Hill, H, H, Jennifer Friend, H, H, H, Audrey Martin, H, Jean Banks 2nd row H, Margaret Tilley, Dinah Thetford, H, H, Shirley Wilson, H, Ruth Jordan, ??, H, seated H, Eunice Edwards, ??, Miss Barnard, French staff, French staff, H, H, Anne Hume.   H = French girl   Joan Gear and Margaret Lockwood are the other English girls.

<u>Jean (Banks) Parrott adds to the story</u>

Jean has her diary to remind her of the visit almost sixty years ago. The sea crossing was calm and they arrived about 5.00pm to be greeted by Marte and her mother. This family took Jean about the town.

She watched three films in French, also going to the theatre to see Tosca and the operetta 'Le Comte de Luxembourg.' The whole party went to Bruges one day, walking over the frontier in the rain but on the way back it stopped raining and the rainbows were magnificent. Ruth recalls the sight of the cathedral spire appearing to move with the clouds scudding past behind it as they crossed the canal. They brought back white bread from Belgium which was a change from the coarse brown bread spread with butter and brown sugar that they dunked into a large bowl of coffee at breakfast. Jean noted that tea at school was without milk, very weak but with sugar. Another morning they all went from school to the Town Hall where they went up in the lift and then climbed six flights of stairs to the belfry from where they could see the whole panorama of Lille set out before them. One day they saw a wedding party in front of the town hall with the bride in white.

After they returned to Beckenham, it was their turn to be the hosts to their friends from Lille. The French girls came in July with their teacher, Mlle Coudron and there was a real international celebration. Margaret Lockwood's mother organised a social which, with a little English here and a little French there, presented no great difficulty. Head Girl, Margaret Lovegrove, was the MC and organised everyone into dancing the Dashing White Sergeant. The competition for making a fashionable hat from newspapers and pins was won by Jacqueline Pois and Miss Rabson, who acted as the model, with second prize going to Ruth Jordan and her French friend, Odile Wurts.

Jacqueline won again in a kind of musical chairs called 'musical fish.' Ann Hume and Jean Kors won the treasure hunt. Sylvia Jane and Sheila Dowsett gave an exhibition of the Highland Fling, so loudly applauded that they had to give an encore.

<u>The Trip to Holland at Easter 1949 by Jean Banks</u>

We left on the Dutch ship 'Prinses Beatrix' from Harwich and then by boat train from The Hook to the Hague, taking all day for the journey. The trip was led by Miss Walters but Miss Henshaw accompanied us, staying at the Hotel Pomona while we all visited our exchange families. Many activities were arranged and just as with the trip to Lille in 1948, Jean has a wonderful record in her diary of the activities.

Each girl was given the equivalent of £1 pocket money to last for twelve days! Jean commented on two visits to museums that she thought would have been appreciated more by Miss Pelling and Miss Stephenson but she liked the trip to the cinema to see Robert Donat and Deborah Kerr in the film 'Vacation from Marriage.'. One especially enjoyable day was when they held a miniature Wimbledon tennis tournament in the morning and then went to the zoo in the afternoon. Two days later they played a table tennis tournament where Jean reached the final. It was on Thursday that she cycled to Delft to see the bulb fields described below by Sheila but she can still recall the unsafe feeling that she was going to fall into the canal from the rather high bicycle with a fixed wheel.

On their last day there was a coach and boat tour of the bulb fields at Hillegom from where they could buy flowers to take home. As for food, Jean remembers the breakfasts of bread and butter spread with multicoloured sugar strands and tea with an incredibly rich ice cream cake.

TWO   MISS HENSHAW 1944-1963

.A visit to the bulb fields of Aalsmeer in 1949 by Sheila Dowsett

Aalsmeer is the centre of Holland's bulb industry near the Zuider Zee. We cycled to the bulb fields along straight, flat roads that occasionally rose up so that we could see the fields of amazing colours on either side. Here you see four of the party enjoying the flowers. *Jean Banks is second from the left next to Grieteke Weiss, her Dutch friend.*

There were deep blue and pink hyacinths, red and yellow tulips and masses of yellow daffodils, laced with the blue reflecting canals and the blossoming fruit trees of the farmhouses. Aalsmeer is on the edge of a lake with the houses along the verge of the water approached by a bridge over the canal. As we cycled back I was still dazed by the overwhelming perfume and the colours of the flowers in the sheds.

How did these exchange visits come about?

It was one of the French teachers who explained what was behind all the exchanges that had occurred since the end of the war. Thirteen year old Cohen Stuart, known as Bertie, met Kathleen Henshaw at a prewar international camp in France. During the war Bertie became a member of the Resistance and lost contact with our Miss Henshaw but after the war they located each other. Bertie was teaching English in a French school and Miss Henshaw asked her to bring a party to London thus starting the exchanges of the last three years. Sheila Dowsett made a presentation to Miss Henshaw of flowers and some pottery at the social in 1949 acknowledging the debt that we all owed to her for our friendships with young Dutch, Swedish and French people.

Readers may be interested that it was during 1948/49 that Mrs Grunspan made an exchange with an American, Miss Chappelle, from a private school in Buffalo. When Miss Chappelle spoke to the PTA she surprised her audience with the remark that the greatest problem she had in her school was with language. Only five of her class of 35 pupils spoke English at home. We must not forget the look at the United Nations by five Beckenham County School girls in the summer holidays of 1949. Joan Gear, Valerie Wykes, Jean Overton, Evelyn Eminton and Joyce Veltom out of a party of about 30 from England spent six days at lectures and discussions about the work of the UN followed by four days climbing in the Swiss mountains.

The Foreign Travel Fund

1956 trip to Switzerland. L to R Misses Handley, Cooper, Pelling, Wiseman and Walters

The Travel Fund grew out of a discussion among the U6 (to which Pauline Crichton belonged) during 1947. It was intended to help towards the expenses of girls who wished to travel abroad with a school party or attend an activity like a field trip in this country. The first money raising effort by the U6 was a raffle but then much hilarity was caused by a 'Baby Show' consisting of photographs of staff and prefects when babies. Not to be outdone, the L6 ran a lunch hour Fun Fair with sideshows, competitions and fortune telling.

TWO   MISS HENSHAW 1944-1963

Miss Henshaw was the question master of Twenty Questions with Miss Wiseman, Miss Preston, Miss Walters and Miss B Taylor. The second form joined in, cleaning shoes and bicycles and running an oddments sale. Wedgwood House sold lemonade and set up a foreign stamp sale. All these activities raised a total of £62 18s 6d. Donations from Victor Thornton and a Parents Association-run raffle and play brought the grand total to £141 3s 8d. Some of the U6 were the first to benefit as a party left on 6 August for Meiringen in Switzerland.

Thereafter, the Travel Fund Bazaar became a regular event on the calendar of the PTA, contributing greatly to the excitement of holidays abroad in those pre-package holiday times. Jean (Kerridge) Hemmings had the reputation of scallywag at school and was not allowed to join in with school holidays abroad. She still remembers having her hopes dashed by Miss Henshaw who told her 'not with this school but in your own time.' Jean says she must have been a terrible thorn in the Head's side. Several times she had stood trembling outside the door wondering 'what have I done THIS time.' The rejection gave Jean the impetus to travel and one year she hitchhiked round Denmark with her sister Marion; recently they were together again fly-driving round the beautiful, magical South island of New Zealand. Jean lives in Victoria, Australia with her second husband Eric but frequently returns to England to check up on her three sons and their families. Marion did even better as she became International Tour Leader with the American Express for many years and travelled worldwide.

Extracts from 'Fifty Years On'

Linda (Hardy) Young says 'Watching my husband's high school reunion in Vancouver, I was struck by a need to be reunited with all my friends who started at the BGSG in 1948. On return to California, I enlisted the help of my dear friends Merrill (Salter) Drzymala from Toronto and Christina (Watt) Rex in UK. After years of faxes, transatlantic calls, e mails and endless letters, they not only produced our handbook but had a wonderful reunion fifty years on in the old school in 1998.'

A touch of nostalgia from Ruth Hixson
Odd things spark a memory, like eating cherries. Miss Kobrak bought a large bag of cherries and on a boat trip on the Thames to Kew we had a game to see who could spit the stones the furthest into the wake of the boat. I loved to listen to her reading 'Little Women' and 'Emma' during needlework lessons. Cooking a roast dinner reminds me of Miss Atkinson. What would she say to today's microwave culture?
How different are our tasty roast dinners from those horrid dinners we suffered at Cyphers and Lloyds! Who can remember 'Thames Mud' and 'Concrete and dishwater?'

Watching a period drama with ladies and gentlemen dancing a minuet, I picture my class of 12 year olds in white blouses and navy bloomers (complete with pocket on the leg) doing their best to look elegant!

TWO   MISS HENSHAW 1944-1963

Playing on the mound by Jennifer (Durell) Elgar
The mound was a very large pile of earth dug out from the foundations when the extension was being built on the school field. It was the size of an Iron Age barrow ideal for hiding behind or even sliding down. There was a smaller mound in Cyphers. Four of us, Glenda, Tessa, Corinne and I would rub our beret badges in the earth to avoid looking like new girls.

Ann (Gully) Patterson and the lime trees
One of my lasting memories of school is wandering along to the station on hot summer afternoons after school with the lovely perfume of those huge lime trees which lined Lennard Rd. I shall be very disappointed if they are not still there as the smell of lime blossom always takes me back to those days.

Brenda (Jelly) Booker and her Golden Years
Was it really fifty years away, it only seems like yesterday!
We all looked the same in our white square-necked blouses, navy tunics and black buttoned house shoes, trudging through the park for House afternoons, getting used to a seven day school week, dressing up for house parties and visiting Cuckmere Haven to discover oxbow lakes. What happy days but, always in a hurry, I married at nineteen with Ann Gully as one of the bridesmaids. Now in our golden years I hope that wisdom and age enable us to make the most of every day.

Maureen (Gillespie) Jordan's memories of a rebel
Climbing trees by Willy Lott's Cottage at Flatford Mill in the dead of night waiting for badgers with Miss Robins; finding ourselves lost in the ice cave in the Trient Glacier on our journey to the Swiss Alps; ogling the boys on our hockey tour down the Rhine with the boys' school. Then there was eating forbidden ice cream on Victoria station and not wearing my beret; being with the boys behind the cycle sheds; trying to walk straight-backed down the corridors to be awarded a posture point----!

Pat (Russell) O'Brien has a paddle
'Patricia Russell, what are you doing?' were the first words ever spoken to me by Miss Henshaw.
I had been at school for two weeks when it rained hard and left deep puddles on the grass in Cator Park. On the way home, I took off my shoes and socks and otherwise in full school uniform including beret was paddling in the water. Sometimes I wonder how I ever learnt anything as I spent so much time outside Miss Henshaw's door. Does anyone remember 'bunking off' to see Frankie Laine at the Penge Empire? By the way, I loved school dinners and always drank my milk!

Valerie (Potts) Baylis) shares a joke
Two grammar school girls were sitting in a local hostelry clutching the price of two half pints of shandy. A large tin-rattling lady bore down on them. 'Dr Barnardo's Home,' she shouted loudly. 'I didn't know he'd been away,' came the quick reply from the girls.

Pat (Logan) Williams and her gems of learning
Aprons we all made in the first form; mirrors to watch ourselves practise French sounds; cooking Irish stew and rock cakes; making those wonderful lawn knickers from personalised patterns; parading up Lennard Rd to games clad unattractively in Navy-blue knickers; the huge significance of wearing house shoes.

TWO   MISS HENSHAW 1944-1963

Elise (O'Neill) Baugh how things have changed!
Privileged to have won a scholarship to a fine school, I remember a relaxed and untroubled time when the most important event in life was the next hockey match and the most distressing was having to eat a pile of grated swede that I'd greedily taken in mistake for cheese! It was a time when competition and winning were not frowned upon and bullying was not part of school life. Parks were safe places for play and cycling to school was fun. 'Grass' grew on the lawn, 'coke' was used to stoke the kitchen boiler, mother cooked the 'joint' for Sunday dinner and 'ecstasy' we felt when exams were over.

Janet (Grant) Ellison in gratitude for
Miss Wiseman's incredible energy during Gilbert & Sullivan productions, Miss Taylor who gave so much time and talent to school plays and Miss Pelling who organised complicated scenic backdrops for both!

Gillian (Foulger) Craven and Miss Kobrak's writing
I certainly didn't want to go to Australia and to leave good old England on 21 March 1950 and so I told nobody, thinking that then it would not happen. We arrived in Aussie via the MV Dorsetshire on 5 May complete with my Art folder. Can you remember the handwriting that we had to do like Miss Kobrak's? At school I had to go from class to class showing it to everyone. I was quite a celebrity. The standard of education was lower than at the Grammar school where I had struggled to be in the middle of the class. Here I was never lower than third!

Gillian (Crewes) Moore-Martin goes from Beckenham to Bristol and back
School turned me into an art student at Bromley College, one of those described by the Kentish Mercury as 'looking as though they were shipwrecked years ago and have only just reached dry land.'

A teacher training course at the Bristol Academy landed me a job with a first year D stream class of 'Fagin's boys' at the local secondary school. Here I learnt about the world when you lived at the wrong end of town where hair was cut short by health inspectors, home life was minimal and where you would be given 6d to 'get lost' whenever 'uncle' visited. I decided to return to Beckenham and took a temporary job as a telephonist at London's Continental Telephone Exchange and stayed over 32 years. My final challenge was to take a course in engineering to install computerised International Exchanges before retiring to enjoy my allotment, grandchildren, music, theatre and exploring the UK by narrow boat.

Ann (Hills) Gamet uses her Maths
How many times do we actually USE any of that stuff rammed into our brains, say negative numbers? I discovered a negative number on my bank balance once I was married. How about the 3,4,5 Pythagoras triangle? Ideal for pegging out the beds on an allotment the shape of a parallelogram except that the tape we were using had been rescued from a skip and its numbers were indecipherable. Comments like 'if you hadn't chosen voluntary redundancy we would have enough money to buy the vegetables' were shrieked across the plot' until we dumped Pythagoras and resorted to guesswork. My favourite was in the days of circular skirts. That's IT! The circumference is your waist measurement from which you can find out the radius of the circle you need to draw on the fabric. If you're smart, the fabric is folded into quarters and only a quarter of the circle is drawn.

We didn't work out VAT percentages at school but that's easy. The present 17.5% has its decimal moved to the left for 10% which is halved and halved again. Personally I use a calculator.

TWO   MISS HENSHAW 1944-1963

Sylvia (Ratcliffe) Bunce on how to avoid sport
I look back fondly on school. Even now I go to classes and love sitting at a desk but the one area I tried to avoid at all costs was SPORT. Oh the horrors of holding up loose navy blue knickers with one hand and wielding a lacrosse stick with the other; the pain of someone tackling and bashing my delicate fingers or having my ankles beaten black and blue on the hockey field. Therefore the main concern occupying the thoughts of me and my friends Linda Hardy and Gillian Withers was how to avoid this torture.

We could take our chances with the spiders under the stage but the best idea was to install ourselves on the ledge of the round window on the way up to the balcony. Our bodies would form half-moons with our feet meeting at the bottom. Once the curtain was pulled we felt safe. We admired those icons of the playing fields like the cricketer Norma (Preston) Izard who became the England Women's Cricket Manager. And I love watching other people play tennis from the safety of my armchair. Happy Days!

Carole (Prichard) Barrs and Norma Preston
I caught up with Beckenham Grammar School when my daughter Caroline began playing cricket for England and began telling us how 'Norma' made them all behave. Those of us who were in Wedgewood House will know that 'Norma' was Norma Preston, our games captain. I still felt like a first former when I spoke to her!

Jill (Stansbury) Thomas and Toto
Do you remember our French text book about the family with the little boy called Toto?
 Perhaps someone in your class also translated Toto's search in the bureau as 'Toto searched in the secretary's drawers.' Then there were the lawn knickers we made in the sewing class with bias facings to the legs. Quite unwearable, but I can still make bias facings today. What about that religious retreat that we went on to Westgate on Sea shared by boys from King's School, Tonbridge? We had a midnight tryst in the grounds and the boys were obviously out for more than a religious retreat but we barred our bedroom door later and saved our souls.

Claire Hardisty and Valerie Dobb get together
Claire Sceats and Val Wilson, as they were, compared their bad moments at school. Among the many they've chosen these three. First there was their secret iagie baigie language that they spoke for about eighteen months to the frustration of parents, teachers and outsiders. Eg

Haigello, aigold gaigirl meaning Hallo Old Girl. Then the class was at Lloyds Pavilion where they had trestle tables. There was one at the back of the room with one end down like a slide. Every time the teacher turned her back to write on the blackboard you were 'dared' to run to the back, have a slide and get back on your chair before you were seen. Finally there was the time when all the five girls in the class called 'Ann' sat together in the front row and spoke in unison when the teacher called out the name Ann.

TWO   MISS HENSHAW 1944-1963

Barbara (Myers) Langridge at Lloyds

I look back on my six years at school with affection where I was taught the value of knowledge and the confidence to follow whatever path I chose.

Perhaps having lived half our lives through a time of war had a great influence on our calm acceptance of our first year at school being at Cyphers and later having lessons at Lloyds pavilion. Who could fail to remember trying to catch tadpoles in the stream at Cyphers and sliding down an escape chute dangling from a Lloyds pavilion window as part of fire drill? I am so pleased that my two daughters both went to the school at Langley Park.

Anne (Mottram) Simmonds 'could do better'

'Could do better' was a recurring phrase on my reports but 'boring and stressed' were words that were never used. We weren't pampered, coached or counselled and friendships made then have stood the test of time. I recall two visits to the Headmistress. The first was despite a letter from my father, having a day's absence from school after spending the night nursing a puppy sick with meningitis was not acceptable. The second was when Dr Schofer detected that my German homework was more like Corinne Golder's than mine! However, I chose one of Miss Henshaw's suggested careers, 'teaching' and rose to the dizzy heights of Deputy Head of a primary school.

Christina (Rex) Watts 'Miss Wiseman would have been pleased'

The further I am from my schooldays, the more I appreciate them. Despite my best efforts I received an excellent education and had my lifelong passion for the human voice nurtured by Miss Wiseman. Post school, I studied singing privately then after 5 years' music study gained LRAM and became Head of Music at a leading Warwickshire independent school.

Jane (Penny) Sackville and her happiest days

The really happy days for me were not at the main building but at Cyphers and Lloyds. At Cyphers we were not given homework except for French vowel sounds and in Maths you could run out of class and go all the way round the building without being noticed. The Lloyds Bank Sports Club was most welcome as sitting in a makeshift classroom using the tables normally used for teas was fun. At break times we explored the building, finding the men's toilets and huge communal baths used by the football and rugby players. The teachers were pretty mad though when one of us missed lessons to watch Dennis Compton batting in a county match in all his Brylcreemed glory. She wouldn't have far to go to watch County cricket today because the ground is now used for Kent County cricket.

Glenda (Thornton) Lindsay and <u>her</u> happiest days

How fortunate we were in our modern and forward-looking headmistress, Kathleen Henshaw, who aimed us at wide horizons and independence. Under her leadership, her excellent staff gave us an all-round education which prepared us for careers in the future, in my case in the world of nursing and midwifery. I have been most fortunate all my life and I attribute much of it to the rich, comprehensive education from the BGSG.

A Summary of June (Potter) Thomsitt's memories

All those shoes!

Making knickers in needlework that split when we bent down.

Walking up to the games field in Navy-blue knickers until the local ladies complained on behalf of their husbands.

Carole Hennessy eating large lumps of bread pudding.

TWO   MISS HENSHAW 1944-1963

Geography with Miss Marshall who always gave A if you copied everything from the board.

Chemistry with Miss Stephenson who had ambitions to be the first woman on the moon.

Peggy Spencer giving us ballroom dancing lessons with the boys.
School dances led by Miss Henshaw and Mr White, stately as two galleons.
Halter necked ball gowns made in the 5th or 6th form. Beryl's father was concerned that her vest would show!
House choir competitions where Blue House sang 'The Trout.'
Glenda Thornton's birthday parties at Thornton's Corner.
Games matches against other schools.

Anne Mottram's amazing skill at cricket.

Three friends send their memories from Malaga, USA and NZ

The three friends are Sandra (Homer) Nash from Malaga, Josephine (Warrilow) Bristol from USA and Pat Braddick from New Zealand. Mrs McPhail's form 1M was one of three classes located in the Cyphers' pavilion in 1950/51, only going to the main school for House afternoons. When they performed Alice in Wonderland in the summer term, Sheila Manning was Alice, Susan Holman was the White Rabbit, Marian Arthur the Dormouse, Sandra Homer the Mad Hatter and Josephine Warrilow the March Hare. The Queen was played by Jacky Scott with Brenda Porrer and Edna Talbot as the guards and Jacky Grimwood and Lesley Perkins the gardeners.

The cast of Alice in Wonderland, 1951 L to R Front Susan Holman, Marian Arthur, Sheila Manning, Sandra Homer, Josephine Warrilow, Back Jacky Scott, Jacky Grimwood, Lesley Perkins, Brenda Porrer, Edna Talbot.

Lunch break at Cyphers was great fun with trees to climb and to sit beneath but we were not supposed to cross the 'Forbidden Bridge' or paddle in the rivers. As time went on, Cyphers was not needed any more as the extension off the dining room in the main building was opened. Those of you who remember Cyphers fondly would be sad to see the remains of the pavilion after a fire in April 2003.

TWO   MISS HENSHAW 1944-1963

On the forbidden bridge at Cyphers L to R Joyce Beckett, Elisabeth Honey, Susan Holman, Josephine Warrilow, Marie Reardon

For the Coronation of the Queen on 2 June 1953, a representative from each form was drawn from a hat. Taken by Miss Wiseman and Miss Hatfield, the group left school at 4.00am to reach the allocated site at the kerbside on the way to the Abbey. While the Coronation was taking place, the party made its way home to watch the last part of the ceremony on 9inch TV screens with magnifiers on the front.

Coronation party, 1953 meeting at 4.00 am at the school

The sixth form made themselves 'comfortable' on the pavement

We had a long wait before the procession started; consequently street cleaners and the like were given a great ovation whenever they appeared. The dark colours of the school uniforms made a contrast between the grand procession when it finally came into view. The brilliant colours of the ceremonial uniforms, the ornamental carriages, the jewels and rich gowns of all involved were wonderful! The generous Queen Salote of Tonga won everybody's heart by defying the weather and insisting on riding in an open coach, but my lasting memory is of our young Queen, looking incredibly beautiful as she turned and waved at us as she passed by in the golden coach. *By Elizabeth Adams*

TWO   MISS HENSHAW 1944-1963

1953 L to R Back row Barbara Tindall, Iris Field, Ann Caws, Margery ?, Sally Crier, Sandra Homer, Valerie Norman, Pat Upton, Elizabeth Honey, Janet Le Warne, ??, ??. Middle row Lesley Perkins, Norma McLeod, Sally Thompson, Margaret Black, Brenda Wallace, Elisabeth McDonald, Pat Howard, Margaret Andrews, Janet Dormer, Susan Holman Front row Diane Ixer, Vivian Hollis, Maureen Moon, Anne Ellis, Mary Thurlow, Jean Bradbrook, Enid Long, Kathleen Sears, Ann McFarlane, Sonia Rees, Helen Sears, Miss Sybil Bell.

Particularly enjoyed was Miss Bell's choir and we knew that she was a former pupil at the school. Sonia Rees was in the Middle School Choir in 1952/53 and we were very proud of her when she became established as singer in the Crazy Gang and eventually in the 1960s played Maria in the Sound of Music at the Palace Theatre, the 'Connie' of our time!

Our favourite teachers were Sybil Bell and Olive Broomhead who must have been good friends because they were always laughing together. They organised our Alice in Wonderland production. We all had a wonderful time at school with excellent teachers.

U15 hockey team 1953 L to R Back row Anne Ellis, Diana Carvell, Sandra Homer, Jean Bradbrook, Ann Jolliffe Middle row Jackie Scott, Susan Holman, Miss Broomhead, Ann Benton, Audrey Seeds Front row Enid Long, Josephine Warrilow, Kathleen Sears

TWO   MISS HENSHAW 1944-1963

The distant figure of Miss Henshaw commanded great respect and affection. We have so many colourful memories in the classroom, on the sports field and of House activities. After more than 50 years we are scattered across the globe but are still in contact and visit each other whenever we can.

The gang leaving in July 1956. L to R standing, Josephine Warrilow, Sheila Crump, Ann Pirie, Pat Braddick, Jackie Scott, Sandra Homer. Sitting, Margaret Wakeling, Susan Holman

An unforgettable sight, by Millicent Oliver

The day was the 6 September 1952, the first day of the Farnborough Air Show. It was progressing nicely and we inspected the aircraft on the runways. We saw the Comet, the first jet airliner, a beautiful shining plane which resembles its namesake when in flight. There was the Canberra, which made the quickest flight yet over the Atlantic, there and back in about eight hours. Then came the most exciting part of the show, the exhibition of faster-than-sound flying by test pilot John Derry in the De Havilland D H 110.

All heads craned upwards as the announcer told us of its approach. The aircraft was a grey machine as the black one had developed engine trouble. We were very thrilled to see this famous airman who exactly this day four years ago, 6 September 1948, was the first British airman to exceed the speed of sound.

The plane looked like a flying wing as it was flying so fast we could not make out the nose and the twin boom tail. It made a power dive from 40,000 ft to pick up speed and crash the sound barrier. As Derry brought the plane down he left two puffs of white vapour behind. We heard the tremendous sonic bangs and then, while zooming above us at about 1,500 ft, the aircraft disintegrated. Over the loudspeaker we heard the announcer cry, 'My God, look out, look out.'

Fragments of the plane, which had been travelling at over 700 mph, hurtled across the aerodrome in a vivid cascade. Part of a wing crashed on to the runway, while the shattered tail fluttered down like a leaf in autumn.. The cockpit with Derry and Richards, his observer, crashed on the outskirts of the aerodrome. The twin engines shot up several hundred feet into the air and then spiralled wildly down like a ball of fire to crash into the crowds on the hillside. There was silence. From the pyre, a slender spiral of smoke drifted slowly on the faint breeze from the great hole in the ground.

TWO   MISS HENSHAW 1944-1963

The aerodrome looked as though a pitched battle had been raging for hours, where really this disaster had taken place in less time than it takes to read this. Crash tenders and ambulances rushed to the scene. Screams pierced the air and people were rushing madly about trying to help the injured. The display was temporarily suspended and we all went home. John Derry and Tony Richards will always be remembered as great airmen who gave their lives bravely in the cause of science and invention. It was a crash that I hope I shall never see the like again.

Ann Weir's Memories of School 1952-58

The first day at 'big school' was fraught with anxiety, as I couldn't get in! I was late and my way was barred into the corridors, so I went home.

My mum couldn't understand what had happened, but next day I was earlier and Miss Parsons (Geography) asked me for a note from my mother to say why I was not at school yesterday. I was quite honest and explained what had happened. She said I was a silly girl, as latecomers were to go in Miss Henshaw's door and write in the late book. I hadn't been told this and certainly would not have even thought of going through Miss Henshaw's door!

My main memory of Cyphers was meeting Marian Barber, now Young, and we are still good friends. She often gave me one of her sandwiches at mid-morning break. Our form went to the 'big school' on Day 1 (we had a 7 day timetable) with Miss Broomhead (PE), and we were the first ones to use the new buildings – classrooms beyond the hall.

I remember buying a school scarf, which I still have, and paid one shilling (5p) a week for 10 ·weeks to a Horne Brothers representative.

At Christmas we sang part of The Messiah at Holy Trinity Church, and I remember feeling special as it did sound good, although I am no singer.

In cookery class I overcame the fear of lighting a match. When I was little my mother had lit our gas oven and it had blown back and caused quite an explosion. Miss Hubble (an Australian) told me to light five ovens at the start of the lesson, and I was so frightened. Marian told me I must do it, so I did, and by the fifth one I was so confident I realised that Miss Hubble must have known about my fear and helped me to overcome it.

I remember outings – one in 1953 when the whole school went to see 'Our Young Queen' and 'The Conquest of Everest' at Beckenham Regal. I felt so proud as we came out of the cinema and marched back to school. Miss Ord (History) took us to London to see Wren's churches. I also remember going underneath Mount Pleasant Sorting Office car park to see Roman remains.

I also went with Miss Rabson to the French church in Soho Square, and though I wasn't that good at French, I still have the French New Testament we were given.

We went to the Old Vic to see John Neville in what they called the 'modern' Hamlet and Richard Burton in Henry V. We all used the theatre binoculars to see these impressive young actors, especially in the romantic scenes.

TWO   MISS HENSHAW 1944-1963

I have seen Yvonne Antrobus in one or two plays on TV and felt proud that she had been at our school. Her parents had opened a special day at school and, as I loved art, I was given the job of painting silhouettes with the aid of a projector [I was tempted to add extra to one of the teacher's noses, but of course I didn't].

We had a recital from an ex-pupil *(might have been Pat Carroll)* who played the Gollywog Cakewalk and Clair de Lune.   *Ann (Weir) Vickery*

The old Langley Lodge and the falling beech tree

Do you remember Hawksbrook Lane when there was still Langley Lodge belonging to Langley House at the end of the lane? The old beech tree seen in the picture came down with a crash one morning when we were coming to school, an event recollected by Lynda Christian in 1963.

Many girls would have walked past it that morning on the way to school, blissfully unaware that it was about to come crashing down. As I turned into the Lane I saw it fall and it was clear that there were girls in its path.

Miraculously, no one was seriously injured but two girls, Marilyn Vowell and Janet Bailey, were taken to hospital. I cannot remember how I and several other girls managed to negotiate our way around the tree which of course completely blocked the Lane, but we obviously did (how dedicated we were to our studies!) as we were treated for shock by staff when we eventually arrived!

After college, Lynda worked in publishing, advertising and accountancy, eventually returning to an educational environment working as a school business manager.

I have been at LPGS for ten years and the school has changed dramatically since my own education when it was Beckenham Grammar School for Girls, not least in that it caters for 1640 pupils and students as opposed to just under 600! My role here is extremely challenging but very satisfying and I feel that I make a real contribution to school life. In the May 2006 Ofsted report the business manager was singled out as 'providing exceptional service' – an accolade of which I am understandably extremely proud. One of my areas of responsibility is estate management. Given my one clear recollection of my own school days, it is probably not a surprise that I set aside fairly large amounts in the annual budget for the maintenance of trees!

TWO   MISS HENSHAW 1944-1963

When the girls moved into their new school in 1959, the birds would fly in and out of the hall during assembly. Ducks were often seen skimming their beaks through the wet front lawn for years afterwards. One morning, in the early 1980s, a handsome pair of Greylag geese was seen on the roof at the front of the school prospecting for a nesting place but in the end they disappeared.

Prefects 1951/52 L to R back row Anne Bowles, Kathleen Watkins, Adrienne Dart, Jane Luckman, Gillian Smith, Anne Guiver; middle row, Hannah Lilian, Shirley Swinyard, Joan Shepherd, Tessa Reardon, Margaret Mackay, Joan Hiller; front row, Beryl Ashley, Gillian Webber, Joyce Long, Hazel Ivil, Gillian Sanford, Tessa Cooper, Shirley Willis, Jean Mantle.

Janet Lambert's braided sixth form blazer and tie with yellow house badge, prefect's badge and cricket colours badge.

Athletics competitions started 1965

Prefect system ended as all U6 had duties under the Head girl with her two deputies

Girls in the U6 were no longer required to wear school uniform

Joan
Chreseson OBE

Jan 1964-Easter 1967

Maintained the excellence of her legacy

THREE   MISS CHRESESON 1964-1967

First Impressions

The editors of the 1964 school magazine decided to interview Miss Chreseson to find out her opinions and impressions of her first year as Headmistress of the school.

Do you think our standard of work would be better if we had fewer outside lesson activities?
Ans: No. The aim of education is twofold: firstly to provide the opportunity to study but secondly to learn to live with the responsibilities and obligations of a community. With increasing automation of the world of work, school must give training for the use of leisure.
What do you think of the House system?
Ans: I have never seen it so well thought out or working so well in a day school. In fact more activities should be House-centred and the seniors should be more adventurous, revealing hidden talents.
What do you think of school uniform?
Ans:It is practical, inexpensive, disguises social differences and gives everyone an equal social start. The seniors could have a certain amount of choice.
Do the prefects and sub prefects have enough authority?
Ans: They have as much authority as the staff but in such a large sixth form comparatively few girls have that authority. The House system gives opportunity for more people to have that responsibility.
Does a girls' school really need a strong games tradition?
Ans: A strong lively school will excel in this field but games like tennis and badminton with their social connotations should be encouraged in the sixth form although those who liked team games should be able to continue playing.
Have your impressions of the school changed during the year?
Ans: Miss Chreseson finished by saying her impressions had not changed radically since her arrival but had been deepened and enriched.

In the foreword to the magazine, Miss Chreseson had remarked on the exceptionally talented and mature group of seniors who had organised the School and House activities with the generous support of the Parents Association. Looking through the magazine you can see something of what is achieved by the Houses. Burrell supported Cheyne Hospital with toys made in house afternoons and helped at Kingwood House. Elwill House had won the House Shield the previous year and spent their House time with practices across the board. Goodhart worked hard to win the Drama competition with Sweeney Todd and had a wonderful House party with a Wild West theme. Langley recorded their year in verse starting with their Spanish theme party and taking presents to the children of Miss Sharman's Home in Dulwich and singing carols in the evening. Kelsey was Miss Rabson's House well known for the Fair that it ran each year for charity, pleased this year to welcome former pupil Miss Caley on to the staff. Raymond House celebrated 'An ugly bug ball' at its house party but also thought of others when they grew hyacinths in home made paper maché pots for the residents of Kathleen Moore Court. They knitted matinee coats for Stone Park Maternity Hospital and a blanket of squares for a refugee family. Their bottle stall at the Barnardo's fete raised a goodly sum, doubling that of the year before. Finally Style house had success across the board in games, singing, drama, winning the Reading competition. They have made a collection of brass rubbings from the local churches and the group carving in soap has become quite proficient. They supported the children's Mayflower Centre with Christmas toys and a summer party.

What to do after the exams by Sylwen Coope and Pauline Chase

The fifth form of the summer of 1964 acted as guinea pigs in an experiment proposed by Miss Chreseson to keep us out of mischief for at least a week after our exams had finished. We were not allowed to leave school as you are today.

THREE   MISS CHRESESON 1964-1967

The English Dept showed us 'The Importance of Being Earnest' starring Michael Redgrave and then we held a formal debate on 'This house deplores the introduction of politics into sport.' It was carried by a large majority. The Art and Science staff then escorted us to the museums at South Kensington which was very interesting but hard on the feet.

The Latin and Geography staff took us to Arundel to the castle owned by the Duke of Norfolk and also round the attractive town. The Latin divisions had visited the Roman villa at Bignor on the way to see the mosaic floors and barely had time for the castle although they made friends with three cows in the field.

Design from the Roman villa at Bignor

After that we stayed at school where Miss Webb showed us superb slides of her visit to Greece and then the rest of the Maths Dept were able to teach us how to sew parabolas with amazing results. We listened to French records with Mrs Trotter and examined a fascinating display of Miss Rabson's French stamps. Mademoiselle Lachavette organised a quiz on France, Mrs Bayley showed us her slides of Southern France and Miss Lewis talked about French food, including snails and frogs' legs.

Ex-pupil Patricia Carroll gave us a piano recital showing us what to look for in the pieces before she played them but we were somewhat daunted by the skill and speed with which she played. Then the German staff played distinctly unmelodious music from Germany and showed us German films after which 'three distinguished actresses' performed two short and amusing sketches.

Finally the Scripture staff invited the down-to-earth speaker, the Reverend Austen Williams, from St Martin in the Fields and we enjoyed his inspiring talk leaving ample time for questions. This week provided something of interest for everyone and we appreciated that so many of the staff had taken part in it.

Miss Chreseson guided the school confidently and maintained its traditions at a time when the school's results were outstanding and probably not matched before or since. Her move to HM Inspectorate came about by a chance remark of a friend who had seen the advertisement by ILEA. At the interview, she was asked why she wanted to leave one of the best Grammar Schools in the country and she realised that it was too good and left her nothing to offer. As Miss Chreseson left at Easter 1967 to take up a position in HM Inspectorate, over half our ninety years had passed but now the school was to see more changes than ever before in its history.

A Message for the anniversary from Joan Chreseson OBE at Shrewsbury

When Miss Henshaw retired in 1964, I inherited a most successful school, one of the best state girls' grammar schools in the country. Miss Henshaw had been a great leader, energetic and innovative. The school was lively and there was excellence in every department. My first task was obviously to try to maintain this standard and if possible to enhance it. It took-time to develop relationships both within and outside the school and to form a view of directions in the future. I was back at school most week day evenings as there were so many activities demanding my presence.

THREE   MISS CHRESESON 1964-1967

The members of staff gave so freely and generously of their time and the parents were equally supportive. Nationally the tide of comprehension was swelling. Obviously great changes were to come in the foreseeable future. At present, the school, situated in a socially advantaged area, was highly selective. It seemed to me that the next stage would require fundamental change and radical thinking.

Local government reorganisation was also in progress in 1965. It was necessary to see what was happening in areas where comprehension was already taking place and to begin to prepare for it. This was when a career opportunity presented itself to me which I could not resist. There followed for me fifteen years of variety and interest with a return to my own subject, English, and a completely different way of working that I did not regret for an instant in my years of working in HM Inspectorate in the ILEA.

I regretted leaving Beckenham so soon. I enjoyed my time there and retain fond memories and admiration for its staff and pupils.

Joan Chreseson was awarded the OBE in the New Year's Honour's list of June 1980 for her work for the ILEA. She says she had a lovely day at Buckingham Palace with her brother and sister-in-law. Her question from HM was 'What do you do?' to which she answered 'I work for Your Majesty's Schools' Inspectorate,' curtseyed and tried not to fall over walking out backwards.

The Red Cross starts up again

On 22 April 1963, Divisional Youth Officer, Mrs Seabrook, set up a new Red Cross Cadet unit in the school with the intention of enrolling the juniors and maintaining their interest. For six weeks they learnt about the International Red Cross and formed into four sections, India, Ceylon, Mexico and Spain. Miss Chreseson was the Guest of Honour at their enrolment on 12 June by Mrs Davies the President of the Beckenham & Penge Division and over the next decade the unit went from strength to strength. A favourite occupation was to satisfy a never ending demand all over the world for To-Do boxes and Disaster Kits. The former consisted of crayons, paper and a game and the latter of a flannel, toothbrush, mug and string. They sent blankets and soft toys to S. Rhodesia (Zimbabwe today), the blankets being made from squares mainly knitted by the cadets' grandmothers. They worked for the Duke of Edinburgh's Bronze Award, ran a trolley shop at the Red House Old Peoples' Home and all passed their exams on first aid and mother craft. Their most enjoyed activities involved training days dealing with a 'bomb disaster' or a 'mock earthquake' where they could try out their first aid and stretcher bearing techniques. Mrs Seabrook left in 1970 when Mrs Lizius came as the new Cadet Officer but Sheila Muir of the L6 became an Assistant Cadet Officer. This was the Centenary Year of the Red Cross and their numbers at school tripled.

Princess Margaret comes to town

It was in April 1966 that HRH Princess Margaret, Countess of Snowdon, came to Bromley to launch a new bus for the elderly. It was presented by the Princess outside Bromley Town Hall on 20 April and Paula Lightfoot represented Miss Chreseson at the reception on behalf of the school.

Avril Smith takes the staff 'Round the world in 80 Days'

The day of departure was memorable with all the school watching from the field. Mrs Rosenberg hastily put the finishing touches to the balloon, while Miss Mead received a shock on changing the light battery.

THREE   MISS CHRESESON 1964-1967

The commotion was even greater when Miss Caley was seen racing across the field, having forgotten the time. Needless to say she was left behind. Some of the tender-hearted first formers burst into tears, thinking some staff might never return.

The balloon landed in the Paris Basin where Mrs Bayley involved herself in an argument with General de Gaulle. She was imprisoned by a French gendarme and Miss Lewis was last seen in a fashion shop. The balloon set off again in the direction of Spain where Dr Schofer was chased by a bull. They then set sail for Italy where unfortunately they lost two more members. Mrs Milburn became engrossed in the Colosseum and Miss Tilbury stayed to sketch the beauty of Naples.

The next step was Egypt where Mrs Lowe and Miss Webb set off on camels to the Pyramids to make some scale models and succeeded in proving Pythagoras' theorem. Working their passage on a steamer the remaining staff arrived in Hong Kong where Mrs Atkins decided to stay to teach the natives how to cook rice. The few survivors eventually reached Australia where Miss Brown became engrossed in a game of cricket and played so well that she was captured by the Aborigines who wanted her to play for them. After much searching, a boat was found going to Los Angeles where Miss Hawkins made a social call on Stravinsky and missed the train to New York.

Soon after this, the train broke down and Mrs Gee left the train to examine a crop of rare bananas. She was last seen being chased by Red Indians. Miss Pye-Smith was lost in the jungle while inspecting Macrodontia cervicornis, an unusual kind of beetle. The journey was finished by paddle steamer when the survivors arrived triumphantly back in England to where the Upper Sixth had kindly taken over their duties. They had proved the theory of Jules Verne and managed to get round the world in eighty days!

Elizabeth Thompson goes skiing with a party of 25 girls and the PE staff

Preparations for our skiing holiday began early in the Autumn Term when each member of the party was handed a vast sheet of exercise instructions and balls of pink and black wool. During the following weeks the exercises were performed daily to the accompaniment of moans and groans. When the art of decreasing had been mastered, pink and black bobble hats began to appear around the school, much to the curiosity of the less adventurous.

Still suffering from the rigours of Christmas, our party assembled at the end of the lane on the evening of 28 December 1965, wearing our now famous pink and black bobble hats. From London airport we flew to Zurich and continued our journey through the Alps by train to Locarno, arriving at our hotel for lunch the next day.

Locarno is situated on the shores of the beautiful Lake Maggiore near the Italian border. Instead of snow-covered slopes with pine trees, we found warm weather and palm trees. Our hotel was comfortable and the food was excellent----- chips with everything! There was no snow until we travelled up Mt Cimetta for our first ski lesson. The journey to Cimetta by funicular, cable car and chair lift was hair-raising at first. Then we overcame our fears and were able to appreciate the magnificent views over the lake and the snow-covered mountains of the Valais and Bernese Oberland.

THREE   MISS CHRESESON 1964-1967

Skiing proved easier than expected although our first attempts ended disastrously. We were shown how to fix our skis and then told to ski down the slope. Most of us chose to fall rather than disappear down into the trees. The next problem which recurred throughout the holiday was to find a way to get up. This was very difficult and many unorthodox methods were evolved.

Gradually the art of moving downhill on skis was mastered and lessons became more enjoyable. We were taught how to turn and traverse a slope and by the end of the holiday many of us could ski all the way down the main slope. Ski lessons took place in the mornings and some afternoons were spent practising but we had several excursions including a trip round the lake by steamer, a session on the ice rink and a shopping trip by coach to Locarno. Our eight day holiday passed all too quickly with only a few large bruises to show for our exertions. We thanked Misses Norvell, Wardman, Plastow and Brooke for taking us and for their help and encouragement.

The PE Dept's 'New Look'

From 1964, PE took on a completely different look. Cricket and lacrosse were no longer official school games but a wide variety of sports became available, especially for the sixth form. Badminton, table tennis, trampolining, and the rather bruising volley ball were popular and judo lessons produced even more battered and bruised bodies crawling round the school. The undefeated British Champion, Greta Stott, took the classes and a sixth form dance raised the money to buy the judo matting.

The greatest advance was the school's progress with athletics and by the summer term of 1966 the school entered an almost complete team for the District Athletics. The Intermediate and Junior teams were placed second and third respectively in their sections. In the Kent Minors' Athletic Championships, our First Year Team was first out of eight schools. Ann Upson and Helen Minting broke the 100 and 150 yards records and Angela Knott in the Long Jump, clearing 14ft 6.5ins. By 1968, Ann, Helen and Angela were competing in the All-England Championships at Portsmouth.

Although few girls played cricket and lacrosse, the school still won the Gravesend Cup and Jacqueline Hodson was selected to play goalkeeper for the Kent Junior lacrosse team. This was to be the last time that the schools played the Beckenham/Gravesend cricket match and the cup stayed in the archives at Beckenham.

Swimming lessons were popular and the school team was second in the District Swimming Gala with Rosemary Lock, Angela Knott, Mandy van Cuylenburg, Hilary Brown and Christine Payne selected for the District Team. Finally the building of a school canoe resulted in growing enthusiasm for outdoor pursuits.

THREE   MISS CHRESESON 1964-1967

<u>To Rupert with apologies for ill-treatment by Anne (Scade) Bambridge of III10</u>

Oh, yellow bear with button eye,
Minus two legs and an arm,
I love you, dearest teddy bear,
You'll come to no more harm.

All day long you sit and think,
And gaze with your one eye,
You remember when I was small
In the terrible days gone by.

I hurled you up and down the stairs
With not a thought for your pride,
Let alone your physical self
Oh you might have gone and died

I pushed you in the oven when
My mother began to bake,
You came out stiff with a burnt black nose,
A yellow teddy cake.

I put you in the bath one day,
'Cos dirty I thought you were,
You came out clean all right my friend
But you hadn't any fur.

I threw you in the dustbin
I'd had enough of you then
But you came back the very same day
Via the dustbin men.

I took you to the seaside,
In the summer the following year
A cheeky crab had a new fur coat,
When he borrowed your tatty left ear.

Then all of a sudden I realised,
What a wise old teddy you were,
You listened to all my grumbles
Without turning the few hairs of your fur.

And now my faithful teddy bear,
These words I say to you,
Please, oh please forgive me,
And say, 'I love you too!'

THREE   MISS CHRESESON 1964-1967

School Uniform no longer for the UVI

Here we see Miss Chreseson's 'new look' for the U6 in the winter of 1965 when they were on a visit to the Daily Express.

Larger picture L to R, ??, Janet Rogers, Pamela Duberry, Janet Batch, ??, Helen Lyford, Jennifer Meads, ??, ??.

Frances (Bates) Boyden 1963 -70 had three Headmistresses

Miss Henshaw Autumn term 1963
Miss Chreseson Spring term 1964
Mrs. Molnar Autumn term 1966

Uniform supplied by school shop Bryant's of Croydon
Winter
Navy tunic, white blouse, school tie (navy with narrow pale blue and pink stripes), navy jumper or cardigan (mine hand-knitted), white socks, navy gaberdine coat with belt, navy velour hat with hat band (navy, pale blue and pink) worn with brim turned down at the front, up at sides and back, elastic sewn on. Black lace-up shoes (outdoor), black shoes with strap (indoor, known as house shoes).

One of the most exciting ventures this year, this gabardine has a sinuous line. In long, lithe proportions, the collar takes an expressive sweep across the chest. The essence of modernism is contained in the double breasted front, its magic sense of balance extending to the slanting pockets. For that lavish peak of femininity, the sleeves should come well down the hand and the hemline well below the knee to give the suggestion of 'I've got to grow into this.'

THREE   MISS CHRESESON 1964-1967

The plain white cotton and simple cut give the desired suggestion of 'no nonsense.' The shirt effect is quite masculine and efficient, and in fact a crisp, efficient male is the ideal wearer. The starched white collar is particularly business-like and adds a scholarly tone. Our conclusion is this is a design for a man.

Summer
Dress made up from material from school shop by my mother (ready made also available, though not as good). Panama hat with hat band and worn as velour hat. Navy blazer with school badge (white horse of Kent), navy, pink and pale blue piping.

Variations higher up the school
Navy skirt instead of tunic, which could be worn in the summer too. Blazer - white piping (forgotten what this signified - age or position e.g. prefect?) Small round hat, not velour, with turned up brim with hat band. Boater with hat band.

Games uniform
White, square necked aertex (?) blouse, navy pleated gym shorts with embroidered initials. Black plimsolls, black hockey boots. Kept in shoe bag with embroidered name.

Satchels/desks
We had satchels to take books to and from school.
We put our exercise books and textbooks etc in our desks in our form rooms. The desks were single and had inkwells. The watery school ink was made up in the room to the left of the left-hand toilets on the bottom corridor and often got bits of blotting paper in them. I bought my own bottle of ink/cartridges depending on the type of fountain pen I had.
 If any writing was found on a desk we had to go back to sit at the same desk we had been in for a particular class, so that the culprit could be found.

First day at school and Forms
We were allowed in the front door on our first day and then not until we were in the VI form. We went to the hall and were told which forms we were in. Roman numerals were used to signify the form, Arabic for the number of the form room. Mine were I 37 Mrs. Milburn (form mistress), II 28 Miss Poole, III 10 Mrs. Bradford, IV 12 Miss Hague, V 8 Mrs. Bayley, LVI 27 (?), UVI 15 (?) Rooms 8, 10 and 12 were on the ground floor, 27, 28 and 37 were on the top floor and 15 was the Small Hall. One-way system, the stairs near the Small Hall were for people going up and the ones near the library for those going down.

Houses
Houses were a very important part of school life. I was in Elwill and the house badge was green. At dinnertime we ate in our houses on the raised area and in the hall. We were assigned to tables of eight and always had to sit with the same girls, who were from different years, first form to UVI. I suppose this was so that we got to know girls of other ages and gave the older girls some leadership responsibilities. When the ruler was passed to our house the first formers had to go the serving hatch for the food. The UVI girl served the main course/pudding and we passed round the vegetables etc. I think the ruler started in a different place each day. On the last day of each term the roles were reversed and the UVI went to get the food for the first formers to serve - a nerve-racking experience trying to make sure that the pie, for example, was cut into equal parts. I have a pale blue serviette with my initials and flowers embroidered in the school colours; however, I do not remember using it at school. My favourite pudding was chocolate pudding and chocolate sauce. There was a very sweet pudding called gypsy tart. We had jugs of a white frothy substance, which we called shaving cream.

Some brave, or foolhardy, girls would turn the jug upside down and upright again before the shaving cream fell out. Some girls brought packed lunches and sat at a table by the notice board by the corridor to the gym.

House afternoons

These were held on Day II after dinner in periods 6 and 7. In 1969-70 House afternoons may have been on Friday afternoons if that is what H.A./P. on my timetable means. According to the Elwill House Report for 1969-70 House afternoon was once a fortnight. We prepared for the various house competitions - singing, drama e.g. a scene from 'The man born to be king'. These gave older girls opportunities for leadership and opportunities for working together for us all.

House parties

We also prepared for the house parties, which were held in the autumn term and to which we invited our parents. We organised the invitations, decorations, food and entertainment. I remember feeling very grown-up at my first one as I had new clothes, shoes with heels and my first stockings for it. I had a green v-necked top and skirt.

Timetables

Until 1969-70 we had seven-day weeks so we did not do the same lessons on the same day of the week. This was to have enough time for all the lessons and activities. Lessons were 40 minutes long from 9.20 to 3.45 with 20 mins morning break and 1hr 25 mins for dinner.

Subjects: First and second forms - Art, English, French, Games, General Science, Geography, Gymnastics, History, Latin, Mathematics, Music, Needlework, Religious Instruction, Speech Training plus House Afternoon and Preparation. Third form - as above except that we had Art or Cookery, General Science was split into Biology/Physics with Chemistry and one Gymnastics session was replaced by Dancing.

Fourth and fifth forms O levels

Everyone took English Language, English Literature, French, Mathematics, Latin or German or Spanish, P.E., Singing and Scripture and we had to choose one subject from each group:

A. Art/Housecraft/Music/Physics/History

B. Chemistry/Religious Knowledge/Geography/Biology

C. Biology/Physics/Religious Knowledge/Intensive German or Russian

D. History/Geography/Biology/Chemistry

We were expected to take one science subject.

I chose History, Religious Knowledge, Russian and Chemistry and did Latin. I dropped Religious Knowledge in the fifth form to spend more time on my Russian. In the fourth form we had one period of Social Studies and in the fifth form Current Affairs instead. I had three free periods in the fifth form We didn't have Speech Training in the fourth or fifth forms.

Sixth form

I took English Literature, History and Latin A levels. Other subjects - LVIth Bio 2 (?), British Constitution (for an O level), General Studies, History of Art, Physical Education, Scripture, Sg (singing?), Speech Training plus House Afternoon and 9 free periods. - UVIth Physical Education, Speech Training and H.A./P. (House Afternoon and Preparation?) and 8 free periods.

Additional comments on subjects

Cookery

Only in the third form. One recipe stands out - that for cheese, onion and potato pie.

Needlework

We had to make a bag from gingham to keep our needlework in.

One year we made baby doll pyjamas then in fashion.

THREE   MISS CHRESESON 1964-1967

Physical education
Gymnastics. Dancing 1965-66 Games Winter - hockey and netball. Summer - tennis and athletics (rounders in lower school)

Those in IV form and above played lacrosse and cricket.
When I was in the III form 1965-66 I remember playing in the house cricket team and was looking forward to playing it again the next year as one of our games. (One of the games mistresses was in the England women's cricket team.) However, we had a new games mistress (Miss Norvell) and cricket was replaced by athletics. I never played lacrosse so maybe that was stopped too in 1966-67.

Swimming
I think we had weekly swimming lessons at Beckenham Baths at some time in the early years, but I'm not sure how long for. It isn't on my timetables, though the first period for gym in the I and/or II form could have been used for it. We caught the train back from Clock House and got off at Eden Park. When we had the swimming gala the whole school went there and back by train. The showers were communal and we had to run through them.

Speech Training One of the things we had to do was to prepare a one minute talk.

April Fools' Day
We did various things: went to the wrong rooms or turned our chairs round so that we faced the back of the classroom. In the III form we planned to balance the waste paper basket on the form room door, but decided not to. Instead we put an upturned beaker full of water on our form mistress's desk. When she picked it up the water went over the desk. In the V form our form mistress played a trick on us and told us that we had to write an essay for English and we believed her!

Break
We bought currant buns at break. This came to an end when a father complained that there weren't enough. After that we could buy biscuits, such as, McVitie's chocolate digestives (milk and plain). They were sold by girls in the area near the hatches. My friends and I asked for the paper from the ends of the packets and taped them together to decorate our form room notice board.

Houses in the Biology Woods
The Bilge Woods, as we called them, were beyond the netball courts near the Small Hall.
In the first or second (?) forms we made houses there. Some people brought pieces of carpet.
Eventually either we were stopped or gave them up of our own accord.

Miss Cutler's death
We missed assembly as our form had been swimming. We came in via the gym entrance and walked up the stairs and were told to sit in the changing rooms. Then we were told that Miss Cutler had died.

The building of the boys' school in 1969
It was very noisy in the gym where we sat our O levels in 1969 as the boys' school was being built. The gym floor was covered so that it was not damaged by the desks etc.

Musical productions
The highlight of the year was the Gilbert and Sullivan production, which was put on by V and VI forms. I was only in The Gondoliers in 1968 as Miss Hawkins left the school, but I sang in the production of Dido and Aeneas in 1969.

<u>Holidays</u>
Russia April 1968. Mrs. Milburn and Mrs Barrett were the leaders.

Holland and Belgium April 1969. Mrs. Langley was the leader. I've kept brochures for the Frans Hals Museum in Haarlem, the Museum Boymans-van Beuningham in Rotterdam and the Musees Royaux des Beaux-arts de Belgique in Brussels. We also visited Amsterdam and maybe Bruges and probably went to other galleries/museums. The trip was for those taking Art A level. There were some spare places so some other girls and I were able to go.

A History Outing to the Commonwealth Institute

A visit to the Commonwealth Institute with Mrs Vanes in February 1967. Jackie Grace and Sally Randall are on the left of the picture which was taken by the Manchester Guardian

Sally Randall today

Jackie remembers the outing to this day as she was captivated by the relief map of Australia and other Australian exhibits. She promised herself that she would go there one day. Although her first marriage did not work out, her new partner had work in Singapore and she left the UK to travel with him: Malaysia, Thailand, Vietnam, Indonesia, Hongkong and of course Australia. She took up water skiing, scuba diving and squash and set up her own business with Hewlett Packard as one of her biggest clients.

Finally she met and married Dick Leitch and lives in Bali with their daughter Katie Grace, born as an unexpected gift on 31 July 1997. Over the past few years, Jackie has taken to novel writing and is very hopeful of finding a publisher, so all you Adremian readers, please look for a novel by Jackie (Grace) Leitch called 'The Unknown Visitors' and help her make the 'big time.'

Pauline Molnar

1967-1973

who initiated the present school badge

Style family brass rubbing from St George's church by Jane Dawson

FOUR   MRS MOLNAR TEMPORA MUTANTUR

Tempora mutantur, et nos mutamur in illis

Let us make sure the changes are always for the better

Pauline Molnar (née Curson) was a scholarship boarder and head girl of King's High School for Girls, Warwick during the 1940s. The King's High School had been established in 1879. Pauline had gone to the school from her native Coventry; she lived in its beautiful, 17th-century house and developed a love of classical literature that formed the foundation of her career.

In 1947, with examination excellence in English, Greek, Latin and French, Pauline won a scholarship to read Classics and English at Newnham College, Cambridge and chose a career of teaching.

Pauline's first post was in Cirencester, followed by London schools. Langley Park was her first Headship where her elegant presence and rich melodious voice will always be remembered.

One lasting change was forced upon us at this time because with the reorganisation of Greater London we became part of the Borough of Bromley, no longer controlled by Kent. Since we could no longer lay claim to the Invicta horse, Mrs Molnar decided that we needed a badge more relevantly ours. Jane Dawson, the Head Girl, researched the history of Langley Park mansion where the school stands, discovering its association with the Style family; she contacted Commander Style of the Watering branch for permission to use the fret and fleur de Lys of the arms of his family for the school badge. The adoption of the new badge in 1969 corresponded with the fiftieth anniversary of the opening of the school and remains unchanged to this day.

Another welcome change of Mrs Molnar's time with the school was the renewal of the association with the Boys' School when it moved from its site in Penge to its fine new building in Park Langley in January 1969.

The school roll was steadily increasing and plans needed to be made to cater for the increasing range of ability and interests as well as the greater numbers in a school destined to become comprehensive. To this end, Mrs Molnar decided to organise the school into six house areas with mixed ages in registration groups similar to that experienced by Miss Fox's school in the late 1930s and early 1940s. True to her Classics background, the houses were to be called Lambda, Pi, Sigma, Gamma, Beta and Kappa (**L**angley **P**ark **S**chool **G**irls **B**eckenham **K**ent). House colours were sought linked to the initial letters so Lambda was yellow (lemon), Sigma was red (scarlet), Gamma was green, Beta was blue, Pi was purple and Kappa was -khaki! In the present school it became Kingfisher blue and Beta was omitted.

When Mrs Molnar left us to become the Head of Mayfield School, Putney, it was the largest comprehensive girls' school in the country. She organised the management of this prodigious school and made a personal impression on all who were there for her consideration, efficiency and of course her fashion sense.

Following her formal retirement to Warwick with her Hungarian-born engineer husband, Alec Molnar, she continued to teach English at local schools and tutored Latin and Greek privately. She was heard reading on Radio 4's 'Poetry Please' in 2003 for the Landor Society of Warwick of which Pauline was a founder member.

FOUR   MRS MOLNAR TEMPORA MUTANTUR

Fittingly, this poem 'Farewell to Italy' was read at her funeral in November 2005 as a tribute to a much loved and respected lady.

Farewell to Italy

I leave thee, beauteous Italy! No more
From the high terrace, at even-tide,
To look supine into thy depths of sky.
Thy golden moon between the cliff and me,
Or thy dark spires of fretted cypresses
Bordering the channel of the milky way.
Fiesole and Valdarno must be dreams
Hereafter, and my own lost Affrico
Murmur to me but in the poet's song.
I did believe (what have I not believ'd),
Weary with age but unopress'd by pain,
To close in thy soft clime my quiet day
And rest my bones in the mimosa's shade.
Hope! Hope! Few ever cherish'd thee so little;
Few are the heads thou hast so rarely raised;
But thou didst promise this and all was well.
For we are fond of thinking where to lie
When every pulse hath ceas'd, when the lone heart
Can lift no aspiration---reasoning
As if the sight were unimpair'd by death,
Were unobstructed by the coffin lid,
And the sun cheer'd corruption! Over all
The smiles of Nature shed a potent charm,
And light us to our chamber at the grave.

Rebecca Abbott's Musical Enjoyment

I was at the school from 1968-75 and my memories of Beckenham Grammar are very positive. In particular, I appreciated the strong musical tradition that it had, and may still have. It helped me develop my personal interest in music, particularly in singing, and I am currently enrolled in a solo singing course at the City Lit in London. Also, I met my husband Paul in an amateur operatic group, which I joined 20 years ago.

I have very fond memories of producing the lower sixth pantomime, Peter Pan in 1974 when we raised money for charity, as we performed it on a Friday evening to parents and friends as well as to the school. I have produced several shows in London since then, in particular a production of Princess Ida in Holland Park, which sold out every night. My amateur operatic society put on a joint production with our sister company, the Village Light Opera Group, based in New York, one week in the summer of 1990. My career has taken me all over the place and all over the world. I have worked in ethical business and human rights, publishing, and in the charity sector, and currently work in the public sector, with the Department of Health's Prison Health programme.

Rebecca celebrates New Year

FOUR MRS MOLNAR TEMPORA MUTANTUR

I live and work in Central London, and have always lived in London apart from short stints in Melbourne and Vancouver.

Back to Beckenham Grammar, it's true to say that the support of my biology teacher, and twice form mistress, Pat Manning, who coached me for a scholarship to Imperial College, will never be forgotten, and is much appreciated.

What really happened at Langley Park School for Girls by Janice Wright (1969-1974)

Firstly there was the uniform. How smart (?) we all looked in our matching navy blue tunics, white shirts, school tie, white socks and choice of two designs of 'house' shoes! We had to wear black or brown lace-ups out of school and change into house shoes when we arrived. This was back in 1969. We also had navy blue school raincoats and a stupid hat with elastic that had to be behind your neck. I didn't really like the winter uniform but loved the candy striped summer dresses and no hat was required either in the summer term, though there was a boater if you wanted but not many girls wore that. Other school rules regarding uniform were knickers had to be named and navy blue, sleeves were to be rolled down, blazers were not to be worn in school, skirts were to be knee length and not longer than 4" below the knee and there was also a beret that cyclists (only) were allowed to wear. In the third form you were allowed to wear a skirt instead of a tunic, but by the time I got to the third form they changed the uniform quite drastically and tunics were no more. It was a navy skirt, a pale blue shirt and a high necked navy jersey. Out went rules for house shoes, ties, coats. The hats were abolished too (I think), and the summer dress could be any summer dress in blue, so we all went off to Etam and bought the latest A-line mini dress in pale blue. After the first year, many of us used to abuse all the rules, skirts would be hitched knicker high, or we'd get shoe grazing length navy skirts. I used to wear silver platform shoes (always put on just round the corner from my house).

My favourite teacher was Miss Swann. She was the PE teacher and PE was my favourite class. Early on in the first year, she decided to run a trampoline club and I duly went along to the selection jump one lunch hour. I loved trampolining and happily I was selected to join the club. I think this was why she became my favourite teacher. Miss Swann also started a diving club which was at 8am in the morning at West Wickham swimming baths, so I was up really early for this as I had to do my paper round and cycle to West Wickham (about 2-3 miles) first. She also ran after-school games. I was very sad the summer day she left; PE was never the same again.

The Trampolining Incident

When I was in the third form, I got together with a girl from the second year who was in the trampolining club too. We used to wait after school for everyone to go home, then we would sneak down to the gym to get the trampoline out. We would jump on it for ages, then fold it up and put it away again. We didn't want to get into trouble if we got injured, so we said we'd drag either of us to the bottom of the stairs if we fell off the trampoline or anything and make out we had fallen down the stairs. We did this many times, and if the caretaker ever said anything to us being in school at 5pm, we just said we were allowed and that we had to practise for a competition. Eventually though we got caught and all hell broke loose. My form teacher or maybe a selection of teachers went absolutely mad at me. I had led a younger girl astray and had risked our necks and therefore I was not allowed to stay after school for any activity (which was a punishment to me because I used to stay after school most nights for hockey/netball/athletics/judo etc).

FOUR   MRS MOLNAR TEMPORA MUTANTUR

Worse though, was the fact that they punished my whole class too, which was grossly unfair because they knew nothing about it. So not only did I have my punishment, I had girls in my class having a go at me because they couldn't go to sports activities either. So I had to go to the PE teachers and beg them to punish only me and not my class mates. I think they probably relented in the end. Then the final bit of my punishment was to stand by the front door and say goodbye to all the staff as they went home, this was so that they could all see where I was and what I was up to. When they had all gone home, I then had to wait for the headmistress to say that I could go home, but I was allowed out of the front door because she needed to see I was off the school premises. I felt that this punishment went on for ages but it was probably only for a week or two.

Last day at Langley Park

July 1974. Many of us were leaving and not going on into the 6th form. So we decided to buy alcohol on the way to school (in our school uniform!) and drink it when we could. I think cherry brandy was the favoured tipple. Of course we all got drunk and I remember about six of us ending up in the sick bay. A couple of the girls were crying and being sick. I remember feeling fine and being indignant as to why I was in the sick bay when I was fine! I begged them not to call my parents (who were much stricter than the school), but to no avail. My father was called and my last journey down the 'lane' was in the back of my dad's car. …. And yes I did get told off at home.

The days of the genetic mice

Helped by her mates Gillian Cornthwaite, Deborah Clarke and Catherine Morley, Geraldine Dudley ran the 'zoo' that lived in room 18. In the autumn term of 1969, they bought three 'genetic' mice whose offspring numbered about eighteen to be used by the sixth form in their genetic studies and sold on to Field Club members. The brown guinea pig, Henrietta, was mated twice with the albino Bumpkin. Of her first litter, only Phoebe survived but all four of her second litter went  home with members. They acquired four new animals; the three hamsters were albino, gold and white and gold and brown and the female jird was bred with a male belonging to a first former. They also had a tankful of guppies, two slow-worms and some fancy goldfish. Eventually they inherited two chinchillas and Flopsy and Mopsy, two Netherland dwarf rabbits. Unfortunately, one of the chinchillas escaped and popped up on the front of the stage during the school play which meant that their days at school were numbered although his appearance brought the house down.

Lorraine Rumph's Impossible Schoolgirl of 1968

There she stands in all her glory: the ideal schoolgirl of Langley Park! Her panama hat is cream and round, with the brim turned down only at the front. Her hatband sports the school colours, clean and bright. Her blazer is not clogged with grime and fluff. No dandruff mars the collar; her shining hair has none. The braid round the edge is intact and the pockets have no unsightly bulges. Her dress is clean, crisp and neat; the hem is the uniform four inches above the knee. Her long white socks are uninitiated to mud or grease. Her regulation black shoes almost dazzle you. Opposite her stands the ideal schoolgirl. Hatless she stands, her hair billowing in the wind. She stares at the other girl. Her ice-cream melts down her grubby dress which barely covers her posterior.

FOUR   MRS MOLNAR TEMPORA MUTANTUR

The dress is almost as short as her blazer drooping over her shoulder, torn and dirty, the elbows sagging sadly, pleading guilty to a long hard life of rubbing on desk tops. Her long socks have slipped down round her ankles, bulging despairingly from want of elastic. Are those shoes under that thick caked mud?

She stands staring at the prodigy in the correct uniform. She turns abruptly in disgust. In the shop window the wax model ignores the gesture and stands stolidly in her perfection.

Jenny Evans cycles on a wet morning in 1971

Coming to school in the rain, girls seldom speak,
Intent on keeping their hats on, their hair dry.
Heads bowed against the rain----
Submission or defiance?
Bootless girls, pussyfooting through the puddles,
Tangles of umbrellas,
Shying from cars as they send up sheets of
Dirty water,
Drowned rats in the classroom;
Putty-coloured socks on the radiators;
Wet gloves at twenty five to four.

But I've got a
Sunshine-yellow rain hat-
I don't mind coming to school in the rain.
Like a North Sea fisherman I brave the storm,
My bicycle dividing a tidal wave as I
Splash through the puddles.

Granted I look like an advertisement to sell kippers;
Granted my hat's too big and falls over my eyes
Granted I crash into parked cars because I can't see---
But my hat keeps off the rain.

Sports Highlights

Carole Gould has belonged to various gymnastic clubs from a young age and is now a member of the Ladywell Gymnastic Club which she joined when it first started three years ago. She came first in both the London and SE Tumbling Championships and the Apparatus Championships and was selected in November 1970 to represent England in Cardiff in the international match, England v Cardiff.

Sixth form games
For the past year, horse riding has been added to the range of sixth form options which already included golf, tennis, judo, swimming, table tennis, driving and trampolining They have the opportunity to follow a term's course in six activities in the hope that they will receive a basic knowledge and skill in a new leisure time activity which they can pursue after leaving school.

FOUR   MRS MOLNAR TEMPORA MUTANTUR

Snippets from Lynne Conolly (née Ainsworth)

Miss Cutler, Head of Lower School, leading the prayers in Assembly to ask for a peaceful resolution of the Cuba crisis. Rows of little girls sitting cross legged on the floor of the Music Hall with upturned faces. We left the hall discussing as to whether Cuba was anywhere close?

Going on a snowy, outward-bound type holiday in Wales. Freezing cold on truckle beds. Being woken on the first morning at 6am by a bagpiper who was in hideously close proximity to the tent. Sandie Mattingly (now Hughes) and I decided we were in hell! Actually the holiday was massive fun even if we had to buy out the local shops' Mars bars to supplement our nutritionally dubious meals. Jamie Oliver where were you??? (Not born)

I played God in the Wakefield Cycle – mainly because it required a strong off-stage voice. I wasn't too keen on the 'off-stage' bit and only agreed to take the part if I was also given '2nd woman' who had a wonderfully purple passage when her child was killed. Great! I also remember in the same play slipping grapes in Lizzy Pote's shoe before she went on stage to do a serious monologue. Hysterical giggles in the wings.

In the Lower Sixth I played Kate Hardcastle in 'She Stoops to Conquer'. This was the first joint production with the boys' school which had just moved on site. Surprisingly there was a huge resurgence of interest in Drama! Everyone getting out of school by 100 yards and immediately repositioning their summer boater or winter velour hat to an illegal and perilously perched position on the back of the head.

Huge navy PE knickers!!! They actually had a small pocket in them to carry your handkerchief. (Please God don't let any boy see me in these). Bridget Jones doesn't know the meaning of 'big pants'!

PS My mother was a strength of the PTA but I think she kept quiet about me!

Duke of Edinburgh's Award Scheme

Starting in 1970, several girls had gained their Bronze Award and were working for their Silver or Gold Awards by 1972. It was not so much the lectures on keep-fit, make-up and social services that attracted members to the group but the expeditions. One group remembers getting lost on the Biggin Hill Airfield and finding themselves on the east-west runway with planes passing them on either side. Their practice expedition on Camber Sands was a catastrophic washout but Canoeing at Cuckmere was more successful. Gillian Briggs, Gillian Watts and Barbara Judge with Mrs Baker and PE mistress, Wendy Manning, were the leaders who kept the group on its feet.

Parminder Bhachu's Langley Park School Narrative

Let me start by telling you about how I got to the school in the early part of 1969 – it was around February or March or so I think, so it was well into the academic year.

I came from Rockhills School for Girls in Anerley which was a Secondary Modern School for "non-selective sectors" of British pupils. I use this highly charged term "non-selective" as it was in the letter my parents had received after I had been tested at Beckenham Town Hall to determine my designation for a school within Bromley. This had happened in the first week of my arrival in London in 1968. I had come from Kenya which had a British colonial education system (Africanized in the 1960s) consisting of O levels (Senior Cambridge as it was called there) and A levels – roughly the same system of examinations that operated in Britain at the time.

FOUR   MRS MOLNAR TEMPORA MUTANTUR

I had done well in school there before migration to Britain at the age of 14. But I did not do well at the multiple choice questionnaires I had been subjected to at Beckenham. Such questionnaires are difficult for most people unless there is familiarity with the local contexts, knowledge, and socialization to the cultural biases that are encoded in such assessment instruments. I had, thus, been classified by Bromley's Educational authority to be suitable for the non-selective sectors of the local educational system. My father had protested this classification vehemently but he had neither any local connections nor any clout to get me reclassified. He had nonetheless written a letter expressing his concerns to the headmistress of Rockhills, Miss Bowles. What brought me to Langley Park was a remarkable intervention on the part of two headmistresses, Mrs Molnar who was then headmistress of Langley Park and Miss Bowles. After I had been at Rockhills for about six months, Miss Bowles noticed that I had excellent grades and was diligent about my work. One day she asked me into her office and told me that she was transferring me to another school. She told me that she hoped that I would never return to Rockhills, an environment that was difficult for me. I came to Langley Park a few days after this conversation. I remember, on the very first day whilst on my way to school I bumped into Mrs. Molnar on the lane leading up to the school.

I did not do well in that first year. In fact I did badly. This was the fourth year, already late in the secondary school trajectory when friendships have gelled and curricular choices made. I was discouraged and found it hard going. Mrs. Molnar invited me for a conversation during this period, of what felt like 'failure' to me, and pointed out the determining factor of this late start. She encouraged me to try harder and persist. I adjusted rapidly the following academic year and for the rest of the time I just about managed to get through the final exams and onto university. I also had some wonderful teachers like Miss Birch who taught me geography; Mrs Manning who was my biology teacher; and Miss Rabson who was so pleased I passed my French Oral exams, despite failing my French O level. She was cognizant of my late start.

I went on to read anthropology at University College London as an undergraduate and then did a Ph.D at SOAS. I studied a multiple migrant community of British Asians to which I belong and later wrote a book entitled *Twice Migrants*, which was based on my doctoral thesis. My first academic job was at the Research Unit on Ethnic Relations at Aston University and later at Warwick University. It was during this period that I co-edited a book *Enterprising Women: Ethnicity, Economy and Gender Relations*. My most recent book *Dangerous Designs: Asian Women Fashion the Diaspora Economies* focused on entrepreneurial Asian women who have created innovative micro-markets of design and fashion from the margins. In 2003, just before this book came out, I was also promoted to a Full Professorship.

My current book in progress '*It's hip to be Asian*' looks at British Asians as globally influentially cultural producers, performers, and artistes.

Comment   'Parminder Bhachu is the most authentic and imaginative intellectual of the diaspora that I have come across . . . on the cutting edge – a sophisticated analyzer of the multilayered identities.'

Gillian (Grimsey) Scales 1973-1978

Chairman of Governors, Leslie Scales, and the Headmistress married 28 October 1977

Head when the sixth form merged with the Boys' School in 1976

UPPER SIXTH 1974 *L to R Back row ??, ??, Susan Nortcliff, Deborah Clarke, Christine Kobrak, Karen Snazell, Julie Duffin, Ann Webb, Diana Stevens, Anne Vineall, Angela Mercer, Jackie Sadler, Tina Shadbolt, Rachael Dawson, Sue Hobbs. Row 3 ??, Joy Vincent, Sally Donaldson, Elizabeth Taylor, Julia Brookman, Janet Knell, Ann Cheale, Margaret Price, Helen Woods, Jane Perry, Lindsey Price, Jane Gilbert, Janet Woods, Caroline Terry, Barbara Myers. Row 2 Deborah Hughes, Geradine Dudley, ??, Madeleine Meakin, ??, Susan Appleyard, Jacqueline Howse, Sally Radcliff, Lynn Yates, Sarah Howell, Helen Atkinson, Janet Hallet, Jean Tinker, Catherine Konior, Helen Baker, Susan Nundy, Marion Wood. Front row Elizabeth Blande, Aileen Knott, Alison Tilley, Mary Jane Charlie, Ann Edom, Alison Browne, Mrs (Grimsey) Scales, Mrs Barnard, Deborah Lee, Sandra Aylen, ??, Judy Thompson, Janet Woosnam, Jennifer Austin.*

FIVE   MEMORIES OF THE 1970s

Mrs (Grimsey) Scales (1973 – 1978)

I was appointed with the brief of turning the grammar school into a comprehensive. Fortunately Bromley had decided that the transition should be gradual, unlike some authorities where there was a sudden change with some children and staff being moved from their existing schools to convert all in the area comprehensives in one fell swoop. The number of girls entering the grammar school each year was 120 and, with the all-ability entry, this was to be increased to 180.

The intention was that the change should begin in 1974, but as building was soon to be started on the 'new block' (not so new now) it was agreed that the school would take its first comprehensive intake of 11 year olds in 1975. This gave us all time to plan and for staff to undertake training and to visit other schools so that they could see how different (and how similar) the teaching and subject matter was for children of an ability range with which they were not experienced. Naturally there was some apprehension, but there was also enthusiasm, and members of staff were, I think, quite surprised at how they adapted to the new demands on them. There was much planning, and the new building was finished just in time for the prospective parents evening. The staff spent all day getting the rooms set out, with displays up on the walls, and we were very pleased with the result, and felt sure that it would impress visitors. As I was going up the stairs I heard one mother say to another, 'Well, I wouldn't send my daughter to a school where the walls were bare brick.' On such opinions are important decisions for a child's future made!

Until we were able fully to use that building, we had so-called 'temporary' classrooms. I seem to remember seeing them for some time after I had left. At the same time the kitchens were being rebuilt and re-equipped to cope with the increased numbers, so we were dependent on food cooked elsewhere and brought in daily. There were also adaptations to the existing building, to provide more practical space, more laboratories, extra classrooms and a Sports Hall. On reading this I wonder now how the staff managed to keep so calm and to keep everything running so normally in the midst of all that turmoil.

The next big change for the staff was the joint sixth form with the Boys' School. Again, this was the subject of much discussion and many meetings, not all of them calm (!). The block for some of the lessons was built on the ground between the two schools, but belonging to the Boys' School. There was a common room for all the sixth form on the ground floor, but there was no space for specialist rooms, nor indeed for all the sixth form to be taught at any time, so it was agreed that some lessons should take place in each school and some in the sixth form block. Timetabling was interesting, to say the least, as the boys had fewer lessons in the morning than the girls and more in the afternoon, with an earlier dinner hour. This cut out a section of the day when lessons could not be held jointly. As far as teaching went, some lessons were taught by each school's staff to mixed groups, and some by their own staff to either girls or boys - a nightmare!

I remember asking some of the girls, after about a term, how they felt that the joint lessons were going. They responded that at first the boys seemed to know all the answers and so they kept quiet, but after a time they realised that the boys just said something to fill the space, and knew no more than they did, so they were encouraged to take more part after that. It would be interesting to know whether the attitude of girls in lessons generally has changed from the time in my earlier teaching days – when many liked to be told and to assimilate knowledge, but were less willing to participate in discussion unless really led out, possibly because they didn't wish to appear foolish if wrong.

FIVE   MEMORIES OF THE 1970s

I also remember something else about the different attitude of girls and boys: Brian Phythian, the Head of the Boys' School, used to speak of the 11 year old boys as 'his tinies'. I was sure that the girls would kill me if I referred to them in that way! I then learned that some of the boys used to cry quite readily if anything went wrong, whereas I felt that the girls might also cry, but would go away and would certainly not wish to be seen doing so. I wonder if this has changed. Possibly not.

When I joined the school in 1973, there were six houses, named by Mrs Molnar, my predecessor, as Lambda, Pi, Sigma, Gamma, Beta, Kappa (she was a classicist), the initial letters of Langley Park School for Girls, Beckenham, Kent. As far as I remember there were mixed age Tutor Groups in each house, making communication difficult - to get information round to a particular age group it was necessary to send a message to a large number of Tutors. It also meant that, if a girl fell out with the girls of her age in her Tutor group, she found it hard to find new friends in that group. In 1974 we decided to have Tutor Groups of one age only, which seemed much simpler all round, and I appointed six Heads of House, with particular responsibilities for all girls in their House, and made for continuity as girls went up the school. At the same time we introduced House badges, with the colour appropriate to the initial letter of the House (or as near as it could be) - lemon for Lambda, purple for Pi, scarlet for Sigma, green for Gamma, blue for Beta, and khaki (actually brown) for Kappa.

There were some very good drama productions. I remember holding up a very realistic and bloody head at a Prize Giving; it had been made by one of the Sixth Form for a play (possibly one of the Greek tragedies?) in which the head was brought in to prove the death. I felt that it was so good that it was worth showing. There were also musicals - one that stands out in my mind is "Sweet Charity", when I commented to another member of staff that I thought some fathers would have their eyes opened by their daughters on stage! There were many excellent concerts, with choir, orchestra and sometimes also parents and staff. A rather different one that comes to mind was a 'Music Pupils' Concert". Two young cellists were playing a Bach duet, in which they very soon got out of time and it sounded more like Shostakovich than Bach. To everyone's relief Miss Tripp went down and asked if she could be of help. We all hoped that she would point them on, but she sent them back in the piece (not to the beginning, I'm happy to say) and they soon got out again, so that one ended and looked amazed that the other was still playing. I hope that didn't put them off for ever. You can see how it has seared itself into my memory!

I also remember that there were some 'fashion parades', showing the girls' work. I can't quite remember how they began, but I know that some of the Sixth Form were involved in the organisation of these. How good they were, and how much they were enjoyed.

The teachers were generous with their time for all activities, not only for rehearsals of all kinds, and for practices and matches, swimming gala and athletics events. There were cruises on SS Uganda, some of these with staff and boys from 'next door', outdoor Multi-Activity holidays and ski trips. As well as these longer trips there were local outings of various sorts - I expect that others will have remembered these and written of them. I count myself very fortunate to have worked at such an exciting time for the school and with such a committed and supportive staff.

In my second year I suggested that the girls should take more part at Prize Giving, and short speeches giving details of events were given by the girls rather than simply mentioned in my Speech. Some editing was needed: in the reports on outings much space was given to the times spent eating and drinking! While they were practising it was hard to make them speak more slowly, and to 'talk to the clock at the back'.

70

FIVE   MEMORIES OF THE 1970s

But the parents were much more likely to listen to the girls than to me (I have no illusions), and I hope that the experience of talking to a large group of people has stood some of the girls in good stead in their futures.

I wonder how many remember the cat that came to the school to have its kittens under the stage? It used to come up during Assemblies and sit on the grand piano to supervise the proceedings. One day I suddenly realised that there was a bit of a stir in the front row and saw that there were little faces peering out from under the curtain - the kittens had learned to climb the stairs. After that some first years were deputed to sit with them under the stage during Assemblies. Fortunately homes were found for the mother and the kittens.

While I was at Langley Park, there was a very good team of Governors, who were always interested in helping the school in any way that they could. Mr Atkins, who had been a Governor and then Chairman since 1946, and also had long association with Langley Park Boys' and Kelsey Park Schools, retired in 1975, and his place was taken by Mr Scales. His two daughters, Kay and Sheila, had been at the school - Kay's first year was in the pavilion which was used by the school when it was still Beckenham Grammar in Lennard Road, after which they came over to the present building. Their father was a lively member of the Parents' Association and, after they had left, a Governor. In the year following the death of his wife he was very supportive of events at the school (I thought), and I think I was more surprised than some of the staff when we became engaged in the summer of 1977! In October 1977 we attended a Governors' meeting the evening before we married, at which he had to tender his resignation as Chairman because of his 'association with the Headmistress'. I was delighted that Ann (Eminton) Handy, an old girl of the school and a friend from my College days at Girton, was appointed to succeed him, as I knew that the school would be in good hands.

We were married at St Mary's in West Wickham, and I was amazed to see so many of the Sixth Form there to support us. That was a real surprise, organised I'm sure by Mrs Barnard. At this time electricity was rationed so that there were three-hour power cuts (we normally knew the times at which these would happen), so after a few days away we got home and managed, between cuts, to paint the pantry - it doesn't sound a very romantic honeymoon!

After that I stayed on for the rest of the school year, and there were all the usual activities and events. It seemed that there was always much going on, with staff and pupils always busily occupied. I thoroughly enjoyed my time at the school.

A footnote: Mrs Herzmark, my successor, had also followed me into the Maths Department when I left in my first teaching post at Queen Elizabeth's Girls' School, Barnet. Such a coincidence. In fact, Mrs Barnard was Acting Head for a term, and Mrs Herzmark started at Langley Park in January 1979.

Some memories from Elaine Kelly and Gill (Manning) Donaldson

We came with Miss Grimsey and left after she became Mrs Scales. We were the first year that didn't have to wear hats and ties to school. Elaine knows as her sister Alison had to and she was two years older than us.

1st year, Mrs Rand checking our names were in our knickers and measuring the heels of our shoes, that was the indoor (Tiffany Start-rites) and outdoor shoes. We had to embroider our names on our PE skirts in needlework in chain stitch and make school dresses that no-one ever wore!

FIVE   MEMORIES OF THE 1970s

No talking in the corridors and the one way system around the old building. We loved Spam fritters and gypsy pie, but did not like the tubes in liver and bacon. In this time school dinners were still served on proper plates, by the sixth form, those silly plastics ones with sections had appeared and chips and hot dogs seemed to be available every day. Mrs Barnard watched us go into assembly making sure we had our top buttons done up, we always used to undo them as soon as we had walked past her, did she know....? We took our dinner money to school in Selotape tins, with our names written on the plaster stuck on the top. We all cycled to school

2nd year - Miss Elcombe told me off for having a nose bleed on my history book; we had Mr Rowland for English. We think the new block was built when we were in the 2nd year. By the second year, Dru (Drusilla Dyson), Clare (Whittaker) and I had braces on our teeth which we cleaned in the cloakrooms every day after lunch, taking a small toothbrush to do it with. Elaine never had one! We had Miss Foster for RE.

3rd Year - Mr Rowland took us on a school trip to see the Rocky Horror Show in the King's Rd, Chelsea, which now has a cult following of which we are members! We had Miss O'Dell for RE who had taught my mother (Mrs Manning), so sometimes called me Pat.

4th year, having taken our options, we all did biology (there were only 6 girls in our year who didn't). The boys used to come down from Kelsey Park at lunchtime to see us, but had to stand the other side of the fence – we were watched closely by lunchtime staff.

5th year, I remember starting our 'O' level exams after Easter with core poetry on May 3rd, apart from Maths which we took in January, well, Elaine, Helen, Gill Tatum and me. My exams finished on Fri June 22nd 1978. We all helped with the tuck shop in the fifth form to make money to buy the red minibus.

6th form, Dru left in the middle of the L6. We went over to the 6th form block and had shared lessons (well some people did). There was always the difference in the boys and girls school timetable, as the boys did a 2-2-3 day and we did a 2-3-2

Charlotte (Campos) Ferreira's memories

On my first day at school in September 1976, I was very nervous. My mother dropped me at the gate and whenever I could pluck up courage I asked someone where I should go. The answer was always 'I don't know,' so I waited by the gates until a bell rang. Eventually I found a board that gave the room numbers and was placed in a class. After a time we were made to line up in the corridor. I thought it was lunch time when a teacher came up and asked 'Pie?' Everyone followed her except me as I didn't want pie until I realised she was asking for the house 'Pi.' My haven was the library where I could sit by the window with its view over the fields. I loved the peaceful atmosphere and the travel books which were an outlet for my imagination and my dreams. English literature was my favourite subject and the teachers were superb; Mr Baker's A Level classes were inspirational and I later went on to study literature at university.

FIVE   MEMORIES OF THE 1970s

Charlotte was the elder of sisters only 10 months apart and both benefited from the joint sixth form classes as you can see from Lola's account in chapter six.

Fiona Shore's Memories of Langley Park School for Girls

I taught at LPSG from 1976 – 1981. What do I remember? I think I was very fortunate to arrive at a time when the staffroom was buzzing with lively, talented people. Oddly I don't remember much about the teaching (!) but I can bring vividly to mind lots of other things. My memories are all good ones and largely revolve around individual members of staff and girls.

I went on two school cruises on the SS Uganda (later used as a first aid ship during the Falklands War) with Beryl Milburn (Classics) Agnes Stickings (also Classics, but at the Boys' School) and Julie Williams (Chemistry). The picture shows Agnes and Julie at the Acropolis in Athens. We had a wonderful time (and hope the girls did too). I am still grateful to the boys who rescued me from some over zealous Italian men and I often think of the opportunity I forfeited to exchange 2 pupils for a couple of handsome camels in North Africa. It was also my first, unforgettable, visit to Israel. I have been many times since.

My other vivid memories revolve around the production of Iolanthe and the more ambitious enterprise of staging 'Noyes Fludde.' Oddly, it was these events which I so enjoyed that eventually led to my leaving school; I became a producer at the BBC. Twelve years later I left to pursue a freelance career which is what I am still doing now, though I can't quite escape my roots in teaching and have returned to the classroom on a very part-time basis to teach A Level Philosophy of Religion at the school which my three daughters attended. I am also a governor of two schools! My husband, Andrew, is back left as

Noah and Governor Anne Handy is front right as Mrs Noah. It speaks volumes for Langley Park that every year a large group of staff meet for a reunion and pick up like old friends with such ease. I feel I was part of the School in a golden era and am lucky to have made so many enduring friendships as a result of being appointed to the staff by Miss Grimsey in 1976.

FIVE   MEMORIES OF THE 1970s

Claire Farrow remembers (Gamma House 1973-80)

I have many very happy memories of my days at Langley Park. At this distance I can truly say that they were the happiest days of my life but I know that I enjoyed them at the time too.

I remember my first day, sitting in alphabetical order in a biology lab and having to learn the School Hymn for my first homework. I still remember it, word-perfect, to this very day.

In fact I seemed to spend the first couple of weeks going everywhere and doing everything in alphabetical order. The first girl I spoke to (after several days of silence) was immediately after me in the alphabet. We are still in touch today. One of my earliest memories was of auditioning for Christine Kobrak's 'Small Choir'. She was a living legend from the Sixth Form with her amazing streak of white hair. I spent many happy lunchtimes rehearsing with that choir in the music room. It seemed to me to be an honour and a privilege to be singing with such a select group!

The annual drama festival was an event which I really loved. Created by Mr Rowland, it became an institution which most of the girls in my form enjoyed and participated in. A whole school day would be set aside for the performances of the various excerpts of plays performed by different classes. Those not performing became the audience – nothing so mundane as lessons on such a special day. A judge would pronounce their verdict and the lucky winners would perform to parents in the evening. A wonderful opportunity and one which I will never forget! I was, and still am, completely ham-fisted at needlework, much to the exasperation of a student teacher. She made me re-do my biased binding example so many times that there was almost no biased binding left to sew in the end. I'm afraid I also failed to excel in cookery but, although I am still no Nigella Lawson, I have improved a little on that front.

I have never forgotten the terror of exam week, lining up outside a classroom with my transparent plastic bag containing pens, pencils etc and clutching whatever lucky mascot was working for me at the time. Of course, ordinary exams were nothing compared to the dreaded "O" levels; sitting silently in the gym, once again in alphabetical order, in rows and rows of desks, listening to our full names being called out and wondering at some people's middle names.

There are hundreds of other memories stored away; Mr Newsome sitting at his magnificent Bluthner grand piano, playing the introduction to "Jerusalem"; the sung amens after the prayers in Assembly; indoor and outdoor shoes (Tiffany Startrite for outdoors!); kneeling on coconut matting for the school panoramic photograph (very uncomfortable); embroidering my name onto my hockey boots (tricky and painful to the fingertips); Mr Jennings, the American exchange teacher who said 'Louis Pasteur' which made us all laugh and called exam week "those little tests" which made me feel a bit better; attending 'House Parties' where the girls performed songs and sketches to entertain their parents; reading 'To Kill a Mockingbird' for the first time. I know that it wasn't all perfect; there were times when I was miserable, hopelessly unable to draw a stickleback or Newton's steam engine, struggling with a quadratic equation or freezing cold out on the Redgra in a seemingly endless game of hockey; but, on the whole I would have to say, definitely the happiest days of my life!

FIVE   MEMORIES OF THE 1970s

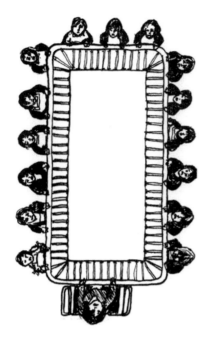

<u>Ann Deacon tries out the new trampoline</u>

The sixth form have trampoline lessons. Unfortunately however inconspicuous you try to look and insist on others going first, sooner or later it is your turn. One way of getting on to the trampoline is to balance on the metal edge and then to somersault into the middle.

You can walk boldly across the bed but if you walk too purposely you bound along and are liable to bounce off the other end. No, it's best to crawl gently to the centre before raising yourself tentatively to the upright position. Next comes the problem of bouncing as you feel that the bed is decidedly hostile and will do its best to catapult you off at the slightest provocation.

You are forced to put an end to your wild cavorting by sitting down. Nevertheless you are told that you are 'depressing the bed nicely' and you feel like saying you're depressing yourself nicely as well but you haven't got the breath to spare. Just as you are bouncing happily more or less in the centre of the bed, there's a shout of 'kill it.' Kill it? Where? What? How? Has a luckless spider ventured forth on to the bed? Suddenly light dawns; it means stop bouncing. You wish you could! Falling over could be dangerous; you might catch your nose in one of the holes. Resignedly you sit down and look as though you meant to all along!

Seat drops sprain your wrists; knee bounces wrench your back and bruise your knees and straddle jumps are impossible unless you are a contortionist.

At the end of five minutes you are reduced to a state of complete exhaustion and weakly bounce over to the edge of the bed. Gingerly you lower yourself to the ground. What's this? You cannot stand; your knees have forgotten they're meant to support you. As your legs buckle when you try to adjust to terra firma, you reflect that kangaroos must be the most unfortunate creatures on earth.

<u>Liz (Bertoya) Sparrow started gliding</u> in 1990, pretty much on a whim. She says: I fancied the idea of flying but knew I couldn't afford power flying, so I turned up at the gliding club to have a go one summer's evening… and was instantly completely hooked. Why? Read on and maybe you'll start to understand.

Most people have no idea what gliding is about, or how it works – so perhaps I'd better explain. I fly gliders – also known as sailplanes – which are fixed wing machines like a very sleek aeroplane without an engine. They fly exactly the same way as a power plane in nearly all respects, all normal controls, we go where we want and land in pretty much the same way – but the key difference is that the engine enables the power plane to climb, whereas I need to find an external source of lift.

In between finding sources of lift, I glide out at a very shallow downhill angle – imagine a bike with no pedals, where you have to keep rolling down a gentle slope else you'd slow down and stop. The better the glider, the flatter the slope and less height you lose as you go.

FIVE   MEMORIES OF THE 1970s

The best gliders will do over 10 miles for 1000 ft of height loss – so on a typical summer's day with 5000 ft cloud base, they will cover over 40 miles before having to find the next climb.

The basics of gliding are pretty simple to learn, and three months after I first flew in a glider, I was sent solo. Wow, that's a pretty exciting moment – all of a sudden there is no instructor in the back keeping an eye on you, you're on your own and doing what most people only dream of – flying silently through the air. Setting up the circuit for your first landing, convincing yourself that you can really do it… probably?!?… check the speed…check the height…everything as it should be?… rounding out and letting the glider settle gently onto the ground…rolling to a stop…YES!!! And leaping out with a grin from ear to ear. Madam, the freedom of three dimensions is now yours!!

Post solo, I progressed through the various badges that are the equivalent of the pilot's licence and let you set off cross-country. On a typical day in the summer, hundreds of glider pilots are doing cross-country flights, many in excess of 300km. Generally we fly round a pre-declared course, exactly where depends on the Met conditions on the day, perhaps from my home club in Hampshire up to Northampton, across the Cotswolds and maybe into Wales, and back. All without an engine and at average speeds of 100kph on a good day. It's a series of climbs and glides. The aim is to find the best bits of rising air – helpfully marked by cumulus clouds much of the time, but not always. And that is where the skill lies in gliding – understanding the sky, flying where the air is going up, and – equally importantly – avoiding flying where the air is going down. Of course, if you don't find the next climb, then you have no option – you will have to land! In which case you find a nice flat field with no crop or stock in and an unobstructed approach, and that will do nicely. Then it's a phone call to your retrieve crew, hunt the landowner and derig the glider once your trailer arrives.

It turns out I'm quite good at this. When I started flying competitions, I found myself doing ok, and all of a sudden I'm the second highest rated woman pilot in the UK – and, a hugely proud moment, a member of the British Gliding Team. My first international competition was the Women's World Championships at Jihlava in the Czech Republic in 2003, where I came 6th in the Club Class (3 different classes for different performance gliders – mine is the lowest performance end of the scale). It was a wonderful atmosphere competing with pilots from around the world, and great fun. I was unable to better that position in 2005 when the World Championships was in eastern Germany, but last year in the UK Club Class Nationals I came 10th, my best position to date so I'm hopeful of a medal at the 2007 World Champs which take place in France in July. By the time you read this, it will probably all have been decided, but wish me luck anyway!

I wish I could show you what it is that makes it the best sport in the world, but perhaps I can give you a flavour of the playground in the sky – launching in your beautiful sleek flying machine, flying silently and seeking out the huge power of the atmosphere; soaring in a thermal with eagles, looking down on the glorious variety of scenery that is the UK. In one flight you might see the Stretton Hills of Shropshire lying like sleeping dragons, and then head east to see the Mondrian that is East Anglia – all geometric shapes and block colours. Then back through the Chilterns to share a climb with those most elegant of aviators, the Red Kites, via a turbulent climb over Didcot power station.

FIVE   MEMORIES OF THE 1970s

Then back onto our own rolling chalk hills for a triumphal beat across the finish line. Being part of nature, taking advantage of the natural energy that's up there if you know where to look, but, just for a while, defying the laws of gravity…

And I thought you might want a short Bio:

Liz Bertoya Sparrow left Langley Park to go to Queens' College, Cambridge University where she read Engineering. It was some years later, after doing a postgraduate course at Cranfield – a university sited on an airfield – that she became rather taken with the idea of flying and started the saga above. When not gliding, she runs a management consultancy and is also a non-executive director of DVLA and DVO, both part of the Department for Transport. She lives in the Test Valley in Hampshire with husband Alan, who happily is also a glider pilot. If there is any spare time left over, she and Alan spend it walking.

Liz and Fiona Bratt

Memories of Langley Park School by Fiona (Croft) Bratt 1973-1980 Gamma House

The thing which stands out in my school time memories is Drama and the confidence that the many opportunities to be involved in drama productions gave to me. We had annual drama competitions for which each class who wanted to entered part of a play; produced, staged, costumed and acted by the girls. It was my first introduction to Noel Coward with Blithe Spirit – 'to hell with Ruth' and to restoration comedy with lines like 'there be two men in t'post chaise at door' said in a West Country accent, see I can still quote from them and lots of pieces of Shakespeare which we studied in class each year. My form always did quite well in the drama competitions, with superb production from Claire Farrow, which probably spurred us on each year.

As we moved up the school I became more involved in the school productions and particularly recall being made to audition for Sweet Charity, the dance and drama auditions were no problem but I could not and still can't sing. I stood at one end of the hall by the piano with the auditioning staff at the other end and attempted to sing, some kind girls who were also auditioning came to my rescue by singing along, only for me to be told that they couldn't hear me anyway! I still got into the chorus.

Two other productions stand out in my memory, firstly when we girls were 'loaned' to Kelsey Park for a rock musical version of Robin Hood (that caused rivalry between the two boys' schools). Secondly when it came to our turn to do the sixth form pantomime, performed for the rest of the school by the lower sixth, the film Grease had been released.

powers of tolerance, quiet firmness and determination. I hope that further hard work will raise her standard to that of safe passes. She will be remembered here for her contributions to performing arts, her pleasant manner, and not least her courage. She deserves every success — I have enjoyed knowing her so much as I have enjoyed dancing with her!

Group Tutor *P. D. Rowland.*
Head of Year *David Blake*
Headmistress *Barbara J. Wezmark*

FIVE   MEMORIES OF THE 1970s

We put on a performance of Mary Poppins during which the characters popped through the pavement into the world of Grease. I landed the Sandra Dee role (miming along to a tape to everyone's relief) and Mr Rowland, Mr Macauley and Mr Blake were very good sports taking the parts of Danny and the Thunderbirds, dressed in our boyfriends leather jackets and dancing to ' You're the one that I want'. I still have my final school report in which Mr Rowland wrote, 'I have enjoyed knowing her as much as I have enjoyed dancing with her!' Happy days!

An appreciation of school by Janet (Mercer) Hagen

Janet now lives in Germany with her husband Helmut and her three children, Jennifer, Alyssa and Dominic but has many fond memories of Langley Park. Being at school from 1970 to 1977, she experienced huge changes from the grammar school of Mrs Molnar, a daunting figure greatly respected if not feared by most girls. Miss Grimsey had to cope with a situation where there were girls in the lower school who could hardly read and found it hard to settle in.

Janet found an old diary with entries relating to the school Athens trip in March 1974 when they flew to Athens from Gatwick on Wednesday 6 March and checked in at a hotel in Glyfada, the millionaire's paradise! Thursday saw a visit to the Astir beach for a swim in the sea and a tour round Athens, including the Acropolis. Friday was the turn of a boat trip to Salamis where they dressed in peasant skirts to enter the monastery. Saturday included a walk up the hill behind the town to see the wild anemones and giant centipedes; the flea market was planned for Sunday and various coach trips for the rest of the time to the Corinth Canal, Delphi and Mycenae.

In June 1975, after O levels, Miss Birch and Miss Henry took a group youth hostelling in the Cairngorms where they swam in the very cold loch (Janet was an enthusiastic Beckenham Ladies swimmer), saw a fell race and watched an international hockey match between a team from Sweden and the Aviemore team. Their guide, Denis the Menace, took them to see the wildlife and they also went skating. Happy days indeed!

Judy Herzmark
Jan 1979 to Dec 1992

Joint sixth form Chemistry with Miss Evans 1988

Fire destroyed the craft hut in March 1987

SIX   MRS HERZMARK 1979-1992

Mrs Barbara Judy Herzmark, Headmistress 1979 - 1992

I came to Langley Park School in January 1979 at a time of fundamental change. After many years as a selective girls' grammar school, the school was in the throes of reorganisation as an all-ability school.

Immediately I had a surprise. Two H.M.I. (Her Majesty's Inspectors of Schools) requested a visit. I greeted them with some apprehension. They were, as always, charming and courteous. Their purpose was to make sure that the buildings could accommodate two extra classes for each of two years who were to be transferred because of the closure of a nearby secondary modern school. It had not occurred to the Bromley Education Authority to inform me of this! Suddenly we had to plan not for six classes in the first and second years, but eight. Not surprisingly the newcomers deeply resented being drafted into another school and this did not help with good order and discipline, presenting a challenge to the teachers. My answer was to establish four Houses, each having two forms in each year group. The Houses were each headed by a very senior member of staff, with a team of Form Tutors. The purpose was to safeguard the interests of each individual girl in a large school and to provide continuity of care for the five years up to the Sixth Form. Sisters were always placed in the same House so that contact was maintained with each family. The Houses provided a structure for competitive sports; older girls helped younger ones and all had a feeling of belonging. We named the Houses Lambda, Sigma, Gamma and Kappa – a relict of a former pattern established from the initials L, P, G, S, B and K for the first six-form entry. The contribution of the House Heads to the good order and happy atmosphere of the school was immeasurable.

My first year saw the first Langley Park Arts and Crafts Exhibition. This was a P.T.A. project planning for which was already under way. Many local artists and some from further afield were invited to display their work, on sale with a commission for the P.T.A. Sculptor Gerda Rubinstein's bronze birds were outstanding, as were Dr Owen Standon's inlaid wood bowls and plates. Former Chair of Governors, Mr Scales, submitted some of his paintings too. Pupils' work was included in the show. A Private View on Friday evening was planned followed by two days of public viewing. The show looked splendid and crowds of people came, looked and purchased. At the last minute – horror – we were told that Borough Bye-Laws prohibited selling on Sunday! A disaster; but we carried on and by the next year the Bye-Law had been repealed. The show became an annual event for all of my time at the school; the artists and the public came year after year. As well as its fund-raising success it was good PR for the 'comprehensive' school which many parents in Beckenham and West Wickham viewed with suspicion. It was good that people came in to see some of the pupils' work in a well cared for building with well mannered girls acting as stewards. As for the profits, they went towards the purchase of a mini-bus, a second-hand vehicle which served the school well.

Head teachers cannot avoid politics and my first encounter came early on. The 1960s and 1970s saw the reorganisation of secondary education from a selective (grammar school and secondary modern) system to all ability schools – larger than before to offer an appropriate curriculum to every child. Some areas embraced the change enthusiastically but others dragged their feet often because of financial constraints rather than educational conviction. In 1965 a government circular 10/65 required local authorities to proceed with reorganisation; by 1978 all Bromley schools, with the exception of Newstead Wood and St Olave's, had developed into all-ability schools and it was the intention that they too would in due course become non-selective. However, the change to a Conservative government in May 1979 soon resulted in the withdrawal of circular 10/65. Bromley declared its intention to preserve the two selective schools serving the whole of the Borough.

SIX   MRS HERZMARK 1979-1992

The Heads of the all-ability schools were united in their disappointment as they realised that many of the most able children would be 'creamed off'. I remember vividly a meeting in the old Town Hall where Head teachers spoke with passion. A meeting of 800 parents of the Langley School boys and girls was almost unanimously opposed to the retention of the grammar schools (four parents were brave enough to raise their hands in favour). However, it was to no avail and the two 'super selective' schools flourish to this day.

The curriculum for the upper part of the school had yet to be developed (no national curriculum then). The lower forms were at first divided into upper and lower bands but the teachers soon realised that the lower band pupils had a poor self-image and lacked motivation. It was therefore agreed that the tutor groups should include children of all abilities and for the first three years most subjects were taught to mixed ability groups, mathematics being an exception. In the fourth and fifth years (now years 10 and 11) option choices prevent setting by ability. After five years of this regime the results at GCSE were excellent; the school came high in the 'league tables'. Every girl took one foreign language and Latin was kept going up to GCSE.

In 1988 the dual examination system with O-level catering for the top 20% and CSE (Certificate of Secondary Education) for the rest was reformed. It had been almost as divisive as the selective school system itself and, although the top CSE grade was supposed to rank as an O-level pass, the examination never achieved parity of esteem. The General Certificate of Education would in future be taken by all pupils with papers of graded difficulty. Finally, it was realised by the 'powers that be' that teachers needed training to adopt new means of assessment and schools were allowed to close some days early to allow training, provided by the Department of Education, to take place. This contrasted with the change from selective to all-ability schools in the 1960s and 1970s for which there had been no structured preparation. In fact there was very little provision for in-service training for teachers until Minister of Education, Kenneth Baker, introduced training days during term time – at first known as 'Baker Days' – when pupils did not attend school.

In 1985 we acquired our first computers, but it was not until 1988 that the Technical and Vocational Education Initiative or TVEI, government funded, enabled the installation of two computer rooms, each equipped for a whole class, and a music laboratory. Finance was always tight but was much eased when in 1990 Local Management of Schools enabled Head teachers and Governors to manage the whole budget. Before then the Local Authority exercised tight control of spending; indeed, unbelievably now, when I arrived in the school I did not even have a cheque book!

Music had always been a strength of the Langley Park schools. There were difficulties in the 80s partly because of teachers' strikes; sometimes the N.U.T and sometimes the N.A.S./U.W.T. withdrew from school altogether.

SIX   MRS HERZMARK 1979-1992

Classes had to be re-arranged and some pupils sent home. In 1987 the new teachers' contracts specified the number of hours teachers could be asked to work; most of the Langley Park staff were generous with their time for extra-curricular music, drama and sport. We had productions and concerts almost every year and the Music Department supported both an orchestra and a band. In 1990 the Fairfield Hall was booked for a musical production – not without risk as the seats had to be sold to cover the costs. Tremendous teamwork produced a splendid performance of a choral cantata 'African Jigsaw', accompanied by the school band and introduced by the school orchestra. The success of this concert encouraged a second Fairfield Hall performance 'Ocean World' in 1992.

It was received wisdom at the time that a six-form entry all ability school would have difficulty providing viable A-level groups for more than a small number of basic subjects. The joint Langley Park Sixth Form could offer a bigger range of A-level subjects and wider choice than either school alone. The combined expertise of the staff of two schools enabled minority subjects to be available. It presented tricky but not insoluble problems to the time-tablers and Mr Phythian and I worked had to make it succeed. Success depended on trust between the two schools as most teaching was shared evenly between boys' and girls' school staff. The Joint Sixth Form recruited a number of students from other schools which was financially advantageous. In my view it benefited the school and I was sorry when Mr Phythian's successor withdrew his support.

Chapters could be written on the sporting achievements, foreign travel, charity work and other activities both in and out of school hours which the girls enjoyed and to which the staff gave such unstinting support. It would be invidious to mention individual teachers because there were so many who contributed so much. School management today is a team effort and much responsibility falls to the Deputy Head teachers. The late Mrs Barnard, who had been at the school for many years, retired in 1982; Elizabeth Blackburn became a Head teacher. They were succeeded by Marian Freeman and Sue O'Neill who both in their turns moved on to headships. Jane Nicholls must be on course to rival Mrs Barnard in service to the school!

In 1991 two enterprising educationalists published the GOOD STATE SCHOOLS GUIDE which gave details of 300 non fee-paying schools in Great Britain judged by the authors to be good examples of state education. Langley Park Girls' School was included and the entry summarised thus:

A school which cares for all pupils and encourages them to reach the maximum of their potential, it has transformed successfully from long-established grammar to comprehensive.

The last half-century has seen many changes in education but none more far-reaching than that from selective to non-selective schools. This was a change not without difficulty and its achievement might summarise my period as Head teacher.   *B J Herzmark*

Linda Williamson's impression of her first year at Langley Park in 1979

To my delight last July, I heard that I had a place at Langley Park. I was a little worried as it seemed such a large school with so many people, rooms, corridors and doors. During my first week, I got lost several times but I soon found my way around. I think the biggest difference between primary and secondary schools is the way you change rooms and teachers for different lessons. In the first few weeks, I walked miles. Another difference is buying dinner tickets on a Monday and having a choice of meals.

SIX   MRS HERZMARK 1979-1992

There are many activities for the first years. I joined the Junior Choir, Recorder Group, and Guitar Group all run by Miss Vandenbrink and a Field Club run by Mrs Manning. I am looking forward to Mrs Roper's Second Year Dance Group.

At my primary school we played netball and rounders but now we do hockey and trampolining as well with athletics and tennis in the summer. The seniors play badminton, volleyball and table tennis as well which must be fun. It would be nice to mix with the older girls sometimes because we tend to stay in our year groups. Although I have only been at Langley Park for two terms, it seems a long time since I last went to primary school.

Cath and Becky remember the 1980s at Langley

Cath and Becky, still best friends after all this time! We had a great time together at Langley in the 80s (1983-1990). We got together to write this excerpt and share a few nostalgic memories of the good times. United by a love of life and laughter and hard work with a little fun and naughtiness at times…

Netball in particular was a favourite pastime of Cath and Becky. We were in the 'A-team' for Langley and often won our matches. Cath was Centre and Becky was Goal Attack. Cath was particularly good at blocking, and Becky was good at scoring and we developed a strategy which worked every time! We remember playing hockey in the mist and the freezing cold in knee high socks and short blue pleated skirts, John Betjeman would have approved! Cath held the Shot-put champion record for years- to her Mother's delight, and we wonder whether the record still remains?

The sporting spirit was truly nurtured by the teachers at the time. We remember Miss Tinham, Miss Long, Miss Watmough (the Champion cricketer) with great affection. They encouraged us all the way. They were also kind hearted enough to give Cath and Becky a lift home after a cross country run due to a dramatic injury suffered by Cath. We would now like to confess that the injury sustained was in fact a gross amateur dramatic affair!

How can we forget the 80s music. Madonna, Eurythmics, Michael Jackson, Sade, Luther Vandross! Jumping around the assembly hall with Miss Theasby, teacher of dance and History. How can we forget our trip to Greece with Miss Theasby? We remember amphitheatres, coach trips along the coast, Greek packed lunches and a night out at a local Greek disco!

We made some lovely sparkly Christmas decorations with Mrs Helt and we do believe we even gave up our lunch break! Our mothers were suitably impressed and still hang these exquisite if not somewhat 'threadbare' ornaments on the tree every year!

We remember being famous even if it was for a day. Becky played the 'Caterpillar' in Alice in Wonderland and emerged on stage from a sleeping bag to the tune of "It ain't necessarily so". We were all slightly envious of our long haired blonde friend, Sam Whatmore who managed to secure the role of Alice! We even got into the local newspaper paper for performing a sketch on how **not** to present yourself at an interview, the *original* Vicky Pollard! It didn't affect our careers too much in the end thankfully. There were some special moments when the intelligence of our year was questioned.

SIX MRS HERZMARK 1979-1992

One of the pupils was asked which cereal would be a suitable grain for crop rotation. Her reply was Weetabix! This left the class in hysterics and the teacher probably wishing he had pursued an alternative choice of career.

Finally, we remember our friends, our teachers and all the fond memories we share both individually and shared about our day at Langley Park.

What happened then... Miss Catherine Bury now known as Doctor Catherine Bury went on to pursue a successful academic career as a Child and Adolescent Clinical Psychologist. Becky Gibson trained professionally as a dancer and worked in musical Theatre as a performer and then as a Resident Director in the West End and on tour in shows such as Chicago, Cats, Fame, Joseph, Grease and Starlight Express.

Careers Day 31 March 1987

Bromley's Poise School presented a very popular careers day that included modelling and interview techniques. Four Langley Park girls acted out situations that showed graphically what could be the right and wrong type of behaviour at an interview. While it is important to be yourself, you must try to come across in the best possible light. Nicola Daley and Michele Stephens, both 15, showed the correct way to conduct

an interview. The interviewer on the left is interested in what the bright, neatly dressed candidate on the right has to say.

Rebecca Gibson, 14, and Catherine Bury, 15, illustrate how not to behave. The candidate is dressed more for a party than for an interview with behaviour to match. From the look on the interviewer's face, she will be glad when the noisy applicant leaves her in peace. The interviewee should have left her sunglasses and headphones at home and whatever possessed her to be blowing bubbles?

Although Catherine has obviously gone over the top in her portrayal of how not to behave, acting out the two situations made the audience think for themselves how they would dress and behave at an interview.

SIX   MRS HERZMARK 1979-1992

A Time for Multiactivities and Skiing with Chris Watmough

England woman cricketer, Chris Watmough joined the school in 1975 and by the 1980s she had encouraged girls and staff alike to take up previously undreamed of activities. Minibuses would be seen driven at correct decorous intervals along the M3 on their way to Hyde House at Wareham. Parties of excited would be skiers would collect in the gym to try on and to hire salopettes, padded jackets, gloves and goggles for their first attempts down the slopes and the Bromley athletics meetings continued to reckon on Langley Park as a school to be feared.

We soon found out that Chris Watmough excelled at everything: she would ski, ride horses, sail, canoe alone (the rest of us had to go in pairs in kayaks), shoot, hit the bull in

archery, water ski and windsurf but after a time some of us discovered her Achilles heel. She never put herself down for abseiling at Durdle Door! One activity that even seasoned downhill skiers found impossible was grass skiing. Each boot had eight wheels that took you down at the speed of an express train (or at least that was what it sounded like). We found that if you baled out, the grassy slope was much harder than snow and left unbelievable bruises and scrapes. Canoeing, sailing and windsurfing were possible on the lake at Hyde House but for water skiing it was the sea or nothing. We would queue up on the beach or in the surf awaiting our turn to pitch nose first into the waves, often feeling overdressed in our wetsuits since the naturist beach of Studland was nearby.

In order to get about more easily, it was decided that it was time that the school had a better minibus instead of the unreliable one always in dock and a converted ambulance was chosen.

Ways of raising the £3,500 needed were devised. The PE dept made a fine start with £1,500 raised from sponsored jog, swim and walk. The tuck shop proved popular and a suggestion by Christine Kobrak that 25% could be made selling crisps raised some £300, only rivalled by her form's sponsored spell with more than £820.

Over £800 came from other fundraisers in the school and donations and so the bus was ours. It was painted bright red but inside you could still see its original green colour.

SIX   MRS HERZMARK 1979-1992

The lengthways bench seats could send the occupants flying at an emergency stop but the bus was tough and reliable. Other departments then wanted to get in on the act and soon a blue minibus was added to the parking space reserved for the red one in the front car park. By 1986, all minibus drivers had to take a special test and it was surprising how many nearly failed because, seeing the end in sight, the driver would exceed the speed limit down South Eden Park Rd.

PE teacher Gill Bull holds the chute down as Chris prepares to go parascending

The first skiing party to Foppolo could have defeated the most determined of party leaders because there was little snow and the beginners had to practise at the end of the only ski run open with expert skiers flying over their heads as they attempted to stand up between the moguls for the umpteenth time.

By the end of the week, the run that had taken two hours on Day One was being completed in three minutes by us all.

The groups were large and enthusiastic with Madesimo, Champoussin and Leysin following Foppolo. Who remembers Miss Jane Bennett arriving at Champoussin with her belongings on her back having skied over the mountains to sleep in a tent among the spring flowers breaking through the snow?

One of the large villas at Champoussin, Switzerland, situated just below the slopes

SIX   MRS HERZMARK 1979-1992

There are several pictures of Chris Watmough's skiing parties to Europe in the 1980s in the section of coloured pages.

Chris never failed to keep the party going. Here she is performing the actions to one of her songs. Could it be 'The Music Man'? Without a doubt, this came from being a member of the England Women's cricket team. Chris had been playing world cricket since 1964 with her first tour to Holland in 1967. In January 1982, Chris left for her third World Cup in New Zealand, confident that they would bring back the cup won by Australia in 1978 in India when England were the runners-up.

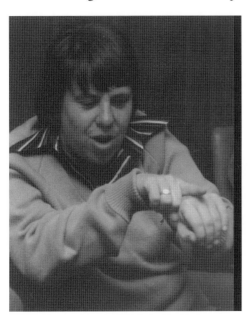 

<u>Lolita Campos-Mascarenhas (known as Lola Campos) 1977-1984</u>

Holding on to my treasured old school scarf and battered but trusty hockey stick I think I am not alone in remembering my school days at Langley Park School for Girls: the daily walk from Eden Park Station up to the school gates on cold winter mornings, noisy, happy groups of girls huddled up near the fence waiting to be the last in!

I remember with startling clarity Mrs Stickings, my passionate and larger-than life Latin teacher. She was so devoted to the Classics, the Trojan Wars and the pangs of love and jealousy of Aeneas & Dido that one could not but fall in love with the subject and endeavour to read all the poems and books she so ardently wanted us to devour in our spare time. Even now I can hear her deep loud voice urging us to learn again and again the dative and future imperfect tense till we were able to recite it from memory. Mrs Newman, a young and cheerful Latin teacher, who was also such a delight, made our lessons so exciting and dare I say fun! I remember another teacher Mr Fairbairn (although I must admit I was a little scared of him) and the formidable Head, Mrs Herzmark. Her voice used to send shudders down the school corridors and if we were told to go her office I remember my friends and I promising to stick to the 'Same Story' in case anyone in our group was called in!! I am so acutely aware, now that I work in a private girls' boarding school in the South West, that times still have not changed in certain areas…

Even now as I look back at the changes that have taken place in the school after so many years, the ethos and principles of the school have not altered: the nurturing and care I was given helped me to gain the confidence and love of the Classics and Romantic Languages that I have now and allowed me to enter the world with a constant love of learning and curiosity.

SIX   MRS HERZMARK 1979-1992

Scrapbook Snippets

When Mrs Herzmark retired in December 1992, she was given a scrapbook of newspaper cuttings covering all her time at Langley. Starting her teaching career as Head of Maths at first Queen Elizabeth Girls Grammar, Barnet and then Woodberry Down Comprehensive, Hackney, she came to Beckenham from Hatfield where she had been Deputy Head.

There was much to find out. In November 1978, our Top of the Form team of Diana Mortimer, Alison Penfold, Marianne Knott and Justine Carter had reached the last four by beating Charterhouse 105 -76.

The school was in the throes of fund raising to replace the school minibus which spent more time being repaired than on the road.

February 1980 saw the delivery of the converted minibus, most of the funds for which had been raised over two years by various school projects like the tuck shop and sponsored swimming, running and spelling.

In September 1979, Sally Reeves won the Nestlés British Junior Girls tennis title with a prize of £300.

Mrs Herzmark was facing the first Artist and Craftman's Exhibition which had all been organised by Bob Mirkellian of the PTA before she came.

In addition to the fine works of Gerda Rubenstein and Dr Owen Standon, there was lovely stained glass by Huldah Romaine Walters and silver jewellery by Susan Campbell. Of the participating pupils, Richard Harris submitted the two pottery pots that have seen service now for thirty years! The following year, impressive work was entered by Sarah Wennink, Alison Hill (porcelain jewellery) and Joanna Reynolds (smocking).

It was the Diamond Jubilee of the school which had opened in 1919 as Beckenham County School for Girls. They celebrated with a garden party at the Langley school when little Helen Adams greatly enjoyed her ride on the pony. This was a family day when husbands and children were invited to spend a happy afternoon.

SIX   MRS HERZMARK 1979-1992

Helen is the daughter of Elizabeth (Mynett) Adams. To commemorate our Jubilee Year, we issued a bone china plate showing the motto and the school's three badges and a coffee mug with views of the two school buildings, Lennard Rd and Langley Park.

Snack lunches became popular in March 1981 as the two Langley Schools were used as guinea pigs to test the popularity of filled rolls, sandwiches, salads and desserts. Five hundred girls queued to try them but Mr Phythian of the Boys School said that his sixth form and staff were still hungry!

Mary Ransford had started on her way to winning several prizes for her art, exhibiting collages at Euston station and, by 1981, illustrating a book of fairy tales. Her mother, Edith, meanwhile had been showing paintings of local scenes like 'The Coach and Horses.'

Here is Mary today with her daughters Clare and Emily.

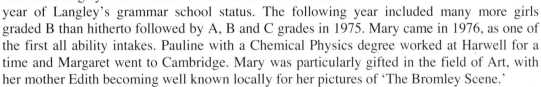

The sisters Pauline, Mary and Margaret Ransford all attended Langley Park. Pauline started in 1973 in the last year of Langley's grammar school status. The following year included many more girls graded B than hitherto followed by A, B and C grades in 1975. Mary came in 1976, as one of the first all ability intakes. Pauline with a Chemical Physics degree worked at Harwell for a time and Margaret went to Cambridge. Mary was particularly gifted in the field of Art, with her mother Edith becoming well known locally for her pictures of 'The Bromley Scene.'

Mary had three collages exhibited at Euston station for the third year running in 1978 with the titles Medieval Jousting, Elizabethan Banquet and Ladies of Astonishing Beauty. By June 1981, she had used her illustrative skill to provide the pictures for a book of fairy tales seen above and she went on to study graphic design at Kingston Polytechnic. After 15 years of working as a graphic designer for various London consultancies Mary started her own business to fit in better with family life. She works mainly for charities and local councils. In the coloured pages there is a sample of her work for Elmbridge Borough Council promoting recycling. More of her work can be seen at www.marygortondesign.co.uk

SIX   MRS HERZMARK 1979-1992

A trip to Russia took place at half term 1984 to Moscow and Leningrad to see Red Square, the Kremlin, St Basil's cathedral, the Lenin Museum, Moscow circus and ballet. They found that they needed to queue three times to buy anything; the first time was to choose, the second to pay and the third to collect. Fiddler on the Roof made the headlines in 1984.

Computers were becoming part of science and technology by 1985 and it was mainly provided by the Biology and the Maths departments at first. A programme called 'Quest' was devised, a database to store personal information like eye colour, shoe size and favourite pets. Dr Winn Allt was in charge. For technology, the first years were set the problem of making buggies moved by elastic bands or propellers. Their completion was celebrated by buggy races in the sports hall. A fire destroyed the technology hut but it was rebuilt in time for September 1987.

In the summer of 1987, Sharon Coombs and her friends in the third year, Louise Laimbeer, Rebecca Brooman, Debbie Howard, Helen Curtis, and Kathleen O'Brien among them, organised a sponsored run which raised £110 for a TV Sports Aid appeal. Another £25 came from selling Sports Aid T shirts, including to their teacher supporters, Jan Hinchliffe and their form tutor Pat Manning.

Twelve of them went to the massive five hour party at the QPR football stadium where Wet, Wet, Wet and Curiosity Killed the Cat appeared.

The Langley Park trampoline team of 24 members swept the board in May 1989 at the Championships held at Orpington where they jumped their way to 16 medals, 7 Gold, 7 Silver and 2 Bronze. PE teacher, Janet Shadick, said it was the highest total any school had won in the four years of the competition. In November 1990, fourth former and yellow belt, Phatthira Mata, won two trophies at the Tae Kwon Do Championships held at the Beckenham Leisure Centre.

SIX   MRS HERZMARK 1979-1992

Jan Hinchliffe and Janet Shadick were back in the news in May 1991 when after three months intensive training they completed the 3-day bikeathon from Westminster to Paris via Portsmouth, Caen and Rouen, as two of the 450 countrywide entrants. Bromley Mayor, Cllr Philip Jones, praised 12 girls from Kappa House who raised £3,400 for St Christopher's Hospice from an 18 mile walk round Chelsfield as part of the Mayor's Charity Walk in November 1991.

Nicola Harvey was one of 12 winners from 27,200 entrants in the Blue Peter Stamp Design Competition in December 1991. She won a camcorder for her design of a bird trapped by a carelessly discarded coke ring pull.

Sharon (Coombs) Koski 1984-1991, sends her news

After her marriage to naval officer Sam Koski in September 2002, Sharon eventually settled in Virginia, USA and tells the following story.

'*So much has been going on with buying a house that I didn't know where to start. First it was a house, then it was land, then that fell through, then it was back on again, then we lost the seller, but we had the builder all ready and waiting, but we couldn't find more land that we liked, then we came across a house.*

It's an old Colonial Greek Revival style home, situated in the historic town of Bowling Green. It was built as a rectory in 1899. Originally it was on Main Street and had a basement, however for some unknown reason (but one we are trying to research into) it was moved in 1959 about 150 feet back from Main Street and turned 90 degrees. Now it has no basement and I don't think it has been redecorated since it moved.

It needs a great deal of work, not to mention new paint. It will need rewiring, new air heating/cooling system, some replacement plumbing, new kitchen, new bathrooms, eventually a new roof, and a huge amount of love. We are both apprehensive and excited. We have so many ideas, but at the same time, know it will take several years and a whole lot of money.

Our first priory is to get running water in the bathroom and kitchen. Then we plan to paint the whole place white to make it liveable. We will work on one floor at a time, starting with upstairs. Now you have an idea of what we have to deal with, I ask you to put your imagination glasses on and just try to picture how this place will look one day.'

She is still in contact with Louise (Laimbeer) Latham, now in Tunbridge Wells and would love to hear from any of her mates in the TV Sports Aid picture. She last met Kate Newman in Hongkong but where is Kate now?

SIX   MRS HERZMARK 1979-1992

Maria Kendrick and Claire Robinson wish to be remembered

L to R back,Sandra Dowdell, Maria Kendrick, Sarah Howells, Jackie McDermott; front Yomi Majekodomni, Tara West and Melanie Batten in the first netball VII 1986

Claire's speciality at the athletics event 1987 was hurdles but she took up rugby at Uni.

Maria and Claire in 1986, year 5 (today's 11)

Maria and Claire were at Langley from 1981 until 1988 but now live far apart. Maria lives in Barbados with her husband and little boy where she works as a Virgin rep having previously much enjoyed being a Dive Master taking out scuba divers every day. Claire still lives in Beckenham and has two small children, Molly and Thomas. She travels to Canary Wharf every day where she works for a leading law firm as a Senior Human Resources Manager. The amazing coincidence is that Claire lives in the same house in Queens Rd where Maria's grandmother used to live. Through her mother, Maria is related to the funeral directors of West Wickham, the well known Killicks and both her mother and grandmother went to the Lennard Rd school. Maria and Claire are still best friends and meet up with the rest of the gang shown on one of the coloured pages of the book. Maria feels that those multiactivities holidays and the opportunities for all kinds of sport at school set the foundations for her present enjoyable job with Virgin having previously won the biennial prize for best representative.

SIX   MRS HERZMARK 1979-1992

L to R back row, Joanne Edwards, Sarah Anderson,??, Sarah Howells, Maria Kendrick; front row, Eleanor Watson, Hayley Price, Sara Powell, Yomi, Nicola?

Life since leaving Langley

Life for **Sarah Russell** has been nothing short of an 'adventure' since leaving Langley Park School for Girls 16 years ago with some GCSEs, A-Levels and the Adremians' school science prize in hand. 'I may have thought that I understood a great deal about the world when I received that prize, but the scary thing in life is that the more you learn, the more you realise how little you know. Today I am living in Salt Lake City, Utah – not somewhere that I necessarily planned to be, but I am a believer in taking opportunities as they knock, so here I am! Rather than provide commentary on each of my various career moves and university courses, it might be more beneficial if I focus on two valuable lessons I have learnt in life since leaving school:

1. **There are many pathways** …
When you are at school making decisions about what subjects to choose and what University course to pursue – don't think of this as your one and only opportunity. Sure, if you are dead set on being a doctor or a lawyer, you need to ensure you make the right choices, but for most of us, we can adapt, learn, recreate and change our pathways on a regular basis. I studied Geology and Mining Geology, which took me into the mining industry. But since being there I have worked in fields well beyond the scope of my original university studies (geology, public relations, government negotiations, CEOs direct adviser) and am now responsible for my company's global mining equipment contracts.
2. **Do things that you enjoy** …
While all of us can benefit from doing things that we don't enjoy and things that we find difficult, as a general rule, I find that people who really excel are those who enjoy what they are doing. Whether it's a passion for cooking, small business, academic study, being a parent, science or art, finding a 'niche' that you enjoy is one of the tricks in life to achieve happiness. It's not easy and will not necessarily stay the same throughout life, but it is one of life's essential ingredients. To all my school friends (some of whom I still see when I am back in England) – thank you for sharing some of my life and helping to shape who I am. I would love to hear from anyone who remembers me and can be contacted via the *friendsreunited* website.'

Sophie Irwin writes in February 2008 (left 2006)

'University life has been very busy. I successfully passed my first year of Medicine. During this time the crew I row with won Sports Team of the Year and won Blades at the United Hospital Bumps Competition last May. I am now on the St George's Hospital Boat Club Committee and hold the position of secretary. Just this weekend I competed in the Hammersmith Head and United Hospital Head race on the river Thames at Chiswick. I am thoroughly enjoying my time at St George's; it has a close knit community which offers great support, similar to that which I received during my time at Langley Park. To this day I still use my A level notes as a learning resource, as the physiology, scientific principles and human geography we were taught are still applicable to my course and of a similar level.'

Jan Sage
from 1993

The Dalo

SEVEN   AIMING HIGH

Jan Sage comes to Langley Park

All new heads want the opportunity to make an immediate impact on their new school, and the saying goes that this is most easily accomplished within their first few years. I was very fortunately placed in this respect. My predecessor, Mrs Herzmark, allowed me to 'inherit' substantial reserves of school funding; she also left me with the exciting prospect of a new Technology building already at the blueprint stage.

So in the next couple of years after I took over in 1993, I had the immense satisfaction of being able to improve the school's facilities. The down side was that staff worked for some considerable time in circumstances of flux and change – which they bore with great stoicism and, in the main, good will. While the Technology Block was being constructed, negotiations with Bromley had already secured some more new build – a wing extension to the main building, still known rather basically as '7 FE' because it was secured at the price of going up from six to seven forms of entry.

With two new buildings simultaneously in construction and innumerable in-house projects and conversions going on, between 1993 and 1998 virtually every subject was rehoused; walls were repainted off-white and grey carpets were laid. Banks of new lockers were installed. The large open space in the Extension was converted into five much needed classrooms. Plants and pictures provided the colour everywhere.

At more or less the same time, the Governing Body and I were nursing plans to make the school grant maintained. Most Bromley schools already had this status which freed them from the Local Authority and gave them greater autonomy and increased funding. I wanted the autonomy and, obviously, any additional funding was not to be sniffed at, but most important for me was that the Technology Schools Initiative (TSI) was only accessible to grant maintained and voluntary aided schools. Clearly it was impossible for us to move on the GM front until we had taken possession of the two new buildings, otherwise work on them would have ceased immediately.

The TSI, I felt, was a priority for the school. My brief was to raise girls' achievement in Maths and Science, and to make Design Technology and ICT realities as required by the dictates of the new National Curriculum.

As soon as the paint was dry and the furniture delivered, the tortuous process of initiating a bid for GM status began. This involved a unanimous Governing Body vote, consulting staff (some very suspicious of it) and balloting parents, with the Electoral Reform Society exercising a close scrutiny and control over the whole process. It was a tense and edgy time, but GM status was secured by an overwhelming parental vote in favour. To the surprise of some staff, terms and conditions of service did not change for the worse; rather they improved with, for example, an immediate increase of at least 300% in our professional development budget alone.

The great irony was that almost simultaneous with our acquisition of GM status there was a change in the rules governing TSI to make it accessible to all schools. TSI was converted into the Technology Colleges movement, and in order to support a good written bid, the school also had to be able to demonstrate sponsorship of £100,000 which the then DfEE would match with a capital grant in addition to the revenue funding which would generate in the region of £160,000 per year.

Writing the bid and raising the money were both very tough tasks and consumed our energies for many, many months. I remember the crushing disappointment of our first attempt being turned down on the basis of a certain degree of fragility about our sponsorship.

SEVEN   AIMING HIGH

The second attempt was successful, and it was only when we had secured TC status that everybody working here suddenly realised that becoming a Technology College was a bonus, not a retrograde step that would turn us into a second class technical school or that would privilege certain subjects over others.

The transforming power of TC status was immediately apparent. Our ICT resourcing and capability increased substantially with curriculum and administration networks embedded rapidly into school use. Developments in Maths and Science led to substantial improvements in pupils' performance and numbers taking up these subjects at A level began, steadily, to grow. D&T took off throughout all key stages and the success rate at GCSE in the five different full Technology courses is phenomenal. And ICT has proved the bedrock of teaching and learning across the curriculum. TC status truly accelerated the pace of improvement throughout the school.

During the course of our time as a GM school (1995 – 1998 until the current Government came to power), we were offered the opportunity to expand to 8 forms of entry with the usual pay off of additional buildings to accommodate the additional pupils. This was my chance to upgrade the last un-refurbished area in the school: Science. Although the 7FE wing had given us two new Science laboratories, the first floor of the main building, given over to Science, was no longer adequate for our needs nor contemporary in style. A new Science Block (yes, that is its name) was built facing the Technology Block, and the old Science floor was converted into much needed general teaching areas and a large Library which would underpin our conviction that the Library is at the centre of the school. Our local MP opened this building for us in 1998.

Class 7GW in the new Science block in January 2008

Towards the end of the 1990s, it became clear that the DfEE (by this time, the DfES) was looking to specialist schools like ours to work in families of other schools in order to spread best practice.

SEVEN   AIMING HIGH

So even in advance of the mandatory community element introduced in 1998/9 we developed a partnership with six primary schools, an infants' school, two secondary boys' schools and one secondary special school. That partnership flourishes today, and all of the schools involved have benefited enormously from the work that has arisen from this collaboration.

Looking outwards towards other schools and sharing journeys with them has been part and parcel of our success at LPGS and an essential ingredient in our being identified in three separate Ofsted inspections as an outstandingly successful school.

Not content with just one partnership, we have benefited from a number of them. Along with three other head teachers of successful Technology Colleges, I enjoyed the venture we embarked on in 1998 (in the bar at the Technology Colleges Annual Conference) to break all the government's rules by forming a virtual education action zone which would attract millions of pounds of additional funding over a five year period. We recruited some 15 other primary and secondary schools in Bromley and Essex, all of which, unlike us, did meet the criteria for socio-economic deprivation and poor performance, to join our consortium, and used all of our political clout to persuade the then Secretary of State for Education that this bid was worth approving. And it was! The four heads travelled to Melbourne in 1998 to research new ways of teaching and learning for our zone, and in 2000 with success looming we employed one of Victoria's most eminent Education Directors to manage our zone for us. The South East England Virtual Education Action Zone (SEEVEAZ for short) had a magnificent five year life with many bonuses for staff and pupils alike, and we really enjoyed the interaction with our Essex counterparts, except for the M25 and the Dartford Tunnel, which we got to know rather too well.

For the Bromley SEEVEAZ schools the end of the zone in April 2005 led straight into a further three year network of schools (known as an 'excellence cluster') called the Bromley Learning Alliance. Again the additional funding this generated led to some excellent initiatives for pupils and staff, ranging from Student Council development and Artists in Residence in schools to lesson observation and middle management training.

We were also invited to apply to become a Beacon School in 2002, in other words a centre of excellence in a number of areas of practice and to work in this capacity with selected other partner schools. No sooner had we achieved this status and begun our collaborations with four other secondary schools than the Beacon initiative for secondary schools was replaced by Leading Edge status – and we had to apply all over again.

This time, in the spirit of good will, we invited LPBS to join us in the bid as the joint lead school. This partnership is still going strong, and has led to some very positive initiatives such as the Lower Attaining Year 9 Science Intervention Project and the Innovations Bidding Scheme. As with the Family of Schools, annual planning is undertaken at a conference hosted by one or other of the partner schools, and it has been a joy to see hundreds of teachers from so many schools sitting and talking and planning with their counterparts. Collaboration like this keeps us fresh and vibrant.

Over the years, we have also chased and acquired a number of kite marks: Investor in People; Charter Mark; Investor in Careers; Arts Mark Gold; the Healthy School Award, Financial Management Standards in Schools and various others. Contrary to the unkind suggestion made once by a colleague that I was collecting logos for our school notepaper (they do look nice!), in fact the pursuit of these standards of excellence has been an invaluable way of compelling us to assess ourselves and improve our practice, and the external moderation of all of these awards has been a confirmation of our commitment to continuous self-improvement – on behalf of our pupils and parents.

SEVEN   AIMING HIGH

Our high performance as a Technology College led to us being targeted in early 2006 by the then DfES to consider applying for another specialism in advance of our re-designation as a TC which was not due until September 2006. Specialist school status until recently has run in phases of three or four years and redesignation has always been a rigorous and time-consuming process of reporting on targets met, or not met as the case may be, and setting targets for the next potential phase. So, early in 2006 we were moving towards the end of our third phase. We considered the choices available and decided to apply for a Languages specialism. We were successful in this, and subsequently the additional funding we have generated has enabled us to enhance our staffing in this area, convert and equip another electronic Languages room, and enhance the curriculum and enrichment offer for pupils. Our main aim is to further drive up results at GCSE (Languages are assessed more severely than any other GCSE and this situation is currently under national review) and to increase numbers taking up these courses at 16+ where currently they tend to be 'minority' subjects.

Towards the end of 2006 with TC re-designation approaching, to my surprise I discovered that we could apply to take on yet another specialism; after due consultation with staff, our choice was Sport with Geography as a supporting subject. We were successful in the whole enterprise and our Sports status was launched with a vengeance in September 2007. Staffing was increased, coaches were bought in, the range of sports on offer has been increased as has the level of participation in competitions and tournaments, and pupils have the opportunity to develop leadership and coaching skills in sports and to gain accreditation for these. Things are moving fast and furiously.

Subjects that are not directly involved in specialist development have nonetheless continued to thrive. Drama, Dance, Music and Art are all powerful and high-achieving subjects within the school, and all benefit from and give much to collaborative work with other schools. The Humanities have a strong profile in the school, and there are rich in-school collaborations, for example between History and French. Geography is instrumental in leading the eco-schools initiative and is now driving our development as a sustainable school, while RS attracts substantial numbers at both GCSE and A level, achieves highly and has equal status as a humanity. English has always been a major player at LPGS in terms of pupils' achievements and it has been active within the Family of Schools since this network's inception, doing valuable work on writing with Key Stage 2 children.

Vocational subjects are well embedded in the school and cater at various levels for large numbers of pupils who benefit, in particular, from the practical and applied approach. And developments in Special Needs and social inclusion have been crucial to our effectiveness. A dedicated Personal and Learning Support area was created by our very skilled site staff at the rear of the main building in 2003 and the PLS Faculty was duly created. It covers a breadth of need from dealing with poor behaviours and pupils in distress, to those with learning difficulties and many more besides. Attendance and absence calls are operated and monitored from PLS, behaviour is tracked and recorded on a special software package, and English as an Additional Language is now a vital element of PLS, supporting a number of Sixth Form students, in particular, with EAL issues, Many pupils have been helped to successfully complete their education at LPGS by virtue of PLS intervention.

The Sixth Form has grown significantly over the years, and we have concentrated much of our effort on providing our 16+ students with really well-resourced self-study facilities: hence the school project which resulted in the Dalo building (haphazardly named after the French manufacturers of this tensile structure which is used for Sixth Form work/talk about work during lesson time and as a whole-school social space at break and lunchtime). A further school-driven project provided a Sixth Form Centre to replace the one remaining rotting mobile left over from that early building phase that began my time here. Our 480 or so Sixth Form students have no excuse for not driving their own learning.

SEVEN   AIMING HIGH

Not only have we all worked hard over the years, we have enjoyed ourselves too. The enrichment activities, charity drives, productions, concerts, cabarets, foreign journeys, expeditions, residentials etc are so numerous that they blur into one magnificent parade of talent, skill and aspiration, enabling the full range of pupils to show what they can do individually and working together and enabled by staff initiative, generosity and good will.

As a result of all this activity, I and, I think, other colleagues have stayed here longer than we thought we might – because there has always been some new challenge, some fresh target to pursue. And a number of us have enjoyed the benefits of our successes, attending award ceremonies and meeting a rich variety of people at them. Our second Ofsted inspection in 2000 which, in the terminology of the time, led to LPGS being pronounced 'particularly successful' led to my being invited to meet Prince Charles at a reception for heads of similar schools at Highgrove. Our third Ofsted in 2006 led to an invitation to meet Her Majesty's Chief Inspector at Lancaster House in London at a reception for heads of schools which had received three 'outstanding' judgements.

A visit by Gordon Brown in June 2007 to hear about the school's anti-bullying policy

The whole journey since my start time here has been enthralling and driven; not always enjoyable but often enough so to make the whole enterprise worthwhile. I am lucky to have worked with so many talented and committed teachers and associate staff members, with senior managers I can rely on, with pockets of fun and humour pretty well every day with colleagues and pupils alike, with a Governing Body that has gelled into precisely the body of people I would wish for – who listen carefully, scrutinise rigorously and let us get on with the job. We never lose sight here of the fact that we exist to serve our pupils' needs, whatever they may be, to the very best of our ability. Currently the DCSF, which has now replaced the DfEE and the DfES, is setting out all sorts of new powers and new constraints for schools, many of them irritatingly badly thought out. But it's still good to be able to enjoy doing our work for the benefit of pupils and to derive so much satisfaction so often from the task.

SEVEN   AIMING HIGH

All those awards!

This is a **Foundation School** that grew from the previous Grant Maintained. This means that it handles all its own affairs using funds supplied directly from government sources and not as formerly through the Kent County Council or Bromley Borough Council.

The Charter Mark is awarded to public services that attain a high level of excellence. It is awarded every three years but only a third of re-entrants are successful. Langley Park Girls School has earned its *third* Charter Mark since its first in January 1999!

Technology College Status was first granted in September 1996 to raise the standards of Science, Mathematics, ICT and Technology. Two years later the school was offering triple science in addition to the dual certification prescribed by Bromley for all its schools in 1990 and in 2001 the school received the Susan Fey award for the most improved GCSE results in Science. Subsequent applications have brought additional funding that helps maintain the level of teaching staff in the face of cuts in the budgets to secondary schools. Maths projects have piloted materials for internet-based learning. It is now in its *fourth* phase.

Virtual Education Action Zone (VEAZ) from April 2000 forms a network for reciprocal learning with other Technology Colleges such as Ravenswood.

The Investor in People Award of 1997 was in recognition of the training available for everyone employed at the school including the office, resources, caretakers, kitchen staff, and technicians as well as the teaching staff.

The Investor in Careers Award is a quality standard for management of careers education in the school that includes careers lessons, a careers reference library, industry days and two weeks' work experience for all year 11. Outstanding in 2005 was the Chinook landing on the Boys' School playing field bringing Deputy Heads Jane Nicholls and Richard Darbourne to focus on the RAF as a career.

The Gold Arts Mark Award was for design, music, drama as well as art, first awarded in 2001 celebrated by masks from different parts of the world but now on its third award.

  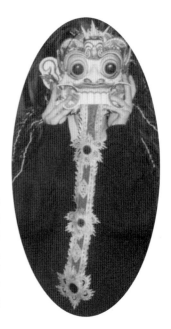

Year 9 pupils investigated the use of masks in cultures all over the world and found that they are worn when people want to be serious, funny, clownish, beautiful, frightening or intriguing as well as influencing twentieth century designers. They give us a chance to be someone else for a few minutes. The girls used papier maché and mixed media to make the masks of their choice as can be seen in the examples here.

SEVEN   AIMING HIGH

Its outstanding success was demonstrated by the performance of 'Encore' at the Fairfield Hall in the spring of 2007 led by Langley's Jazz Orchestra of forty of Langley's best musicians.

Leading Edge Status grew in 2005 from the previous Beacon status (2002) of high performing schools that are encouraged to work in partnership with other schools, not necessarily in the immediate neighbourhood. It has enabled the school to build on its work with the Women Unite Organisation in South Africa. Katie Shanahan of Year 8 in December 2007 wrote this account of a visit by a group of ten girls to Cator Park School for a language festival. *Once we arrived we had a French session where we introduced ourselves. Unfortunately for us, we were learning German! Then we had croissants which we asked for in French. After that we were put into groups and learnt some Russian, Turkish or Italian. After we had learnt two languages, we had lunch. We had to ask for the food in the language of the country it came from-France, Italy, Spain, Germany, Turkey and Russia- which was very difficult. Then we went to the studio to learn a Spanish dance and then sang songs in German, French, English, Russian and Italian. Finally we were given certificates and notebooks for our work. We all found this trip enjoyable and I found that learning new languages was quite a challenge but still very pleasurable.*

It was the turn of modern languages when **MFL Status** was conferred in 2006. The school was approached by the Dept of Education to develop a second area of specialisation in addition to Technology. Now Modern Foreign Languages are funded by almost an extra £130,000 per year and teaching has been extended to local primary schools. Mr Gonzalez teaches Spanish at Marian Vian. Since the beginning of the autumn term 2006, Mandarin is one of the languages offered at Langley as an enrichment activity at lunch time and after school. *'Ni hao, wo jiao Sha man hua'* is *'Hello, my name is Samantha'*

One of the most recent accolades was **Sports Specialist Status** awarded in April 2007. Success in many areas such as cross country running, athletics, netball, hockey, trampolining, swimming, gymnastics and multiactivities over the years suggests that perhaps this recognition is long overdue. Girls have progressed to England athletics, National trampolining and the Olympic swimming squad from Langley.

Healthy School Status for nutrition, exercise, mental health, school atmosphere and effective anti-bullying was awarded in June 2007. Visitors to the school frequently comment on the impeccable behaviour and neat appearance of its pupils and Gordon Brown visited in the summer of 2007 to speak to the girls with respect to their peer listening roles in the school's policy against bullying.

Peer Listening by Sarah Bowes (2000-2007)

I was a student at LPGS since the age of eleven and spent the Sixth Form studying A levels in French, Religious Studies, English Literature and Classical Civilisation Studies. I really enjoyed my years at the school which were happy, interesting and rewarding. I was an active member of the Music Department, singing with the choir and visiting the Black Forest and Belgium on Concert Tours. I completed the Silver Level of the Duke of Edinburgh Award and was appointed a Senior Prefect.

In 2006, after GCSEs, Year 11 girls were given the opportunity to attend a day's workshop with the Beat Bullying Organisation. Having completed the course they were then appointed as Peer Listeners. Two or three Peer Listeners are appointed to each form in Years 7, 8 and 9. They speak to the girls in small groups or individually if they have been made aware by staff of a particular need for extra support.

SEVEN   AIMING HIGH

Problems range from bullying, loneliness, lack of friends to difficulties with schoolwork and homework. The conversations are confidential but if they feel that a student is at risk of being harmed or harming others around them then the situation is reported to senior staff. The School's Peer Listening Network has been recognised with a Diana Memorial Award. The Rt. Hon. Gordon Brown, subsequently Prime Minister, visited the School in June 2007 to learn about the success of the scheme. In August 2007 GMTV featured LPGS and interviewed students and Peer Listeners in a programme which looked at issues concerning going back to school. I think my position as a Peer Listener was very worthwhile and rewarding. It has given me the interest and confidence to study for a degree in Applied Social Sciences, focusing on Criminology, and possibly to pursue a career in the social services field.

In case the reader thinks this is a school of all work and no play and is in serious need of 'happiness' lessons, take a look at the balloons and the three foot square cake that was shared out to celebrate the first Charter Mark and the fun of the egg and spoon race.

Jane (Pearson) Bowes and the Langley Park Girls Parent Staff Association

As an old girl (1964-71) I can clearly remember the first time I walked into Langley Park School for Girls (or Beckenham Grammar School for Girls as it then was). It therefore felt

rather surreal when my daughter started at the school in September 2001. I joined the PSA in 2002 (will I never learn!) and was elected Chairman the following year. The PSA Committee is a small group of very friendly parents and staff who meet approximately once every half-term to organise social and fund raising events. The biggest annual event by far is the Fireworks Evening in November in partnership with the Rotary Club. The fireworks are always spectacular and hundreds of people attend every year whatever the weather. Other recent events have included wine tastings, salsa dancing, a craft fair and quiz nights, both Music and General Knowledge. These quizzes are hugely popular, with up to two hundred attending, and the last evening made an incredible £1,100 profit.

102

In addition to these fund-raising events the PSA also provides refreshments at parents' evenings, the uniform sale in July, the Open Evening in October and hosts a Wine and Cheese Evening each September for new parents.

The money raised in the last few years has been put towards a new school minibus, text books, teaching aids and additional studio lighting for the drama department but the highlight for me was in January 2006 when the PSA was able to hand over to the school a cheque for £20,000 towards the new Dalo Building (a dining and social facilities extension) which has proved to be an enormous asset to the school and students and is a marvellous setting for quiz nights! Since then we have managed to raise a further £10,000 for the new Food Technology room which needed computers, smart board, projector and furniture. This room will benefit every child in the school and contribute to improving and developing their knowledge and understanding of nutrition and the role it plays in life. These substantial amounts of money have been achieved through much hard work by quite a small committee and great support from parents, staff and friends.

I will be resigning at the AGM in November 2007 as my daughter is hopefully off to university in 2008. I have really enjoyed my second 'career' at LPGS and I wish the PSA and my old school every success for the future.

Joanna Sanderson tells of her months in Malawi

Joanna Sanderson (1999-2006) left school after taking her A Levels in 2006 and the following January went to Malawi to teach in a girls' school until the summer. The subjects she was teaching included PE, science, remedial English and she started a creative arts club after school. She said materials were scarce but she was excited about teaching the girls to be artistically creative, which was not previously given any time in Malawi, probably because of lack of resources. Joanna also

gave Bible lessons at a local orphanage, including games and other ways to overcome the lack of material. She left behind pictures for the children so that they can talk about the stories any time they like. Part of her stay in Malawi included travels round Zambia and Malawi and the picture shows her on Chisomulu Island in Lake Malawi.

Hannah Doherty (2000-2007), School Captain

Everyone always says your school days go too fast; any Langley student will know this only too well. It may be a cliché but it does feel like only yesterday that I was a nervous eleven year old, apprehensive, but excited to begin my time at Langley, unnecessarily large rucksack in tow and a skirt that skimmed the ground. 'You'll grow into it!' my mother promised; I never did. So many wonderful experiences have been bestowed upon me in the last seven years, from adopting the position of an MEP at the European Parliament in Strasbourg to trekking through chin-high foliage on Dartmoor as part of the Duke of Edinburgh's Award. The time I spent in school wasn't half bad either! Lessons were vibrant and relevant, making full use of the excellent technology and resources on hand to enrich our learning.

SEVEN   AIMING HIGH

Belonging to LPGS does not mean merely turning up for eight periods each day and completing the work which is required, although don't get me wrong, attendance and hard work are important! However, there are many students who take pleasure in doing so much more. There are numerous extra-curricular activities for budding athletes, actors, musicians, linguists, the list goes on. Moreover, there are opportunities to contribute to the school community, particularly in the Sixth Form, by assisting other students through the provision of pastoral support, or as a prefect, for example. As School Captain, I was proud to be involved in a school with a strong ethos on community and comradeship, a sentiment that I am confident will withstand another ninety years.

Readers of the school newsletters will see that Hannah after a visit to the Blue Circle cement Works in year 7 was heading for a career in computing. In year 8, attending a three day course at PGL (Peter Gordon Lawrence activity centre), her favourite activities were the zip wire and the quad bikes. By year 11, work experience saw her destined for garment design. She commented, *'I had an amazing time; it exceeded all my expectations. I enjoyed the whole experience of going to a workplace and working with adults. The main thing that I learnt was being able to get on with things without being told exactly what and when.'*

In the event, Hannah departed for Bristol to study Economics and Politics. Perhaps we have not seen the last of Hannah Doherty!

What would you put in a time capsule?

In 1996, Pat Cordner, teacher of RE, decided to have a time capsule buried in the front garden, not to be dug up for one hundred years. You can see the plaque on the wall outside the Headmistress's study.

There are photographs showing Miss Sage digging the hole for the capsule, watched by a crowd of enthusiasts but nobody has any recollection of what the box looked like and what it contained. The teacher and her class have long left school.

Coins, poem written in Mandarin, weather forecast, picture of a car, train, plane? Would they be able to read our CDs in 90 years time? Will our school still be here when another 90 years has passed? Can anyone solve the mystery of what's in the capsule?

SEVEN   AIMING HIGH

Is there anything not provided at Langley?

Although it may be hard to believe, Neshe Olson, Maxine Yawson and Lucy Perrett had to say 'Yes' when they wanted to find out how to make a brick wall. They went to Lewisham College on a construction project and made a start on bricklaying, plumbing and carpentry.

Do you know your preferred learning style?

One of the main differences that can be seen in the teaching methods of today and of say 30 or more years ago is the broadening of the range of study so that it has become less traditional, more topical and with greater sharing of experiences among educational establishments. In May 2001, year 8 were guided by 24 trainee teachers from Goldsmith's College for a whole day. In the first workshop session they discovered their learning style from inter or intra personal, linguistic or mathematical/logical, visual/spatial, musical, naturalistic or kinaesthetic. Hope Cowell found that she was most intelligent in kinaesthetic. She was quite successful at learning to count to ten in Japanese by making up a story but hopeless at drawing her hand without looking at the paper, only watching her hand.

In Memory of Felicity Langford

On 1 May 1998, the school, led by Y12, celebrated the life of Felicity, who died of meningitis when only 16 in August 1997, by planting a memorial tree in the school garden.

At lunchtime, money was raised for the Meningitis Trust at a Teddy Bears' picnic by means of a balloon race and the planting of sunflower seedlings chosen as potential winners of the tallest plant by the end of term. Miss Sage's sunflower outstripped 50 others by a foot!

SEVEN   AIMING HIGH

The next year, they had a Mad Hatter's picnic that made £390 for the Trust from eleven stalls selling books, balloons for another race, cakes and chocolates donated by Beckenham Sainsbury's. Felicity's friends did not stop there. Leigh Davies, Sarah Knibbs and Katie Jefferson made a collection outside Sainsbury's over two weekends and collected £1,175 for the Meningitis Trust. Miss Sage and Leanne Benford are shown here wearing their 'mad' hats. Miss Sage's hat resembled a purple spider

'Annie' at the Churchill theatre

Successfully auditioned in July 2007, six LPSG students appeared in a cast of 34 in 'Annie' at the Churchill theatre between 30 October and 3 November. They were Grace Liston, Amy Godden (Pepper), Ellen Gauntlett (Duffy), Abigail Runnicles, Vicki Smith and Karen Mortby.

The Memorial Garden

The year 2003 was a sad one for Langley and has been remembered by the memorial garden on the front lawn that provides a quiet area for contemplation.

The rabbit plaque on the wall is in memory of Jalpa Patel who died when only 13 years old. A book of memories exists written by her friends.

The bench is in memory of Mrs Sue Repper, teacher of special needs who died from cancer in October 2003, sadly leaving her family and greatly missed by her classes and fellow teachers at school.

You will notice Jalpa's panel on the wall has five rabbits. The school had three rabbits, all named Buddy. The last school Buddy became ill and was cared for by Mrs Morrison (from catering) and her daughter Cherie. The rabbits were dearly loved by successive years 7 and 8, including Jalpa, and deserve their place in the memorial garden.

BUDDY BOOKING LINE

020 8663 4199

(please ring if you could offer to look after him on a weekend or in a holiday)

Book early to avoid disappointment!

SEVEN   AIMING HIGH

Both Miss Sage and Miss Carson were seriously ill during 2003 but fortunately they recovered.

Suzy Payne's message today

My name is Suzy Payne and I was a student a Langley Girls School between 1996 and 2003. I am currently (2007) an undergraduate studying English Literature at the University of Kent in Canterbury, which has increased my passion for drama both on the stage and the page. There is no doubt in my mind that the enthusiasm I have for the arts was found with the help of the keen and memorable teachers at Langley.

I remember Langley as being a school at which I'd felt very much a part of the action. I spent the majority of my seven years at the school in the drama studio – the room I'd spent an entire open evening in on my first ever visit. Drama continued to be my favourite lesson from the first time I'd taken part in the lower school drama festival, to the finale of 'Oh What A Lovely War', which had been the school production of my final year in 2003. We were lucky at Langley, to have an exceptional teacher in Brigid Doherty, who reminded us that Drama was a subject just as challenging as any other, if not more so. As a result, the hard-working drama classes and casts of the many productions and cabarets remained a close-knit bunch. Miss Sage was also an inspiration in her support of the school as a whole, but especially in terms of the arts. We were always grateful for her frequent visits during the rehearsals taking place in the hall and she would often comment on the singing she had heard from her nearby office. While I chose drama to dominate my time at the school, my interest grew in many other subjects such as Religious Studies and English, and this was almost always due to the quality of the teachers there.

In my experience, Langley was a place where students were given the benefit of the doubt, and were constantly encouraged to push themselves further and to achieve more whilst enjoying a good mix of hard work and recreation. I have always appreciated what the school brought out of me, and look back with affection at my time there. I hope it remains a place of similar memories for many more students in the years to come.

SEVEN   AIMING HIGH

L to R 'Oh What a Lovely War,' 'Once in a Lifetime' and 'The Chalk Circle' from a collage of Suzy's roles.

My first day at Langley Park School for Girls by Eleanor Farley in 2007

The night before my first day at Langley I felt very excited. I was usually excited after the summer holidays but this was different. I could find my way around Oak Lodge easily but Langley …it's HUGE!! I've always worried about its size but now it really started to bug me. What if I couldn't find the classroom? Also, my friend had told me some people were bullied. What if I got bullied about the length of my skirt? Or the number of key rings on my bag? But my mum told me not to worry and to go to sleep.

In the morning I woke up at about six o'clock which was much earlier than usual! I felt a bit apprehensive but very excited. I quickly got dressed and got my things together. To get to school I walked. I walked with my mum to my friend Lottie's house. My mum dropped me off there and then Lottie and I walked from her house to school. On our way we talked mainly about what Langley would be like! When I first got to school we were taken straight to the main hall to have a talk with Miss Sage and Mr. Chilton-Higgins about what they expect of us and what for us to expect now we're in Secondary school. After that we went straight to our form rooms and the day began. When we got to our form rooms there were a lot of things to do. First we were told a lot of information about school rules, where to come in and go out and lots more! We were also given our lunch card, our planners, a map and our GNBs. We went to top up our cards and see if our parents had put any money on them, then it was break time. After break we had History. Our teacher is called Miss Manville and I thought she was a bit scary! For our history homework we had to cover our books which wasn't too bad! It was lunch after history and after lunch it was maths, my least favourite subject! But once the lesson started it quickly turned into my favourite! Mr. Jenkinson, my maths teacher, is incredibly funny! At the end of the day Miss Hamlett, my form tutor, took the register and then the bell went! We will all have a heart attack by the end of the year because of that bell! Looking back, I don't really know what I was so worried about. I've stopped jumping out of my skin every time the bell rings but I haven't quite found my way round yet but I soon will. I hope!

I'm still a bit scared of Miss Manville though!

EIGHT   MEMORIES OF THE WAR

When the war started in September 1939, only the fifth and sixth forms were allowed to attend school as there were insufficient shelters. The third and fourth forms stayed at home working with the help of staff visits, the first form met for lessons at the Holy Trinity Church House and the second form assembled at the school pavilion in the two changing rooms where it was very cramped and cold. Miss O'Dell and a new PE teacher, Miss Williams were in charge. The third and fourth forms returned to school in October and the others did not use the school until November.

In this picture where Pat King and Mary McIntosh are playing Audrey Handy and her partner, the pavilion looms inhospitably on the right but the tennis courts were always available. Today, although the hard court area is still there, the tennis courts have gone. The old wooden pavilion has been replaced by a smart new brick built one and the field is used for athletics and cross country.

Stella Martin's memories of starting school as the war began

September 1939 was the time when lots of happy eleven year old girls were preparing for their new school with proudly ordered Gorringe's uniforms and trips to Frost's, the little shoe shop in Penge. So far they were unaware that instead of satchels they would soon be carrying boxes containing gasmasks. Then on 5 September, letters arrived at home (letters because few families had telephones) postponing the beginning of term now that war had been declared until the windows had been taped against flying glass and the trenches on the playing field were ready. The school was considered vulnerable due to proximity of light industry and vital railway networks.

Our school soon continued but in a surprising place. We were given rooms at Holy Trinity church hall working at bare wooden tables which seated eight on each. We met the teachers. We met each other and our strange situation quickly became normal. Arithmetic became Mathematics, drawing became Art, singing became Music and writing became Literature. Out went our laborious cursive writing with its extravagant loops and in came simple print, styled by national handwriting expert, Marion Richardson. We had to write on every inch of every line and our best books had to be covered in brown paper so that they would last for several years.

After a few weeks we were allowed to start at the real school. After the friendly, if dusty, church hall, school seemed huge with its long corridors, stuffy cloakrooms, stark toilets and big classrooms. Now we had a form room, a desk and changed rooms and teachers for every lesson. We had to concentrate to have the right books in the right place. Homework was set and homework was done. No excuses!

With the retreat from Dunkirk in 1940, the Battle of Britain began as a prelude to the Blitz. All the time we made our way to school, even though we had spent the night in air raid shelters listening to bombs falling so that we cycled through the debris and dust from bombed houses with broken toys in the front gardens. Then we faced a day underground in the trenches unless it had rained and the shelters had flooded. Then we sat in the corridor by the Headmistress's room as this was thought to be the safest place. Girls lost homes, possessions, relatives, pets and form 3A lost a classmate. Air raid sirens wailed day and night but Algebra homework was still set-and done!

EIGHT   MEMORIES OF THE WAR

A diary of the time records, 'As we were having dinner we saw the wing of an aeroplane with a cross on it swoop over the playground and heard the ack-ack-ack of machine guns and the bullets hitting the asphalt.'

Extracts from the log book of the Beckenham County School for Girls on the use of trenches

10 January 1940 There was now accommodation in the trenches for 300 girls and staff but the new forms would not be put in the trenches until the pumping difficulty had been solved. Water was coming up through the sumps and automatic pumps were to be installed. Two lamps were to be kept in each teaching room with tins of biscuits and wrapped barley sugar. Elsan toilets and screens would be placed in the trenches and gas curtains for the entrances.
2 September 1940 Mistresses would have to use their own judgement when to take the girls out to the trenches. Miss Fox said she would think over whether the girls should take their dinners out with them.
11 September 1940 The school would open for half-time education only from 23 September and staff could arrange to take classes of under 15 girls in school if they wished. Miss Broadhurst and Miss Atkinson were to organise staff into sticking on window protectors.
Tuesday 24 September 1940 The question of reopening the school was discussed as **time bombs** had fallen on the trenches demolishing them and the Royal Engineers were expected that afternoon. It was proposed to recall a section of the school on Thursday.

Pat Ridler's memories of that time

I was the only one walking down Lennard Rd from New Beckenham station on Wednesday 25 September 1940 but I came on the train from Lower Sydenham by myself. With the place deserted I waited outside the front door, too scared to do anything else thinking I was late, when I saw Mary Hayhow enter the gates. She was the only girl in the whole school known to me, as I came from out of area but she went to my church. She knew a thing or two as she was in the Prep so she rang the bell to find that we had been missed out from the frantic messages sent to warn everyone to stay at home until next week.

Back in due course to start at the new school, my form seemed to get no further than the entrance hall where we were crammed together while some of us read 'A Midsummer Night's Dream.' Why do I remember Kathleen Agate and Jean James reading their parts? Then it appears we were all sent home again.

Looking through the magazine of 1941, I found out why. On Wednesday night, 3 October 1940, the school was showered with **incendiaries**. The studio and room 26 were damaged and so we were sent home with some work while the staff mopped up after the firemen. By the following Monday we were back at school again for half days, rather tired by this time of having our term interrupted and spending hours on end down the trenches. The middle staircase and those rooms were out of use for some long time but cloakrooms were bricked up as shelters so that the wet trenches were no longer needed. From time to time, windows were shattered and doors came off their hinges when bombs fell close by but there were no more direct hits. There was one serious incident however when the school playground was machine-gunned and the wall of the dining room hit, fortunately at the middle of the lunch break when most were inside. I think that this may have been in January 1943 when the Catford Primary School was bombed from aircraft that had flown up the Thames and continued to fly over Beckenham chased by fighters. This is confirmed by Margaret (Lovegrove) Watson who was in the dining room and saw the staff duck beneath their top table as three planes with black crosses machine gunned the playground and bullets struck the dining room wall. Marjorie Sear dived under a privet hedge to avoid the machine guns.

EIGHT   MEMORIES OF THE WAR

Knitting for the Merchant Navy

Since January 1940, the school was busy raising funds for wool to knit garments for the Forces and it was felt that the Merchant Navy's need was greater than the Royal Navy as the men had no uniform grant. We bought wool at cost price from the Merchant Navy Comforts Service having raised nearly £37 in this first year.

The finished garments were 33 pullovers, 20 pairs socks, 25 pairs seaboot stockings, 44 pairs of mittens, 3 pairs of gloves, 3 pairs of wristlets, 57 helmets and 27 scarves.

In addition we had 52lbs of wool to knit during the summer holidays. Money was raised through efforts like raffles, guessing the beans in a jar, sale of felt flowers, money from the gate of the staff v girls netball match and various competitions eg dancing and advertisements. A small group of devoted knitters continued throughout the war.

Evacuation to Exeter in WWII by Pamela Daymond

On 2 January 1941, eighteen of us said 'Goodbye' to our parents and accompanied by Miss Preston and Miss King we boarded a London bus for an unknown destination.

On the train, we 'acted daft' so if we saw a cow we would say 'look milk' and so on! We were served a cup of greasy soup and a pasty on the journey and when we arrived at Exeter we were taken to a local Children's Home. We had a medical examination and slept two in a 2ft 6in bed with a dip in the middle. The next day, the WVS drove us to our billets and after a few days, Miss Preston and Miss King were recalled by Miss Fox and replaced by a young mistress, Miss Rabson. She listened to all our moans and groans and we assembled each morning by the stationery cupboard at the Bishop Blackall School for a talk. Miss Rabson undertook her duties very seriously and we all felt very comfortable with her.

At weekends Miss Rabson would take those who wanted to go on hikes in the country and the two springs we were there, she took us to pick daffodils to send home. The Baedeker raid on Exeter came after we had been there for 17 months.

Several of us were bombed out and all we could think of was to get home. It did not occur to us to contact Miss Rabson or tell the Bishop Blackall School that we were safe. We now know that she mounted her bicycle and visited all our billets, finding to her horror that one was gutted by incendiaries and others badly blasted. It was twenty four hours before she heard that all her girls were safe. In 1969, the evacuees finally managed to gather together on the school's 50th anniversary at the Adremians lunch to say 'Thank You' to Miss Rabson. We all had a laugh at the time that had elapsed and presented Miss Rabson with a small gift.

In January 1991, ten evacuees met again with Miss Rabson (by now known as Rab) at one of their houses, that of Nancy (Banks) Tonkin, well known as the Adremians Secretary for many years. It was not until that meeting that Miss Rabson revealed her horrific cycle ride round Exeter looking for us after the raid. Of course lots of family and wartime photographs were passed round and after that the group continued to meet annually.

EIGHT   MEMORIES OF THE WAR

In 2000, five of the evacuees went to see Rab at Wantage for coffee, a buffet lunch and afternoon tea in spite of her advancing years.

In June 2001, Rab acknowledged how touched she was by the faithful friendship of her girls for so long.

The Exeter party was as follows: Nancy Banks, Barbara Barker, Sheila Bates, Betty Bleay, Jean Cocking, Pamela Daymond, Valerie Dill, Gwen Fairhead, Joan Field, Wendy Jones and her sister, Freda Long, Christine Parker, June Ridout, Yvonne Sheldon, Kathleen Tichner and Grace Turner. Sadly although they all survived the Exeter bombing, Joan Field and another County School girl, Pat Peters, were both killed on 2 July 1944 when a V1 fell on Trenholme Rd in Penge. Pat's friend, Jean (Upfold) Snazell remembers seeing a school house shoe in the rubble.

A Well-Travelled Evacuee, Betty (Bleay) Godson, 1939-46

My memory of evacuation is mainly of the freedom I enjoyed and the amazing variety of people whom I met. Like many during the Second World War, it completely altered my horizons and gave me a far wider view than I could ever have had living in Beckenham.

I was lucky enough to be evacuated to Exeter in January 1940, aged 11. I say 'lucky' because the people with whom I was billeted were mostly very kind and had pleasant homes. On Saturdays in the spring I would set off on my bike armed with a huge pasty. I had found a great friend in another evacuee from a school in North London and we spent the whole day in the glorious Devon countryside cycling, clearing streams and riding horses... I shall never forget the honeyed smell of whole banks of unpicked primroses along the roadside.

I was learning the piano and at a later billet I joined another evacuee, who was a violinist, and the daughter of the house, who was a cellist, and we spent many hours practising trios together.

It never occurred to anyone that, as girls, we might be in any danger. Men were away at the war and we were free to roam as we pleased. However, at one billet, the husband, an unpleasant man who frequently berated his wife in front of me, making me feel very uncomfortable, attempted to force his attentions on me. I very quickly reported this to Miss Rabson, our French teacher, who telephoned Miss Fox, our then headmistress. Miss Fox was a rather formidable figure, short and stout with a ramrod back, Eton crop and pebble-lens glasses. We were a bit afraid of her but on that occasion she was kindness itself to my poor father, who had been summoned to the School and given the reason for my return. Within two days I was home again and a few days after that I was despatched as a lone evacuee to Stafford to join the local High School there along with girls from the Ramsgate High School in Kent. When I think back on it, the sheer logistics of moving all those thousands of children to different schools and homes was an incredible achievement.

I eventually returned to Beckenham to prepare for my GCEs (General Certificate of Education exams) in the Fourth form. I know I felt somewhat of an expert on Australia as I studied it in Beckenham for the third time, having already done it in Exeter and also in Stafford! I remember spending a lot of time in the shelters (dug into the School lawn) having dimly lit lessons, but the crunch was having to take an oral music exam with V-bombs droning overhead! Fortunately they droned on further north so we were able to continue with our exam. I understand that special dispensation was given by the examiners for pupils taking exams under these conditions...in any event, we all passed.

My last experience as an evacuee was especially interesting. My mother arranged for my sister and me to go to our great aunt in Yorkshire.

EIGHT   MEMORIES OF THE WAR

She lived with her husband in a stone cottage on the Neasham estate, near Darlington. My great aunt had once been personal maid to Lady Wrightson, the wife of the owner of the estate. When the Nanny of her grandson was taken ill, Lady Wrightson invited me to go to the Hall to look after the little boy as what we would now call an 'au pair'. I was to have one French and one Music lesson a week and was allowed to practise on the grand piano in the ballroom, in which, sadly, the furniture was covered in dust sheets.

Nevertheless, despite the fact that there were few staff, only one maid, a cook and one or two elderly grounds men, due to the war, I was able to learn something of how the estate was run and of the caring and practical attitude to their staff and ex-employees shown by the estate owner and his wife.

However, at the end of the summer holidays, the Schools Inspector was knocking at my mother's door when I had not registered at school in September, so I was reluctantly obliged to return and take my place in the Lower Sixth.

Rosemary Davidson tells us the sad tale of Mary Helen Whayman

Mary Helen Whayman, also known as Mollie, joined the school in 1922 at about the same time as Nancy Wiseman and when Nancy was moved up into the upper III, Mary took on the position of form captain of the lower III in Nancy's place. There are not many records of Mary as she went through the school but she is shown as having passed Drawing and English with credit. In 1929 she went on to a London polytechnic and passed the preliminary Science and Druggist exams. Then she did a three year apprenticeship in Pring's in Bromley eventually finishing as the Head of Pharmacy at Croydon Hospital.

Rosemary lives in Australia and wrote to tell us of how Mollie was killed on the last night of the blitz, 10/11 May 1941 when a number of bombs fell on Kendall and Sidney Roads, killing seven people among whom were Mollie, her mother Mildred Alicia Whayman and her mother's sister, Miss Tonge. Neighbours said that they had stayed in their Anderson shelter all night and had just returned to the house having decided the attacks were over.

Transform your rubbish...

recycle
for Elmbridge

SOME FORMER PUPILS — —

GIFTED & TALENTED

FASHION

Recycled materials and computer-aided printing

Key to the BCGSG 1948 reunion of 1998

Standing 1 Margaret (Taylor) Phillips, 2 Jean (Woodward) Runciman, 3 Carole (Prichard) Barrs, 4 Miss Margaret Cooper, 5 Valerie (Wilson) Dobb, 6 Claire (Sceats) Hardisty.

Back row 7 Pat (Russell) O'Brien, 8 Valerie (Batten) Lines, 9 Marian (Heale) Smillie, 10 Miss Muriel Uglow, 11 Joan (Russell) Hardy, 12 Janet (Grant) Ellison, 13 Anne (Woods) Gordon, 14 Linda (Wood) Zerk, 15 Pamela (Brooks) Anderson, 16 Elaine (Johnson) Oldham, 17 Kathy (Madgwick) Jackson, 18 Miss Nancie Pelling, 19 Miss Margaret Henson, 20 Molly (Sears) Oakleigh, 21 Jill Jones (Adremian Secretary), 22 Gillian (Crewes) Moore-Martin, 23 Gillian (Ansell) Lusty, 24 Maureen (Gillespie) Jordan, 25 Mary Hardcastle, 26 Janet (Coling) Woods, 27 Jennifer (Coppard) Hargreaves, 28 Corinne (Golder) Older, 29 Janet (Elam) Burrell, 30 Patricia Kenny, 31 Sheila (McKail) MacKenzie.

Centre row 32 Ann (Hills) Gamet, 33 Pat (Logan) Williams, 34 Ann Bartlett, 35 Anne (Mottram) Simmonds, 36 Joan (Dell) Finch, 37 Jennifer (Berriman) Mead, 38 Christina (Watt) Rex, 39 Sylvia (Ratcliffe) Bunce, 40 Glenda (Thornton) Lindsay, 41 Jane (Penny) Sackville, 42 Jennifer (Durell) Elgar, 43 Jill (Stansbury) Thomas, 44 Brenda (Body) Hazelton, 45 Edith (Pullen) Worthington, 46 Jill (Alcock) Whalley, 47 Merrill (Salter) Drzymala, 48 Jill (Ford) Moxon, 49 Sheila (Barclay) Howden, 50 Gwen (Smith) Pritchitt, 51 Daphne (Roberts) Brook, 52 Linda (Hardy) Young, 53 Carole (Hennessy) Gear.

Front row 54 Barbara (Myers) Langridge, 55 Mrs Sybil (Bell) Cox, 56 Joyce (Clarke) King, 57 Vivien (John) Smith, 58 Millicent (Oliver) Snoding, 59 Ruth (Hutchinson) Stobart, 60 Ruth Hixson, 61 June (Potter) Thomsitt, 62 Tessa (Edwards) Kail, 63 Beryl (Huke) Reid, 64 Elise (O'Neill) Baugh, 65 Sylvia (Kirk) Harrison, 66 Jill (Cowham) Simpson, 67 Shirley (Porrer) Bradley, 68 Brenda (Jelly) Booker, 69 Ann (Gully) Patterson, 70 Margaret (Trim) Mould, 71 Madeline (Beech) Lightfoot.

The 1948 entry met 50 years later in 1998 for this photo stretching across from the facing page.

Below is a similar meeting of some of the 1952 entry
L to R Kneeling:
Jill Bury, Maureen Wyard, Rosemary Bentley, Christine Parry;
standing:
Margaret Dossor, Gillian Shelley, Ann Weir, Suzanne Roe, Marian Barber, Ann Everett, Pat Finn, Elizabeth Mynett, Valerie Martin, Jackie Mead, Elizabeth Wilkinson.

Multiactivities at Hyde House

Top L to R, Abseiling at Durdle Door, water skiing at Studland, snorkelling at Lulworth Cove, long boat

Middle, Hyde House, Wareham, archery with Steve, grass skiing.

Cheers from Chris Watmough.

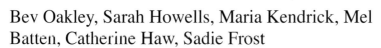

Bev Oakley, Sarah Howells, Maria Kendrick, Mel Batten, Catherine Haw, Sadie Frost

LEAVERS 2007

Dixie Queen

Leavers' breakfast

LEAVERS 2008

Leavers Breakfast Morning

Cheryl and Charlotte

Addington Ball

CAPE TOWN 2005

Leysin

1980 LAKE COMO

1983, COLLE DI TENDA

DAVID BLAKE

Skating 1989

Polybagging

CYPHERS

Two fires, the first just before the 1987 storm, the second in 2003, left Cyphers desolate and ripe for development by Waterside Developments, Sept 2007

FELICITY LANGFORD

The tree was planted in Felicity's memory by her friends in May 1998. Various activities were run, also in 1999, to raise money for the Meningitis Trust

The balloon race, sun flower competition and teddy bears' picnic

Mad hatter's tea party

TECHNOLOGY 2007

EIGHT   MEMORIES OF THE WAR

Rosemary has Mollie's autograph album where there are entries by Mary Cox, K Millington and R Payne including a drawing made of stick figures keyed to the names of the 30 girls in her class and their teacher, Miss Darling.

Key

1	A. Jesshope	11	M. Dryden.	21	A. Grassby
2	W. Arnold.	12	M. Whayman.	22	J. Peet.
3	D. Bristow.	13	G. Bartlett.	23	K. Millington.
4	M. Purfield	14	Miss Darling	24	R. Payne.
5	G. Millwood	15	S. Carwardine.	25	R. Harrop
6	M. Smith.	16	G. Vince	26	M. Rudderham
7	W. Balmforth.	17	L. Richards.	27	E. Lawrence.
8	M. Elliott	18	P. Ashton.	28	S. Barron
9	B. Parker.	19	A. Burden	29	A. Weaver.
10	I. Rabbets.	20	M. Cox.	30	J. Beale.
				31	M. Edwards.

Flying bombs and the great divide by Yvonne Ames, Phyllis Jutton, Sheila Briggs and Pat Ridler

Yvonne writes, 'For many of us, the appearance of the pilotless planes, the doodlebugs, in the skies over Kent brought the worst of the war which by June 1944 we thought was nearly over. Within three weeks, the option of being evacuated by the school appeared on the notice board and a party of over fifty girls, some with younger members of the family, chose to go. Miss Rabson and Miss King were in charge. Others accompanied their brothers from the Boys' School.

On 3 July, we climbed on to London buses waiting at Alexandra school for our journey to Kings Cross and then destinations unknown. Rumours spread that we were going to Scotland and by way of war time train journeys this could have been true because it took us all day to get there. The train was so long that our coaches didn't reach the platform and after humping our cases along the train, we found ourselves at DONCASTER. Most of us had never heard of Doncaster but as we had been half expecting beautiful Yorkshire dales where we could spend our summer holidays we were cheered to see 'Yorkshire Traction' on the sides of buses waiting to take us to Goldthorpe.

This is where our education started as we waited in a school to be 'chosen' by the local people.

EIGHT   MEMORIES OF THE WAR

They thought the evacuees would be five year olds, not great galumphing, disagreeable teenagers who were old enough to be at work. We could not understand what each other said and we certainly did not realise that our hosts would often have to give up their own beds to accommodate us. They usually lived in rows of small terraced houses, often back to back and normally impossibly close to the pits. We were seeing slag heaps for the first time and men returning home from work covered in coal dust because there were no baths at their pitheads.

Phyllis lived with one such family, Mr and Mrs Fellowes, where she was billeted with her friend Thelma Gyi. The back to back house was at Highgate and was owned by the colliery. In addition to the parents, there was Harold, their son of 17, and an older daughter with a boyfriend in the RAF. The house was small and opened directly into the parlour which was only used for high days and holidays. The other room where they all lived had stairs leading up to three small bedrooms and a door off to the scullery where all the washing was done. The toilet was a basic affair in the yard and a zinc bath was produced on Fridays for a bath in front of the fire. Phyllis's brother, Peter, stayed in Thurnscoe with Mr and Mrs Webster, who were relatives of the Fellowes. Thankfully they had a proper bathroom where Phyllis and Thelma could have a bath!

Mr Fellowes worked at a mine where there were baths provided but his son Harold came home dirty and exhausted every night from working at the forge, frequently falling asleep under the table before he washed.

Yvonne's experience was similar but she was told by her mother that she must stay with her brother. Eventually Mr and Mrs Lunn said they would have them if the WVS could provide their bedding. They also were living in Thurnscoe that Yvonne found an incredibly dreary town. Mr Lunn worked at the Barnborough Main Colliery and his son, Ronnie, had just left school that summer to work in the local colliery Hickleton. He was in the local Sea Cadet Force and longed to join the Royal Navy. His sister, Mavis was 13 and not very friendly because she thought us snobby (which we probably were!). Their house was a modern one with a bathroom and looked out over the fields. This was something that I realised about this part of Yorkshire. Although the villages were small and plain, they were surrounded by countryside, not housing estates like our Beckenham.

Yvonne's memories include proper Yorkshire pudding served with gravy before the Sunday roast and the mushy peas that accompanied the shop bought fish and chips with vinegar. Sometimes when she came home from school there was a huge pile of free coal outside in the street that had to be moved in. For the first three weeks, she and her brother were given no clean underclothes, but she told Miss King who visited Mrs Lunn and put the matter right. After Christmas, Yvonne's host, Mr Lunn, went on night shift and Yvonne began to find her bed was gritty with coal dust and sometimes warm when she went to bed. She realised that Mr Lunn was sleeping in her bed during the day when she was at school!

Sheila and Mary Hill were billeted with a middle aged couple, Mr and Mrs Ryan, who had no children.

They were shown up to a very comfortable room with a double bed and walnut bedroom suite. After a bath and a change of clothes they were given a good supper. They discovered that Mr Ryan was a miner and that Mrs Ryan had been a cook. The Ryans were devout Roman Catholics and they encouraged the girls to go to church with a neighbouring family, the Myers, and their three children. Both the Myers and Mrs Ryan were very musical and owned pianos. When they found that both Sheila and Mary could play the piano, Sunday evenings became great fun as they played all the songs from musicals of the 1920s and some Gilbert and Sullivan.

EIGHT   MEMORIES OF THE WAR

Pat was billeted with Valerie Curtis in the house of a pit manager, Mr Grace, complete with a bathroom and all mod cons but every Saturday they were told to amuse themselves all day until the evening so they caught the bus to Doncaster. Of course they had very little money but could spend the morning at the swimming baths and the afternoon at the cinema. One day they watched 'The Desert Song' with heart-throb Dennis Morgan first and then ran up the road to see 'Fanny by Gaslight' with James Mason.

Many returned home once the frequency of the flying bombs died down and the September term started and there were fewer than 200 out of the 351 girls on the roll to start the school year. They had all started at Wath Grammar School bemused that the term began in the middle of August and some could not wait to return home to the familiar school certificate syllabus, gradually joined by most of the other evacuees.

Thelma went home at Christmas and Yvonne with her brother stayed until the spring but Phyllis and Peter remained for ten months until the end of the war. Peter who attended the local primary school came home with a thick Yorkshire accent. All the girls were popular with the boys at the Coed Wath Grammar School (although they mocked the Southern accents) but their girls were none too pleased with the evacuees from the South. However several lasting friendships were formed, some lasting for years.

Phyllis had a particular friend, Arthur Walker, who subsequently went to Bristol University and shared a room with an Old Beccehamian, Alan Mead. Some years later, she discovered the same chap was a very good friend of folk she met in Holland. A small world indeed but without a doubt they had all learnt a valuable lesson on how the rest of the world lived!

Wath Grammar School (that became Comprehensive) was of course the school attended by William Hague.

Wath on Dearne Evacuation Party (may not be complete)
Yvonne Ames and her brother, Barbara Andrews, Evelyn Andrews, Heather Ansell, Barbara Barker, Pat Billinghurst, Joyce Birkenshaw, Sheila Briggs, Mary Bristo, Maisie Browne, Cynthia Brownlee, Pamela Cable, Christina Champion, Annie Cheetham, Lily Cooke, Mollie Copper, Hazel Cope, Pauline Crichton, Margaret Cummings, Valerie Curtis, Margaret Dungay, Olive Elton, Dorothy Fields, Jennifer Friend, Joan Gaved, Thelma Gyi, Mary Hill, Margaret Hurford, Julia Hurford, Kathleen Hyde, Joan Hyde, Mary Jones, Phyllis Jutton, Peter Jutton, Stella Martin, Audrey McPhun, Mildred Miles, Audrey Mitchell, Joy Newell, Audrey Nicholls, Joan Norris, Margaret Paige, Yvonne Penn, Dorothy Percy, Daphne Perkins, Ida Pleant, Joyce Poupard, Isobel Reid, Pat Ridler, Audrey Rivett, Beryl Robbins, Pamela Robbins, Janet Skinner, Eileen Skues, Muriel Sudbury, Dawn Sullivan, Pamela Terry, Margaret Tilley, Sheila Thompson, Heather Waterfield, Pamela Webb.

Miss King and her dog Billy

EIGHT   MEMORIES OF THE WAR

A party of 21 from Wath Grammar School made a return visit to Beckenham for a week in September 1946. Miss King and Miss Henshaw arranged a timetable to include Regent's Park Zoo, the National Gallery, the Houses of Parliament, the West End shops, Madame Tussaud's and the City with St Paul's cathedral where the damage inflicted during the blitz was still apparent. Then the Wath visitors made up a scratch hockey team that beat our school hockey XI one afternoon which made them enjoy the party in the evening even more.

Digging for Victory by Marjorie (Sear) Davy formerly Snell

Miss Stephenson and Miss Rabson organised a gardening group in the garden of the empty house next to the school, later the caretaker's house. Diggers, planters and weeders would go before and after school to grow vegetables and maintain the fruit bushes. Marjorie's memories are of the spiders' webs and blackberry thorns but she cannot recall where their produce went!

Sheila (Thompson) Hocking recalls wartime school 1939-1946

I can well remember the excitement of going up to London to Gorringes to buy the school uniform. Hmm the new smell of it all but the huge disappointment that because of the outbreak of war we were not able to go to school until safety arrangements were in place.
Eventually we were accommodated in the Church Hall further along Lennard Road, with the Church as our air raid shelter. At play time a huge tin of custard creams appeared and we were able to buy some. I still love them!

Front to back, left, Monica Duncan (née Weeks), possibly Betty Bleay, Eileen Spalding and Marion Kerridge; right Margaret Rees, Rowena Lewis,??

Once the shelters were ready we did get to the school with regular air raid practices; then the raids began and we had lessons in the shelters; wonderful Mrs. Wright the school cook actually served our lunches in the shelters, even tureens of rabbit stew! We were advised to take iron rations each day in case we were held at school late because of air raids. I think we ate them during our first visit of the day to the shelters! We had gas mask drills - ugh the smell of it still lingers in the memory. Girls who were taking their School certificate exams in July 1944 were put in the surface shelters converted from the cloakrooms at the back of the hall. Marion Kerridge remembers trying to work out notes in a music exam when waiting for the drone of a doodlebug to pass overhead.

EIGHT   MEMORIES OF THE WAR

Gwendoline Strachan is at the front left and Marion Kerridge right at the back of the left hand row. In the centre on the right are Barbara Costidell and Betty Curtis. These examinations were taken in early July at the time of the worst of the V1 bombing in Beckenham.

Hilda (Trowbridge) Hannaford took school certificate in 1940 and remembers being told by Miss King to get under the desks that had been put out in the hall when a dog fight was going on overhead during their French exam. They were only the flimsy folding desks used solely for exam purposes, completely useless for protection, but they all passed French so probably the examiners were told of the interruption.

A Red Cross Cadet Detachment was formed in the School under the command of Mrs. Alexander, starting on 27 November 1942. We were trained, sat exams and received certificates. Rowena Lewis and I were selected to represent us at Buckingham Palace on 16th May 1942. What a day! Assembly at Wellington Barracks, soldiers whistling from the windows at the older nurses, marching to the Palace garden where we all lined up on the lawns. It was a VERY hot day and quite a few fainted and were carried down to the lake where it was cooler. The Queen (the late Queen Mother) in a lovely heliotrope dress and hat gave us all permission the sit on the grass until it was our turn to be inspected. I was so nervous when she actually reached us, if she had spoken to me I couldn't have replied, my mouth was so dry. George VI joined her on the steps later and we all then had to march past, back to the barracks and dispersal. Prior to going to the Palace we were given marching instruction by a member from the RAF. I think he must have despaired of us, poor chap.

EIGHT   MEMORIES OF THE WAR

As we got older we undertook duties at Beckenham Hospital on Saturdays and during the holidays. We really felt we were doing something even if it was rolling bandages. In the VI form I became Detachment leader with a very smart outdoor coat and cap. The poor Sister I helped one holiday nearly had a heart attack when she asked what I would be doing after the holiday as she signed my 'black book'. I told her I was going back to school. 'How old are you then?' Sixteen was my reply. 'If I'd known you were so young I wouldn't have given you some of the jobs I asked you to do. I shall certainly ask the nurses their age in future!' I had been giving bed pans and blanket baths.

Mrs Alexander left after five years to be replaced by Mrs Dixon. Pamela Sands became the new section leader and the unit went from strength to strength until 1952 when all the founder members had left and the school's House system demanded much of the senior's time. It was ten years before it started up again in a slightly different form.

Miss Atkinson was my Yellow Group 1 teacher and also Housecraft, Cookery and Needlework teacher - all my favourite subjects. I still do a lot of craft work. I have happy memories of my time in the choir and Miss Wiseman taking us through Hiawatha, my first show; The Gondoliers, The Mikado, Pirates of Penzance and Trial by Jury. The walk up to the playing fields with Miss Edwards in her very short sports skirt and being whistled at was quite an event. Lacrosse was rather painful on the knuckles I seem to remember. We had after school sport then as well as Saturday mornings.

Of course there were two lots of evacuation, the first to Exeter at the beginning of the war and the second during the doodlebugs after we had sat our School Certificate exams in the shelters at the back of the hall in 1944. We didn't know where we were being sent, our parents just waved us goodbye at the school as we left by coach. We went to London and then train to Yorkshire. The first billet I was taken to with Evelyn Andrews the woman said she could not cope with huge great girls like us, she thought she would be getting younger children. So we sat in our coats and hats, eating what were left of our sandwiches, waiting for the billeting officer to come and collect us. We finished up with a miner and his wife, young daughter and miner lodger. We shared a bedroom with the daughter. Eventually Evelyn was moved to be with her sister. I used to come home from school and all the day's washing up was waiting for me to do so that we could eat later, also the ironing and mending. We also had our fun times and eventually attended Wath upon Dearne Mixed Grammar School; a very new experience for us.

Then there were the Harvest Camps in deepest Kent, mainly fruit picking. Some were under canvas, we had a hilarious time. Dear Mrs. Wright came to cook for us so we certainly didn't starve. I do hope we weren't too much of a chore for the staff that were responsible for us!

I well remember my prize giving when I received my School Certificate, school geography prize, school needlework prize and the Elgood Service Prize - Anatomy books for my future nursing career.

In my last year in 1946 a party of 28 of went to Sweden for three weeks. Miss Henshaw had a Swedish friend who I expect made all the arrangements over there. We had been going to school early to learn some Swedish and we had gained Swedish pen friends. 21 of the 28 were sea sick on the voyage from Tilbury to Gothenburg, despite some taking sea sickness pills! We were accommodated well down in the hold in ranks of bunks. We sang songs on deck at night. A floating mine was sighted and some of the crew had long poles at the ready to keep it away from the hull in case it came near us!

We then travelled by train from Gothenburg to Stockholm and came across yogurt for the first time, their national dish.

Also we found that we had to say when there was enough on the plate or the waiters continued to load us up. At Viggbyholm station we were met by a horse and cart for our luggage and we all followed behind in the dark like refugees. We were accommodated in a boarding school on the edge of a lake amongst woodland where swimming before breakfast was de rigeur. We each shared with a Swedish girl. At our first meal we were asked if we always swayed at the table in England. We hadn't realised we were still feeling the motion of the ship! Those of us with pen friends were able to spend a few days with their families and what an eye opener the food was; Sweden had been neutral during the war so hadn't suffered from rationing. The shops were full and brightly lit; it was a job to take it all in. Most of us went home with cases packed with food and other goods. It was a good thing my mother met me at Tilbury as I couldn't lift my case and I had about tuppence halfpenny left.

I can honestly say that despite all the vicissitudes of the war, the school being machine gunned, the home going train also machine gunned on another occasion and we had to go back to the school, evacuation after nights spent in our Anderson shelter in the back garden meant we slept in a bed without disturbance, I really enjoyed my time at the school. Why can't all schools have the discipline we had; the respect for the staff and prefects and each other?

Pat (Dickson) Cross remembers school at the end of the war

I should have entered the school in September 1944. It was then the Beckenham Girls County School; the Grammar School title followed the implementation of the 1944 Education Act in 1945. I passed 'the Scholarship' at Anerley Junior School (Preliminary, Written, Oral) in the spring and early summer of 1944. The term '11 plus' came later. In fact we took the exams in our 11th year, so most of us, including me, were 10. In late June 1944 the V1 attacks on London and the South East began. All the schools closed. Our street in Upper Norwood was destroyed by a V1 and I was evacuated to Somerset. I came home in October and belatedly started at Beckenham. There were only enough girls for two first year classes, 1X and 1Y and girls came and went until V weapon attacks petered out in early 1945. A V2 explosion close to the school delayed the start of the Spring Term, the dining hall had been damaged and many windows blown out. I do not recall any particular alarms over V1 or V2 attacks; they were a fact of life and we got on with attending school.

There was even a large scale school Christmas production 'The Knight of the Burning Pestle', an early Jacobean comedy. In July 1945 I saw my first G&S opera at the school, 'The Mikado', produced by Miss Nancy Wiseman. I thought the production wonderful. Many of us, me included, travelled quite long distances to and from Lennard Road, by bus or train, notwithstanding fog, raids etc. No one had a car.

Registration 1944-45 was still based on the vertical House system, each House group (I was in Blue 2) comprising about 25 girls from Years 1 to 5. This allowed friendships to develop across year groups and in Blue 2 there were 2 second year girls also from Anerley Junior, Joyce Long and Lily Cook, who became close friends and I was also very friendly with a 4th year, Pamela Graveney, who left to start work before the end of the year. House registration was dropped in 1945 for the year group system required by the law. There were enough girls in my year for 3 classes by the Summer Term 1945 and September 1945 saw the full complement of 4, which our year group retained until the end of the 5th year. L stood for Latin, teacher Miss Walters, who became our Form Tutor in 5L to our general delight. I can still recite the names of 5L in alphabetical order: Andrews, Anning, Archer etc. finishing White, Wiffin, and Williamson. My years at Beckenham were generally very happy and I made friendships which I still maintain. When we get together we still talk about school and remember teachers, mostly affectionately. Having moved from London in 1959 I still visualise the school in Lennard Road and still see myself cycling down on that unmade surface. Oh, the punctures, especially when we had to go on to whole days of lessons in the Lloyds Bank Pavilion from 1948-51.

EIGHT   MEMORIES OF THE WAR

Life in the Wrens by Effie (Denis) Brampton

Bubbling over with glee, proud in our new uniforms, we, a party of newly fledged Wrens, entrained for Dartmouth. The journey was long but never tedious as we were anxious to savour life to the full. It was a glorious day and the sun shone as if it too shared our excitement. Imprinted indelibly on my mind is the first glimpse of the sea, blue as blue and the sharp contrast of the green, green grass with the red Devon soil. On to Kingswear, across the ferry to Dartmouth and so we reached our new quarters, trying to look like old hands at the game.

Our work was to maintain small vessels as mates to the electricians, gunners and chippies and we had our first glimpse of the gallant little ships of the coastal forces, the motor launches and gun boats. They had not long returned from their heroic attack on St Nazaire.

The men were of the 'Old School' and had never worked with women before. To see their efforts at withholding bad language was a sight in itself and on the whole we got on very well together. We learned shooting with .22 and .303 rifles although we were non-combatant and not expected to use them against the enemy.

There was the lighter side of life with dances, cinemas, long walks in the countryside that ended in a tea of boiled eggs, Devonshire splits with cream and rowing up the river to Dittisham.

At frequent intervals we had to attend Divisions at the Naval College where we joined the young cadets from thirteen years upwards in the march-past where the Captain of the college took the salute. With the music stirring our blood, we felt proud and yet humble to be part of the Royal Navy. Then we were posted to an entirely new category of 'Torpedo Wren' at Gosport for two years. Our work consisted of supplying torpedoes to the MTBs accompanied by regular 'scrub-outs' when we would be up to the elbows in filthy oil. All categories of Wren were at this base; gunners, chippies, radio mechanics, transport, clerical and the much envied boat crews, who went out in all weathers. After a three month course at Roedean, I emerged as a Leading Wren Torpedo woman and was able to put up the coveted 'crossed torpedoes.'

When I returned in December 1943, it was to see the build up to the invasion of Normandy.

Our job was to maintain the fleet of small boats in fighting condition as D Day approached. Shipload after shipload of men went out, whistling, cheering and singing and we waved and cheered back as they passed. What a lump it brings to the throat to think of the many who did not return to that well known shoreline again.

Finally I took up my duties at the Admiralty, Whitehall thinking in terms of aircraft as war continued against the Japanese Forces. It was at a joint meeting of the Navy and RAF that I met my future husband for the first time.

In every way I count myself privileged to have been a member of the W.R.E.N.S.

EIGHT   MEMORIES OF THE WAR

A visit by Odette Marie Celine Churchill 1912-1995

French woman, Odette Churchill, the British agent in France who was imprisoned by the Germans and suffered torture and solitary confinement, kept a capacity audience spellbound at a meeting of the PTA in November 1954. The gallery was packed with senior girls.

Her description of fortitude in the constant face of death could not fail to be an inspiration to all who heard her.

Odette Brailly, born Amiens, had married an Englishman, Roy Sansom in 1931, moving with him to England where they had three daughters. The War Office requested all French-born residents of London to supply photographs of their home town and Odette volunteered her family album which contained photographs of the Channel coast. She had experienced some of the heaviest air raids in Britain until 1942 when she was asked to go to train under Colonel Maurice Buckmaster and return to France to act as a radio operator in the Resistance in a part of France that she knew very well. She landed near Cannes in 1942 when she met agent Raoul, aka Peter Churchill.

He remarked that no one would look at her twice and that she might be useful! Later of course in 1947 they were married because her husband Roy had died during her time in France.
.

When Odette (called Lise) and Peter Churchill were betrayed by a double agent and captured by the Italians, Raoul told them that he was Winston Churchill's nephew and that Lise was his wife. This may have saved her from immediate execution and she stuck to her story under torture. She was kept in solitary confinement in Fresnes prison in Paris during which time she had nothing to do. With no books and no way of writing, she spent the time imagining designs of clothes for her children.

Odette was condemned to death in June 1943 and sent to Ravensbruck concentration camp. She survived the war and testified against the prison guards at a 1946 war crimes trial.

One day during her imprisonment she found a leaf and managed to hide it. As a little girl she had been blind for over two years when she would wrap her arms round a tree in the garden and confide in it. The leaf gave her strength as she thought where there is a leaf there is a tree and where there is a tree there will be hundreds of trees.

When she received the George Cross from the King, she said that she was accepting it on behalf of all her comrades who had not returned. Although she had been condemned to death, she was the only one who came back. 'Now, every day, I marvel more and more at the gift of life. Odette and Peter were divorced in 1956 and Odette married for the third time to Geoffrey Hallowes. She was awarded an MBE, was the first of three WWII First Aid Nursing Yeomanry (FANY) members to be awarded the George Cross (gazetted 20 August 1946) and was Chevalier de la Légion D'Honneur.

Miss Fox and the terrier

A great tragedy for the boys' school occurred when Headmaster, Mr Gammon, was killed during the blitz with his wife and son by a direct hit on his house in Foxgrove Ave. We discovered only in 2007 that his daughter was not at home at the time. Her son told us that the family terrier was left homeless by the bomb and was taken in by Miss Fox as the Headmistress of the neighbouring school.

EIGHT   MEMORIES OF THE WAR

Harvesting apples at Brenchley 1945 L to R Top Elise Beeton, Pat Duplock; middle Elizabeth Evans, Ann Hurford, Jeanine Warman, Thelma Gyi; front Sheila Thompson, Jenifer Jennings, Margaret Jay.

The Victory Parade by Eileen Wiffin

The trumpets were sounding, the people drew near,
The procession had started at last.
The horses, the cars and the tanks were all there
As the planes in formation flew past.
The mechanised column came by with a roar,
The guns and the searchlights as well,
The lorries and jeeps, AFS to the fore,
The commanders, 'It's Monty,' folks yell.
The Navy, the Army, the RAF too,
The Marines were all present as one.
The pilots looked down from their planes as they flew
And their silver wings shone in the sun.
A word of praise for our friends overseas,
From the Empire, the whole world, they came.
Such noble and dauntless allies were these
Who won honour and glory and fame.
The people all cheered as the land girls passed by,
So smart in their brown and their green.
The ATS and WAAFS with their chins lifted high,
And the WRENS, they all marched as a team.
The workers, the miners, the WVS,
The nurses had answered the call.
The men on the home-front were there with the rest,
And the housewives, most honoured of all.
Through all the long years,
Through trouble and strife
I'll remember that day
To the end of my life.

NINE   SCHOOL UNIFORM

In all the reports about school uniform through the years, there is no agreement over the length of the skirts. Being females, they managed to let them go up and down with fashion. In the earliest days of the 1920s, the tunics were 4 inches above the knee, but by the thirties new uniforms were measured to make sure that they did NOT come above the knee. The shortest 'pelmets' worn in the days of mini skirts measured 12 inches but they were followed by long droopy skirts trailing along the ground.

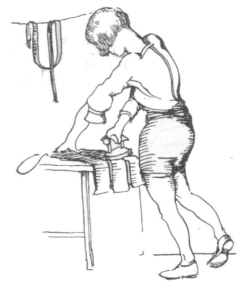

Tennis team of 1928 L to R Back row: Mary Cox, Muriel Forrester, Eileen Andrews. Front row Kathleen Buckley, Marjorie Forrester, Marion Morris.

The first official uniform was strictly adhered to with its square necked pleated heavy serge tunics and girdles and matching square necked white blouses. The best way to keep the girdle flat was to dampen it each night and to wrap it round a jam jar.

The tunic was long and it was not until some years later that this cumbersome garment could be removed for PE lessons. Some girls were still too modest to be seen in just blouses and navy knickers even in school! During the summer by the 1930s, the uniform was somewhat lighter, consisting of a white cotton dress with long sleeves and of course the regulation black stockings.

NINE   SCHOOL UNIFORM

Jean (Piggott) Ridout remembers that her mother had a hard time providing a clean white dress every day for herself and her younger sister with no modern laundry aids such as detergents and automatic washing machines. The dresses were very impractical since the girls had to use pens with nibs and liquid ink for writing, which invariably found its way on to the white dresses. Prefects would stand on duty at the school gates to check the uniform at the end of the afternoon. Woe betides any girl who tried to sneak out without such essential items as school hat and white gloves.

Representatives of forms 1 to 6 1944/ 45. L to R Rosemary Johnson, Evelyn Eminton, Elise Beeton, Ann Barber, Johann Kitchen, Pat King.

Decorous behaviour outside school hours was a must and eating in the street was strictly forbidden, even a few sweets. The boys at the neighbouring Grammar School left later than the girls to prevent contact between the sexes but Jean managed to meet a boy with whom she fell in love and married during WWII. They were married for over 60 years.

In 1936 the tunic changed to a straight pinafore style top with an A line skirt that had pockets in the side seams where you could keep a purse. The black woolly stockings were changed to fawn, lisle ones but these went out during the war to be replaced by white ankle socks. Hats were worn always when out of school, blue velour in the winter that lent itself to being twisted into new designs and panama hats in the summer with such tall crowns that we would unfurl them until the hat would only stay on with a hat pin. As velour became unobtainable in the 1940s, we changed all the year round to a navy beret worn with a school badge.

Also in the 1930s, the summer dresses were in a range of sweet pea colours, very pretty indeed as the girls came out of school although the effect was ruined by the awful thick fawn lisle stockings. Mary (Stewart) Hockey started school in 1943 when clothing coupons had been in force for two years so that she is uncertain how her mother managed to provide her uniform.

NINE   SCHOOL UNIFORM

Certainly the uppers of her house shoes seemed to be made of painted cardboard which showed through when they began to wear. Her friends were Pamela (Prynne) Saunders, Jean Barnes, Kathleen (Etheridge) Reardon, Betty Tolhurst and Eunice (Austen) Hewitt. She remembers Pam giving an excellent portrayal of Victoria Regina and going on to teach drama.

After the war Miss Henshaw would have liked to have seen a change to a butcher blue skirt suit but parents and girls alike were too conservative. At least the tunic was phased out and replaced by a collared shirt and tie worn with a skirt. Also by the early 1950s, the piping cheered up the blazer and the Invicta horse of Kent had grown on to a light blue background.

The youngsters wore blue and white checked summer dresses made to specific measurements such as four inch sleeve seams and Miss Henshaw was annoyed when the size of the checks varied. Subsequently a dress from candy striped material was introduced in white, pink and two shades of blue for £2 13 6d from Horne Bros, Croydon, although you could make one for just over £1. The pockets were supposed to be in the seams and not patch pockets as you can see in the picture. When the wearing of the boater became optional in 1969, it died an instant death followed by the winter hat so that since then there has been no school hat at all.

The picture shows the 1963 swimming team all dressed the candy striped dresses.

The wearing of a summer dress became unpopular especially when the girls were encouraged to make their own in needlework. Instead they wore the winter uniform but in lighter materials. A blue blouse with a navy skirt became the all year round uniform.

By 1973, the new girls wore a blue blouse and a round necked jumper with blue and pink stripes round the neck replacing a V-neck. They wore knee length white socks and a special style of shoes called Tiffany Start-rites bought from Ayling's in Beckenham. The blazer remained much the same except for the new badge with the Style arms.

NINE   SCHOOL UNIFORM

Finally the blue blouse and navy skirt were phased out in the late 1990s and the present day uniform of white open necked blouse and V necked pullover worn with a pleated check skirt and navy tights would have met with Miss Henshaw's approval to be sure. **If you want to know the six summer dresses that were worn over the years they were:** all white, white spots on red, green or blue, pastels with white collars and cuffs, blue and white check, candy striped navy/blue/pink and any blue dress when the manufacturer discontinued the stripes in the 1970s.

The three school badges are portrayed on this 60th anniversary plate produced by the Adremians when Nancy (Banks) Tonkin was their secretary

It was not until Miss Chreseson's time that the sixth formers were allowed to school out of uniform but there were always those who preferred fashion to sensible clothes suited to a formal business environment. The picture on the left shows the Head Girls in 1960.

In 2004, Miss Sage issued rules for the sixth form banning trainers, jeans, combat trousers, shorts and cut-offs, strappy tops, bare midriffs, sportswear, mini skirts, logos, body piercings except for earrings, tattoos and unnatural hair colourings and styles.
The sixth form leavers in May 2007 seen below left show how they compare with the U6 in the winter of 1965 with Miss Chreseson.

L to R, Valerie Yorston, Iris Kennedy, Desirée Dubois, Margaret Lang, ??, Maureen Collis, ??, Janet Mosedale, Maureen Ratcliffe.

NINE   SCHOOL UNIFORM

Back to Basics: Dress Code Reminders July 2007

Please, parents, remember that **we** prescribe the uniform for this school and that **you** are responsible for ensuring that your child conforms to it.

I am becoming increasingly irritated by the current abuses of the Dress Code. The four most common areas of frustration are:

- **Skirt length**. Many skirts currently being worn are too short because pupils have outgrown them. They are in fact hipster minis. **Please replace them.** Alternatively if your daughter's school skirt suddenly becomes mysteriously shorter, check if she is rolling it over at the waistband and **stop her**. This is your area of responsibility.
- **Shoes**. We stipulate flat black shoes but are flimsy ballet pumps with or without straps or ribbons really appropriate? I think not! Please equip her properly.
- **Bags**. Are you really allowing your daughter to use an imitation of the latest 'it bag' as a school bag? Why? Do you think it is a good trend? **Stop her!** Please provide her with a plain canvas holdall suitable for large text books, files and A3 folders. She can use the 'it bag' in the 138 hours per week she spends out of school.
- **Make up.** Do you not see your daughter's face when she sets off for school? The Dress Code says 'no make up.' Please **insist** that she does not wear it. We have been wasting school money on providing pupils with face wipes and make-up remover. **No longer!** From now on, any pupil who turns up in school with foundation, eye make-up, lip gloss etc on will be required to wash her face with soap and water. If this does not work effectively, she will be sent home to remove it and will make up the time after school.

I urge parents not to let their daughters become fashion victims in school time. Please give us more help in this. Uniform should be UNIFORM! My thanks to those of you who do so much to support us in respect of it. Sorry to sound so hectoring.

Plus ça change!

Helen, Alan and Elizabeth Mynett 1955

On holiday in Cliftonville, school blazers and all!   *The girls have blazer braid and blue badges*
Edith Ings, Muriel Forrester, Eileen Andrews
in 1927 with the first navy badges.

NINE   SCHOOL UNIFORM

School Hats by Glenys Dunderdale, V26

Shaped like a basin, a dish or a cone,
And each with a character all of its own,
The seven hundred school hats from pegs suspended,
Were really, I'm certain, never intended
To be individual. Varied, unique,
Pleated or stretched, shapeless or neat.
As I passed by, a haughty straw boater
(Which it certainly seemed had an over-sized quota
Of new stiff white snobbery), said to a velour:
'I'm sorry old chap, but I find you a bore.
Your personal appearance is not very neat,
I mean for example just look at that pleat!
Your hat band is twisted, your brim is quite bent,
And right in the middle, there's a simply huge dent.
Your elastic has broken, you're old and unbrushed,
And as for complexion-you're covered with dust!'
The velour shrugged its hatband and hopelessly sighed;
After due meditation it coolly replied:
'If you knew of the treatment I often receive,
Of what terror I go through, you cannot conceive.
I'm screwed up and squashed, left unbrushed every day
And thrown in a corner, should I get in the way.
Of this great big cloakroom I've oft made a tour,
By being kicked over the hard, dusty floor.'
I next heard a beret, faded and flat,
Deeply conversing with a panama hat:
'To a bird's nest of hair each day I'm attached,
By kerbi grips I'm incessantly scratched.
When I was new I had a big peak,
And the felt I was made of was both soft and sleek.'
'Oh', sighed the panama, 'to be back with the others,
In my cardboard box at the Croydon 'Horne Brothers'!
This cloakroom is certainly getting me down
And exposure to weather is turning me brown.
On Thursday last week I was out in the rain,
Without any hood to protect me, again.'
So I beg you dear comrades be kind to your hats
Don't bend them or pleat them, or use them for mats,
And they'll be quite grateful, I'm sure of these facts.
Signed: Society for Prevention of Cruelty to Hats!

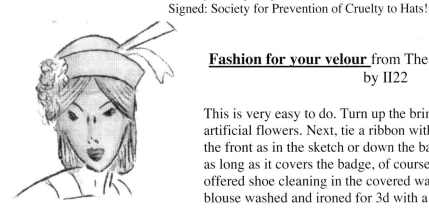

Fashion for your velour from The Daily Orbit 4.3.1960 by II22

This is very easy to do. Turn up the brim and add a dangle of artificial flowers. Next, tie a ribbon with the ends dangling over the front as in the sketch or down the back. Either way will do as long as it covers the badge, of course. This publication also offered shoe cleaning in the covered way for 2d and your gym blouse washed and ironed for 3d with a 48 hr service

Field work by GC

Farningham

A bootful

Juniper Hall

Box Hill

TEN   REPORTS FROM FIELD TRIPS

As soon as Miss Robins and Miss Burton appeared on the scene teaching sixth form Botany and Zoology at the end of the war, field trips to places like Malham Tarn, Flatford Mill and Dale Fort became part of the course.

Dale Fort near Milford Haven in Wales is never to be forgotten with the red sandstone cliffs, bright yellow gorse, pink thrift and deep, deep blue sea. At night it would be so truly dark that the sky would be filled with millions of stars. First timers were always amazed at the diversity of flora and fauna to be seen on Castle beach right beside the fort.

Sea pink by Barbara Munro formerly Mrs Smith, Bio dept

Margaret Hughes wrote in 1953 of when she stood on the wind-swept beach of the tiny village of Dale and caught her first sight of the grey stone walls of Dale Fort that seemed to be built into the sides of the cliffs. Originally built to protect the coast from the impending invasion by Napoleon, it now has an excellent position on the rocky coast to act as a marine biology field studies centre. It was used as such by successive groups of Beckenham girls (and boys) for thirty years all of whom realised that this was work-with-a-difference. In a week they picked up an amazing amount of specialist knowledge and enjoyed every minute!

Eleanor Harrington remembers many trips with Miss Robins and Miss Burton including days at Dale Fort followed by a visit to Slimbridge, where Eleanor experienced the coldest night of her life sleeping on a 'narrow boat.' As she was the last to step on board she ended up sleeping on little more than a shelf, really a tiny short bunk in the bulk-head. The Constable country of Flatford Mill was their destination in 1952 where they slept in Willy Lott's cottage. They went on the river in boats and Eleanor caught some leeches but no fish.

TEN   REPORTS FROM FIELD TRIPS

Ann Harrow described the cottage with its steep red roof, white walls and tiny lattice windows opened by ancient wrought iron catches. There were low beams, sloping floors and the window panes rattled with the wind. There were two huge Tudor fireplaces burning wood and lighting at bedtime was by candles, there being no gas or electricity laid on. The laboratory was where the grain had once been stored. The wheel of the mill was gone and all that remained was a rushing mass of water curling through the lock gates, its seething strength contrasting violently with the calm motionless appearance of the flooded river.

The terra-cotta coloured stone of the mill remained as it had been when painted by Constable in 1817 but it remains very much alive as a busy ecological and artistic centre.

Willy Lott's cottage

In 1951, Eleanor Harrington went to Oldenburg, Germany on a joint trip with the Boys' School. In the picture at either end are Myra Gray and Peter Keats who were destined to marry. In between are Judy Nicholl, Anne Bowles, Mary Gardner and Margaret Harrington.

One of Eleanor's most vivid memories was nearer home when they visited the Natural History Museum in South Kensington. Crossing Westminster Bridge, Miss Burton pointed out the building site of the 1951 Royal Festival Hall. The Festival of Britain was a revelation to those of us who had grown up during the war. Eleanor says, 'We seemed to go from Black and White into Technicolor. The high light of my biological career was when the Natural History Museum took some of my drawings of fungi from a weekend at Juniper Hall.'

Margaret Mackay described a fourth form visit to Juniper Hall, an old brick house with wings added at different periods. The library was a stately white, blue and gold Adam drawing room and other rooms were set out for mapping, with the Biology laboratory housed at the back. They looked for fossils, studied the farms, heath, woodland and ponds and the highlight of the week was at Cuckmere Haven to see the floodplains, under-cut cliffs, sea anemones and saltmarsh, all leaving them with many happy memories.

A contrast in means of transport is shown between the fungal foray by bike to Petts Wood led by Miss Robins in 1945 and the flights over Biggin Hill and Westerham by the Environmental Studies groups led by Mr McManus and Mrs Manning some forty years later.   True, the plane was something of a sardine can where we all sloped sharply backwards in the seats before take off but it was exciting to make out Sir Winston Churchill's memorial at Westerham and see all the bright blue swimming pools in the back gardens of the wealthy.

TEN   REPORTS FROM FIELD TRIPS

L to R Margaret Friend, Audrey Nicholls, Kathleen Stedman, Barbara Stanyon, Thelma Flack, Doreen Chambers, Pat Ridler and Dorothy Percy.

In between, most of the field centres were reached by train and land rover. To the eight sixth formers and two staff who set out on the trip in 1951 to Wales from Paddington early in the morning, they felt like early pioneers.

Through the Thames valley, the Goring gap and the Cotswolds, the steam train then plunged into the long Severn tunnel and they saw the coal-filled Usk River bubbling down from the hills. At Swansea, the rows of dreary slate houses and derelict steel works were hemmed in by huge black slag heaps, all dominated by Swansea's heather-topped hillside. From Haverfordwest, they careered in the Field Centre's truck through the twisting lanes with windswept bent trees to the far corner of the St Anne's peninsula in Pembrokeshire.

Christine (Stenning) Dolman's memories from her school days include the geography trips. She writes: The first of these was with Miss Marshall when our class went to Box Hill for the day. We caught the train to Dorking and spent the day walking along Box Hill. Miss Marshall's enthusiasm for the subject instilled in me a life long love of the countryside. It was a lovely outing and I feel we all thoroughly enjoyed it. Other visits included a steel works which was an amazing experience. I can remember standing in front of the furnaces and feeling the heat and the deafening noise as the men worked as they handled the molten metal. In October 1950 as a member of the Geography society we visited Croydon Airport, now long gone. Among the many planes and air lines we saw, were Strato Cruisers, Convair Liner, Constellations, Cloud Masters, Sky Masters, Canadian North Star and French Languedoc. The Airport officials were very friendly and we again thoroughly enjoyed the experience.

TEN   REPORTS FROM FIELD TRIPS

The last visit took place in the lower sixth in 1953. As part of the Geography A level course we visited Llangollen in Wales. We were studying land formations and each day left the youth hostel where we were staying to explore the surrounding countryside and mountains. On our journeys out we carried in our satchels, books, pencils, pens, notebooks, macs and food to sustain us through the day. The scenery was spectacular but it was very, very hot and we were surrounded by flies. Climbing up the mountainsides was exhausting and even the sheep were surprised to see us there. One day we sat high up the mountainside drawing the land formations in our note books when a very impressive thunder storm hit the surrounding mountain tops. It was amazing to watch the lightning hit the rocks and hear the loud peals of thunder. One day crossing a small mountain stream I managed to fall in and became very wet, in due course I caught a very heavy cold. In the youth hostel we all shared one room with bunk beds. I chose the lower bunk bed and my friend took the top. This was not a very sensible choice on my part as the bunks were very old and rusty and every time my friend turned over I was sprinkled with rust dust. Apart from my friend's blisters, and me catching a very heavy cold, taken as a whole, the trip was exciting and very educational.

In the summer of 1963, Latin classes made two visits to digs, one at Eccles near Maidstone and the other at Bignor near Arundel. While helping with the early stages of a dig, Margaret Bourne was lucky enough to discover a previously un-revealed wall with her trowel. The picture shows Latin staff Mrs Phyllis Barrett and Mrs Beryl Milburn doing their best to make another discovery. The finds so far at the villa site at Eccles included copper brooches and bone pins but our girls were thrilled to find red Samian ware from Gaul as well as the more usual black pottery.

TEN   REPORTS FROM FIELD TRIPS

Geography field work has always played a great part in the study of the subject and the geographers have always been the toughest of all the field workers, walking miles to view a ridge of Greensand or cycling in all weathers from one Youth Hostel to another in between studies. The lower sixth geographers in the April holidays of 1963 made their way to Westerham with Miss Burrows and Mrs Gee, only to find that Mrs Gee's daughter was ferrying her mother about in her car! The rest of the party walked (or took the bus) to find the chalk escarpment, the origins of springs, the local brewery and the farms of Edenbridge while lodging at the Crockham Hill YH. Oh for the future with the minibuses!

The school's first minibus is parked over the road on the right about 1980

Because of the enthusiasm of Miss Chris Watmough when she joined the school in 1975, we put together the money to buy a converted ambulance. The old bus was not in school colours at all, being bright red with a wooden luggage carrier on the top. Although it was not the fastest vehicle on the road, it was trustworthy and much loved by the PE and Biology departments. In the picture, you can see it parked by the roadside while the sixth form biologists listened intently to the Warden from Scadbury. Having its seats as benches running lengthwise, there was plenty of space for all the nets and other impedimenta required.

TEN REPORTS FROM FIELD TRIPS

WE CYCLED TO PARIS 50 years ago in 1959 by Pat (Finn) Roberts

I recall being astonished when my mother suggested I cycle to Paris during the Easter holidays of 1959. I was in the Upper VI at Beckenham Grammar school This was an era when money was still scarce, foreign travel was relatively new, and I was female and young (17), an unsophisticate and lacking in street wisdom compared to today's youth.

 True I had bicycled around the south of England the previous Easter of 1957, staying at Youth Hostels, but then my parents must have been assured that we were only a phone call (albeit using a phone box) and a car ride away should things go wrong. I had enjoyed a school trip to Switzerland and an Austrian pen friend exchange and was full of enthusiasm about what I had seen abroad that was different.   In 1959 neither parent had ever been out of England, but must have seen what a pleasure foreign travel had given me.

Not believing my luck, I talked it over with my school and cycling friend Margaret Williams and unbelievably her parents also accepted the idea of this adventure. I remember a lot of preparation by us, what to take, discovering ferry times, estimating our travel distances- writing to French youth hostels to book our accommodation, and working out how to meet the costs in French Francs. A lot of this was done by silly notes in the classroom. We were studying for our A levels at the time too.

When I read my 'photo album come diary' of the trip I am slightly embarrassed about how 'boy mad' we were and the language we used. What is a 'chile' person? I suppose we were 'flexing our flirting-skills'! However reading today about where we stayed, what we saw, and the impact some things made on us overrules the immaturity of silly teenage girls and their inane comments.

We left England on the first day of April after over-nighting in Dover. We were using our everyday bikes on which we cycled to school and in and around Beckenham. Each had 2 panniers, one either side of the back wheel. We wore trousers and anoraks and little head scarves. Luggage was minimal.

We watched anxiously as our bikes were lifted by crane onto the ferry. Would the wheels buckle? But we were excited and delighting in the fact we were 'free'. Was school really that bad? In Calais we found the youth hostel shut and moved on to Arques YH. We had a miserable night sleeping under damp blankets. The next day we set forth to Amiens. There were not the motorways of today, only the long straight national routes – smooth tarmac until you came to a village or town and then COBBLES!

Our English bikes with their narrow wheels couldn't cope and neither could our derrieres. Direction signs caused us to make several wrong turnings and an extra 2 or 3 miles were not welcome when we were forced to return to a crossroads and start again.

We were also noticing ruined buildings, piles of rubble, and many wooden crosses. We know now that France, like England, was still recovering from the war, that damaged properties were commonplace and that the Commonwealth Graves Commission and the French counterpart were still hard at work managing the graves of dead soldiers.

TEN   REPORTS FROM FIELD TRIPS

Amiens Youth Hostel was a converted warehouse with comfortable beds and we slept in late before heading for the cathedral which impressed us very much. The sun came out and it became very warm, so much so that we changed into shorts to cycle on to Beauvais. We caused quite a stir in our short shorts, much like I suppose wearing a bikini to go shopping in Tesco today.

On Saturday 4th April, en route to Beauvais, I took a photograph of Margaret sitting at the base of a memorial. It was built to remember the R 101 airship that crashed in October 1930 with great loss of life. Later in my life I was to read about the competition between a privately built airship, the R100, and the Air Ministry's R101 in Neville Shute's book 'Slide rule'. Nevile Shute was a senior engineer with Barnes Wallace working on the project. Later I was to marry a 'half Australian' and Shute's books gave me a love and understanding of Australia. Barnes Wallace of Dam Buster fame was also of course the designer of the bouncing bomb and my RAF husband and I are only too aware of 617 squadron's history as it is based up the road from where we live today!

On to Paris where the YHA is described as a 'dump' in my diary, closely resembling a 'bus shelter'! However the atmosphere was excellent and we didn't allow the close proximity of the traffic to spoil our sleep. I read in my post cards to my mother that we planned to hitch hike to the sights surrounding Paris, and in the next few days we saw Versailles, Fontainebleau and Chartres as well as Paris which we thought was so exciting. It is notable that the sightseeing spots in these old photos have very few people in them, unlike today's tourist crowds where one queues for an hour or so to gain access. We visited all the top spots in Paris and visited the Louvre to see Venus and Mona. We spent our spare money on presents for the family – I departed UK with about £20.00 and returned with change. The exchange rate must have been very favourable. The YHA only allow a certain length of time in each hostel so 4 days later we were leaving Paris for Rouen and during the next few days travelled via Neuchatel and Fervent –a YHA hut with straw mattresses- but we slept well. Back to Calais and then Dover. A lorry driver gave us and the bikes a lift to Southend Ponds and we were home by 4 pm. I had sent a post card in advance asking for sausage, chips and pickled onions to be my welcome home meal!

Within a few months of this trip we had left school and had either started nurse or teacher training (there was little choice of careers in those days it seemed to me) but with a sense of confidence and achievement. It was a good experience for 2 girls about to leave home and become independent, to learn to make decisions and be responsible for them. I have retained my love of travel and history, throughout my life, and remain fit to cycle to get around our local market town.

Others setting off in 1948 for a YHA hike

TEN   REPORTS FROM FIELD TRIPS

Snapshots from Iceland, the land of ice and fire, Easter 2000

Led by Miss Aspa and Miss Orr, 22 Geography students from years 10 and 12 made their way to Iceland. Here are comments from four of the party.

Claire Jackson's first impression was how empty it was with hardly any people and no trees; one of the most amazing sights was Gulfoss, a huge waterfall with masses of ice everywhere. Victoria Moore was struck by the geysers of which only one, the Churn geyser, erupted after she had waited for a full five minutes with her camera pressed to her face. Sarah Smith enjoyed walking along the snout of the black glacier and the black sand beach, black because of the ash from volcanic eruptions. Victoria loved the geothermally heated blue lagoon where she even managed a faint tan although they were surrounded by snow, ice and incredibly bright water. Dotted round the edge of the lagoon were buckets of exfoliating face scrub. So there they were, floating with white gritty rock hard faces when a group of men from Shirley and Crystal Palace walked past and made rude remarks. They were left with matted hair from all the minerals in the water.

Miss Aspa summarised the visit saying that the landscape is the most striking thing about Iceland, miles of black lava fields with little or no vegetation, snow-capped mountains and smoking volcanoes. Only 280,000 people live there, half of them in Reykjavik and there is virtually no pollution since energy is from hydroelectric or geothermal sources. The girls were delighted to find that their rooms in 'Vik' were en-suite!

The trip to Iceland became a regular excursion in the years following.

Geography Field work at Durdle Door, Dorset and a trip to Strasbourg (in the snow) were taken by the VI form in 2007.

L to R, Sarah Taylor, Will Kiln, Laura Kincaid, Lydia Bryant, Laura Boccadamo and Charlotte Symes on their trip to Lulworth Cove and Durdle Door, Dorset

L to R James Fletcher, Laura Boccadamo, Josh Robertson, Kaja Vasanthakumar on a bridge in Strasbourg

Below, Laura Boccadamo, Josh Robertson, Andrew Gummer, James Fletcher and Kaja in the shop.

ELEVEN   SCHOOL DINNERS

Mrs Wright,
Brenchley 1945

Doris, back row second from left, 1946

Canteen staff Jan 2008
L to R back Martin,
Michelle and Jane; front
Wendy, Kim, Linda, Marilyn

Dinner in 1950s at old
school

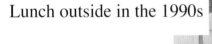

Lunch outside in the 1990s

Dinner at
Langley 1959
with the hall
crowded, girls
sitting in Houses

ELEVEN   SCHOOL DINNERS

School dinners were never compulsory as the lunch break was long enough to go home and back. You could have 'cold' dinner where you took your own sandwiches to eat in the housecraft room. Many girls did not stay to school dinner because it was said that you had to sit until you had eaten everything. Some girls enjoyed the three course meals for ninepence with two desserts but Betty Capon remembers the day when plaster fell from the ceiling on to the staff sitting on the platform in the dining room and turned all the teachers into ghosts. In any case, in the early days, milk, or cocoa with sticky old penny buns and chocolate biscuits were available at morning break.

Two weeks of menus in 1937

Mon Jan 11 Roast mutton, gravy, potatoes, treacle pudding, fruit salad.
Tues Jan 12 Stewed steak and carrots, dumplings, potatoes, rice pudding, fresh fruit.
Wed Jan 13 Steak and kidney pudding, greens, potatoes, baked apples, blancmange.
Thurs Jan 14 Stewed mutton and carrots, potatoes, jam tart, fresh fruit.
Fri Jan 15 Fish cottage pie, cauliflower, steamed chocolate pudding and sauce, milk jelly

Mon Jan 18 Roast beef, gravy and potatoes, bread and butter pudding, fresh fruit.
Tues Jan 19 Stewed rabbit and dumplings (or fish cakes), apple pie, raspberry blancmange.
Wed Jan 20 Roast mutton, gravy, potatoes, semolina pudding, fresh fruit.
Thurs Jan 21 Steak and kidney pie, potatoes, jam sponge pudding, jam sauce and jelly.
Fri Jan 22 Fish cakes, cauliflower, custard sponge, fresh fruit.

As the war started in 1939, the school was not available for dinners and girls having free dinners went to Miss Fox's house, terrified that she might be there. Fortunately the housekeeper coped with them and neighbours took in the girls who brought sandwiches. Ask anyone in decade three of the Adremians if she remembers school dinners and it is likely that she will say 'chocolate pudding with chocolate sauce' accompanied by a faraway look in her eyes! The dining room at the old school was rarely used for anything else other than for feeding the hungry and this was war time. The tables were set out ready to receive the daily orderly queue. Eight per table with a prefect at the head, unless you were very lucky (!) when you would have a member of staff instead; one girl would be allocated as waitress. This gave us the excuse to wander around as we would collect the cutlery, jug of water, the vegetables in dishes (eat your heart out Jamie Oliver) and the main dish. This was to be served out by the head of the table watched keenly by the other seven to make sure that it was served out precisely into eighths. Odd though that a favourite was sliced roast meat warmed up in gravy and we cannot recall anyone suffering from food poisoning. My best meal was a thick slice of cheddar cheese served with a mound of mashed potato and cooked beetroot and the worst was a beef stew because there were always too many carrots (one was too many for me).

Almost all the staff had their meals with us, seated on the raised area at the front and we would watch to make sure that they had the same as we did. They did not always enjoy sitting with us; Miss Rose did not like vegetables and hoped that the dish would be nearly empty by the time it reached her. Unfortunately a particularly efficient waitress would return to the hatch for vegetables especially for Miss Rose! Having washed the first course down with a glass of water, we craned our necks to see what was for pudding. I can see the readers' noses wrinkling with disgust for the days when set cold semolina was on the menu but it was decorated with eight mounds of whipped 'cream' that our sugar deprived systems craved. Usually it was some form of sponge pudding with the appropriate sauce and fruit dishes in season like plum tart, rhubarb crumble and apple pie.

Both staff and girls benefited from after school clubs like choir practice because Mrs Wright would leave fresh baked rock cakes for us with any bottles of milk left over from the day.

ELEVEN   SCHOOL DINNERS

We even took our beloved cook, Mrs Wright, to the harvest camp at Brenchley in Kent in 1945 but found that she gave us grated apple sandwiches to eat for lunch after a morning spent apple picking, taking surreptitious bites! Mrs Wright left school in 1946 and her place was taken by Miss Sutherland who married Mr Braby the greengrocer, Birkbeck Rd.

There was a favourite little dinner lady called Doris who was Miss Fox's personal maid and a wonderful concert was performed some years later where the dinner ladies presented a kitchen symphony played 'a la washboard.'

Dinner in the Chemistry lab in 1945 at the time of the V2s from a painting by Miss Pelling

This euphoric state of affairs was to change for the entry of 1948 when overcrowding meant that the school kitchens could no longer cope and meals arrived in metal containers.

Jean (Woodman) Runciman summarises as follows. 'Among my memories of BCGSG in the early years is the daily ordeal of the school dinners. Sometimes we had to eat in the science laboratory where the strong smells of sulphuretted hydrogen and formalin did little to tempt the appetite or aid digestion. We had to queue up to be served really dreadful food from huge metal containers. It was a school rule that each girl had to take a portion of everything (anorexia nervosa would not have been tolerated).

It often proved difficult to eat the stuff but Carole Pritchard and I devised an ingenious system to dispose of it. We always carried a large paper bag (polythene or cling film had not been invented) and proceeded discreetly to fill it with dollops of soggy cabbage, dehydrated potato and other abominations. The bag was then placed in the gym slip pocket to be thrown into the River Beck on the way home. On one memorable occasion, we were shovelling a chunk of meat into the bag when Miss Stephenson caught us. Looking positively apoplectic, she grabbed the bag, now dripping with gravy, and stormed, 'What is this?' A long acrimonious interview with Miss Henshaw followed and stern letters were sent to our mortified parents.' Others recall the pink and green blancmange and rhubarb pudding as the worst dessert ever encountered.

ELEVEN   SCHOOL DINNERS

Another era when dinners were much in favour was when past pupil, Johann Davey (née Kitchen) 1939-1945, was the school cook at Langley, a position by now known as 'Catering Officer'. The girls sat at the tables in the hall at Langley in House order with one from each form and the senior girl at the head. It was hard for the dinner ladies to set up and clear the tables away every day. When Jo started as Catering Officer at Langley Park in September 1975, it was to provide the girls with a well balanced meal every day. She had to submit four weeks in advance of balanced menus within the allowed costings.

She had first worked as a very humble dogs-body at Ravenscroft School for Girls in January 1970 but having obtained her City & Guild's certificate in Catering at Lewisham College, she worked her way up the ladder in school kitchens throughout the borough until the Langley vacancy occurred. The old kitchen had been made over and was equipped with new stainless steel appliances including a dishwasher. But, when they tried to wash up the very large roasting trays, the sinks were too small to take them. A typical male design fault!

Jo says that she gets very cross with people who say that school meals of her day were terrible. Each meal was as good as the dinner ladies could manage. They experimented with recipes and did things like jam and cream slices, crème brulée, curries and home made bread rolls. The greatest kick was when a child would say, 'That was lovely, are there any seconds?'

On a sweltering hot day, the girls were doing their O and A level exams and the railway banks were catching fire so they supplied both girls and firemen with long drinks of iced lemon or orange squash. One day, they found that a squirrel had got in overnight through the water gullies of the old kitchen and caused havoc over all the equipment that had to be cleaned before cooking could start. Don't forget that everything was cleaned and samples of all food served refrigerated before the staff could go home every day. Once, at a hygiene lecture, a food inspector said that the cleanest kitchens he found were at light-houses and school kitchens!

Frances and Sally, Jo's cooks

At first, Cook Sally and Assistant Cook Frances were determined to gang up on their new Catering Officer, Jo, if they didn't get on, but they remained friends for years. They were providing 400/500 meals a day and Christmas lunch was a full house.

Lola Campos and her sister, Charlotte, remember lunch times as great fun: queuing by forms, girls jumping in the line, a little scuffling and name calling before they were ushered into the Dining Hall with their dinner tickets. The dinner ladies used to dish the food out on to their trays and they remember a voice shouting 'Anyone for Seconds' before all hands went up for second helpings of rice pudding and jam, lemon meringue pie and jam tarts with custard!

In the spring of 1978, they were told that the Borough was to stop providing school meals and would introduce snacks of rolls, fruit and yogurt. Jo decided that it was not the cooking of her training and so she left on 30 September 1978 to pursue another career in accountancy.

ELEVEN   SCHOOL DINNERS

Healthy Eating in the Cafeteria from 2006

As part of the present school's ongoing drive towards healthy eating and living, they have been working with the caterers, Scolarest, to implement the government's new standards for school meals. Scolarest ran a nationwide competition in October 2006 by asking pupils to create a healthy eating design. The winner was Sarah George of year 7 who received a £20 gift voucher for her slogan 'Be a Cool Dude----Eat Healthy Food' that was reproduced on balloons for a race on 20 October. All the balloons were bright red and it was announced later that Langley was doubly lucky because a year 10 pupil, Charlotte Boyd, had won the race. Her balloon landed in Southwold, 156.2 km away. Charlotte's prize was in the form of four Red Letter Day Purple Experience vouchers worth nearly £800 for her and her family to choose from a variety of adventures such as hot air ballooning. The event also raised money for 'Children in Need.'

With effect from September 2006, a new and exciting range of nutritionally balanced meals and snacks has been offered. These range from tasty soups, fresh salads, wok and pasta dishes to traditional main meals, yoghurt and fruit bars. Today's standards require that all pupils should have at least two portions of fruit and vegetables or salad a day and the new food choice reflects this. Food which does not comply with the new government standards will no longer be sold in the cafeteria. At first only 40 school dinners were taken up, rising to 150 to the delight of the catering team.

Year 8 talks about lunch in 2008

The canteen is open for breakfast, morning break and lunch. There is always a choice of food including vegetarian options. A hot lunch is offered, pasta, jacket potatoes, pizza, salad or sandwiches although sometimes a choice may run out. Kerryanne said that most of the food is fairly priced but they all agreed that drinks can be quite expensive. Katherine said that they

have a daily limit to spend. Most meals cost between £1 and £2.

Emma said that they don't like asking parents for more money on their smart cards which are used to pay for meals.

Emeline liked the good choice of fruit and healthy options and Sanjidah was happy with her jacket potato with cheese although she would like to see more vegetarian options. As an onlooker it seemed quite difficult to eat a jacket potato with plastic disposable cutlery! Time can be tight if they wish to go to lunchtime clubs such as table tennis or Latin and this can mean that they miss lunch completely. Lunch can be pre-ordered early in the morning but they would like a system of first come first served instead of year by year as they are often last in the queue whereas last year they were first!

TWELVE   SCHOOL HOUSES

Red, Orange, Yellow, Green, Blue, Wedgwood

Wedgwood I with Miss Hawkins
1954 and Blue House staff early
1950s Misses Cooper, Burton,
Broadhurst, Barnard, and Moore

L to R Janice Harding, Margaret Williams, Janet Anson,
Anne Roberts, Helena Robertson, from Wedgwood House
that changed to RAYMOND 1959/60

Lambda, (Pi), Sigma, Gamma, (Beta), Kappa

TWELVE   SCHOOL HOUSES

Miss Fox's school had existed for fifteen years when in 1934 the school house system began with six Houses named after the colours red, blue, green, yellow, orange and wedgwood. Within the houses the girls were arranged as in a boarding school with girls of all ages and forms in the registration group. The idea was that girls of different ages would associate and share their interests but a girl could be the only one from her form in the group and become very isolated. This was particularly the case if the girl came from out of area or was a late entry. Everyone wore an appropriately coloured house button so that past pupils invariably link a girl's name with her house. There were many competitions for the Houses: apart from the obvious netball, lacrosse, cricket, tennis and eventually hockey matches there were the Reading, Drama, Gymnastics and Singing competitions also Cups to win for Deportment, Charity, Diligence and General Knowledge.

The Houses were taken very seriously with a House motto and song. The first Captain of Orange House was Daphne Turner and the comments that follow were made years after she left when she was a lecturer in Physical Education at Bristol University. *It is a long way from the platform of the school hall to that of Bristol University and a far cry from studying social reform with Miss Grice to lecturing on Health Education to post graduate students. Yet my roots at Beckenham County School as House Captain under Miss Grice have given me strength and inspiration. What comes to mind is the boundless enthusiasm for the new venture in the life of the school and the endless work to be done if Orange House was to be the first proud winner of the House Shield. Two happy years of bullying and coaxing went into the winning of that shield, persuading each member of the House in turn to be a poet, dramatist, singer, gymnast, games player and party hostess. The House parties seemed like a wonderful dream as we piled high the bowls of jelly, fruit salad and masses of cream but House matches were a grim reality of calling for maximum effort. There was fun too in choosing the house motto, 'Up and at 'em' and the house song, 'Cheer, o' cheer for the House!'*

When Miss Henshaw came in September 1944 with the new Education Act, the vertical house system was abandoned. As we returned to Forms, we were able to make lasting friendships with our peers while retaining membership of Houses for competitions. After the war, numbers increased rapidly and Miss Henshaw saw the need for House time to be included in the timetable. This would provide girls of all ages with the chance to take on responsibilities otherwise denied them. She devised a seven day timetable to supply Day II and Day IV afternoons for House activities and space for a wider range of subjects. At the same time there are other advantages like no 'Friday afternoons' or the loss of Monday's lessons on Bank holidays. Where a whole day was needed for an event like a drama competition, that day could be missed from the timetable so everyone could enjoy the event without feeling the lessons had been lost. The success of this brilliant idea was proved by the length of time that it was part of the school's working from the late 1940s to 1969/70. The return to the five day timetable in 1969 was forced on the girls' school when the boys moved next door.

TWELVE   SCHOOL HOUSES

Certain lessons like Latin, Spanish, RI and Craft were shared. A House afternoon remained as one afternoon per fortnight.

The move to Langley had been marked by the Houses acquiring local names: Langley (blue), Goodhart (yellow), Elwill (green), Raymond (light blue), Kelsey (orange) and Burrell (red). Styles (white) was a new later house eventually amended to its correct Style, named after the 18th century residents of Langley House.

It was in 1350 that the Langley family took over the land and from 1510, John Style, a London Alderman, developed it into an estate, building the mansion. Subsequently Sir John Elwill moved in from Exeter, followed by Hugh Raymond of Great Saling in Essex. By 1765, the Burrell family who already owned the Kelsey estate had extended its lands to include Langley. When Peter Burrell died in 1820, both Kelsey and Langley were auctioned and Emanuel Goodhart purchased the 423 acres of Langley House. All these names were used for the Houses of the Girls' School as it took over the Langley land. Langley House burned down on 5 January 1913.

MURDERS

Back in 1824, there was a murder in the peach house where the school stands today. Thomas Morgan was fatally injured on the night of 16 August when attempting to guard Mr Goodhart's greenhouses situated in a walled garden. Dr Ilott and Sir Charles Farnaby were called but Thomas died in the afternoon and was buried at St John's churchyard, West Wickham, the next day. A man called Thomas Coombs who was selling peaches and pineapples in Kennington was executed in December for the crime although he did not confess.

Mrs Molnar needed to plan for a further increase in numbers that would accompany the

transition from grammar to comprehensive. She decided to return to the vertical system of the 1930s and 40s although many old girls wrote of their disquiet at its disadvantages; also the school building was not really suited as it lacked six areas that could be used equally by the Houses. They were named in Greek according to the initial letters of Langley Park School for Girls Beckenham Kent as Lambda (yellow), Pi (purple), Sigma (red), Gamma (green), Beta (blue), Kappa (orange). At this time of turmoil there was a brief return to registration in forms in 1971/72 before the new Houses were set up for September 1972.

Gamma Upper 6 last day at school 1977 L to R standing Jenny Parrott, Miss Birch, Sarah Dillane, Anne Crouch, Mrs Manning, Pauline Bird, Julie McKnight, Alison Broome. Front Janet Mercer, Hilary Roden, Vicky Furbisher, Sue Churchus, Jenny Bickmore, Carole Knight.

TWELVE   SCHOOL HOUSES

At Speech Day on 15 November 1972, Mrs Molnar said the following.

'When we suspended the old Houses, we did so partly in order to give ourselves the opportunity to think and plan for the larger community that re-organisation would bring. A vigorous House system has been part of our life for over 25 years and before that the school was organised into vertical groups. The combination of the two will, we hope, provide the continuity of support and concern which is necessary for each pupil to achieve her fullest development intellectually and socially, where older pupils can help younger ones'.

The main disadvantage of Mrs Molnar's system became apparent to Miss Grimsey because it corresponded with the development of the joint sixth form with the boys' school in 1976. With many of their lessons and registration held in the sixth form block, senior girls lost interest in their Houses although some Houses continued to succeed, notably Gamma House under Miss Birch.

The keen competition that had existed throughout the school fell away and the House Shield was no longer awarded. Overall, Wedgwood (Raymond) House had been the most successful, winning it in successive years as particular groups of dynamic members moved up the school.

In 1974/75, the benefit of an elastic timetable was recognised again when a two week timetable returned and once more girls saw the advantage of the different lessons on Monday mornings and Friday afternoons.

Another factor in the loss of House interest was the spread of public examinations and permission for the girls to leave school after their last paper. Some lack of interest in societies and Houses had been apparent several years before in the time of Miss Chreseson when in the magazine of 1964 the editors had commented on the 'limp, damp inertia and anti feeling beginning to permeate the school i.e. why should we care about anything else other than coming to school to work.' Perhaps such House systems are most effective in boarding schools. As Mrs Scales (née Grimsey) left in 1978, it was left to her Deputy Mrs Barnard to run the school in Forms once again until Mrs Herzmark took over in January 1979. The Greek House names were retained for competitions. Eventually the Houses were reduced to four: Lambda (yellow-lemon), Sigma (red-scarlet), Gamma (green) and Kappa (blue-kingfisher) and this system remains to the present. The mathematical among you may be able to count eight House systems that have operated since the school began in 1919.

Dramatic Interludes by Mary Hardcastle of Red House 1948-1956

Dramatic interludes were the lollipops of school life: they acted as a sweetener in the continuous round of academic slog. They certainly provided a competitive focus for the House system, which may otherwise have appeared somewhat pointless. Reminiscences of the annual Gilbert & Sullivan, school plays and concerts remain etched in my memory, providing not only immense enjoyment but generating inspiration which had a positive influence on my career. At a later date, I was to become deeply involved in the production and staging of school events. My first experience was through the House Drama Competition in the Spring of 1954. Although there were six plays, we were only permitted to watch three, hence my intimate knowledge of some and consummate ignorance of others.

I knew something of the preparations of Red House for their excerpt from Twelfth Night but nothing of the brilliance of the actual performance. Watching Shirley Handy as Sir Toby and Shirley Mackay as Maria setting a trap for the unsuspecting Malvolio played by Pam Mitchell, I was transported into the world of the theatre. Costumes, lighting, music and dramatic intrigue, it was all there. Wedgwood's excerpt from Hamlet was announced by a magnificent Gertrude played by Audrey Colthorpe.

TWELVE   SCHOOL HOUSES

The curtain was raised on a play with Christine Knight as Claudius, Shirley Wilson as Hamlet, Evelyn Eminton as Polonius et al. But who played the ghost of Hamlet's father? To

complete the trilogy, we had yet another Shakespearian play within a play as Orange House presented Pyramus and Thisbe from 'The Dream.' A talented second former, one Celia Antrobus, executed the hero with the 'bloody blameless blade' and took an unconscionable time a-dying.

Orange house rehearsal of Pyramus & Thisbe from A Midsummer Night's Dream in the library in 1948. L to R M. Henderson, Pamela Preston, Gillian Robotham and Celia Antrobus

We viewed this with delight and it was noted that a future star was about to rise. The scene was performed before a dazzling Hippolyta, Pat Thompson, as she reclined upon a gorgeous couch. I was hugely impressed, hooked! Shakespeare was 'it' and drama was for me! Not destined to tread the boards however, I was to push others to their limits to create and recreate this magical experience for themselves and the audience who watch, vicariously savouring the smell of greasepaint.

In later years we were introduced to playwrights such as Christopher Fry, T S Elliot and Shaw. My memories are biased towards Red House and maybe details have become distorted with the fullness of time but please share the following:
Murder in the Cathedral with Betty Luff as Beckett, Hefina Davies and Sonia Rees (later in 1965 Maria in the Sound of Music)- those Welsh accents!
The Escape of Lord Nithsdale with Gillian Grellier; super costumes, good story line based on fact.
The Boy with a Cart - Pam Goodwin and a cast of 'thousands.'
The Merchant of Venice with Christine Harrington as Portia and Jennifer Crier as Nerissa. Did they become professionals?
Richard II with Betty Luff as Gaunt and Jen Durell as a stylish courtier.
Richard III and The Inca of Peru with Gill Smith, Ann Spackman and Gloria Morgan.
King John with Gill Brown and a diminutive Prince Arthur.
Pygmalion with Daphne Brown as Mrs Eynsford Hill. Wow, who said the naughty word!
Henry VIII with Daphne again as Katherine and Gillian Whittle as Henry
Arms and the Man and so on ---not to forget Vivien John as St Joan

There's no space here to mention the host of major productions including 'She Stoops to Conquer' that no one called Hardcastle could forget. In recent years I was shown round the old school in Lennard Rd by Year 7 pupils of Cator Park where the school hall was the library and the stage a computer bank. However I paused to revisit briefly those 'dramatic interludes' performed by eager schoolgirls and once again I applaud their memorable achievements.

Orange house staff at the same time, 1948.

L to R Miss Pelling, Miss Thompson, Miss Rabson, Miss Marshall, Mrs Kaye

THIRTEEN   KEEPING THE SHOW ON THE ROAD

ADMIN

CHARTER DAY

CHEMISTRY PRACTICAL

Lap tops for all;
L to R Herjit
Dehal, Robin
Crosley, Albin
Wallace (Zone
IT director),
Bob Small,
Jane Buckland
June 2000
(from Kentish
Times)

THIRTEEN   KEEPING THE SHOW ON THE ROAD

There are so many people in the school without whom pupils and teachers would be unable to carry on. Perhaps our caretakers must come at the top of the list. Mr Nash with his ever increasing family of little boys kept the school in Lennard Rd going throughout the war and Charlie Jewell took over when we moved to Park Langley. What a favourite he became! Nothing was too much trouble, opening the school so that we could feed the animals on Saturday mornings, using his carpentry skills to construct a gondola for the performance of the Gondoliers and dealing with all the bags of metal milk bottle tops that were brought to raise £250 for a Guide Dog for the Blind. The sixth form rewarded him with a shield ornamented with flattened, polished milk tops. Charlie Jewell was very touched. On his

retirement, his place was taken by John Clarke. For a few months in 1973, John Evans worked as the assistant caretaker to John Clarke but then went to St Bernadette's. Fortunately for us, the post became vacant again here and John Evans returned in 1979. He not only has a talent for carpentry, fondly remembered in 1980 when he built a sentry box for Iolanthe but he has always been there ready to help, putting up and making shelving galore. He also helped the lab techs with things that stuck, leaked or were too heavy for them! He opened the school for weekend rehearsals and loaded the minibuses when we went on our field trips and multi-activity holidays. He grew a great variety of orchids and chrysanthemums in his greenhouse and entered successfully in the flower shows. It is with great pleasure that we see him there to this day as the school Site Manager with continuous service at Langley of some 30 years by the time this book is published.

The Science Department could not function without their laboratory technicians who like the school secretaries worked for most of the school holidays, not shutting down when we all departed. Starting with Lois Brooker, an old girl of the school in Miss Fox's time, she was the technician keeping the Chemistry Department going during the war while she studied for a Chemistry degree. Those who knew her were pleased to learn that she not only gained her degree but became a teacher at James Allen, followed by Sevenoaks and Whyteleafe Grammar School.

When she left in 1947, she was followed by Lesley Foster, Irene Kinisson (Ginty), Heather Cameron, Phyllis Harris, Joyce Jarvis, Mrs Fulton who came to us from Wellcome's as a Chemistry graduate, Marjorie (Sear) Davy (formerly Snell), Ann Lack, Frances Longbottom, Jackie Smith, Mavis Trodd and Lyndsay Williams.

L to R Back row Lyn, Frances, Ann. Front row Jackie, Mavis, taken in the 1980s

THIRTEEN   KEEPING THE SHOW ON THE ROAD

Since holiday times are when the builders and decorators come to do their tasks, the technicians would find their equipment would go missing, especially their electric kettles. Lyn stopped this by tying a label to the kettle which read 'kettle used for boiling fish bones only.' After nearly twenty years working at the school, Lyn left to work in the clinical measurements department of Bromley Hospital from January 1992 until February 2002.

What may be thought today as an incredible event occurred when the Science department's increased use of visual aids required the full time service of a technician. You may have noticed that all the technicians named here are ladies but the Borough thought that such a job could only be carried out by *a man who would have to be on the highest scale* and this was in 1973! Needless to say, our ladies carried out the job with their accustomed efficiency and aplomb at their lower rates of pay.

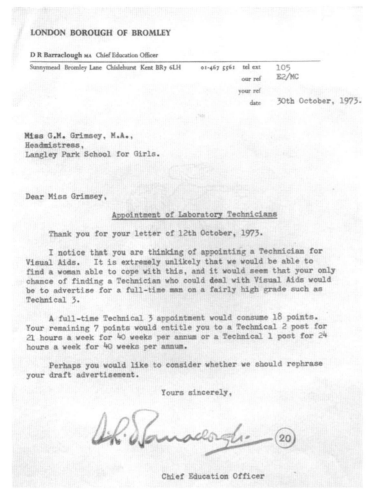

LONDON BOROUGH OF BROMLEY

D R Barraclough MA Chief Education Officer

Sunnymead Bromley Lane Chislehurst Kent BR7 6LH   01-467 5561   tel ext   105
                                                    our ref   E2/MC
                                                    your ref
                                                    date   30th October, 1973.

Miss G.M. Grimsey, M.A.,
Headmistress,
Langley Park School for Girls.

Dear Miss Grimsey,

                Appointment of Laboratory Technicians

        Thank you for your letter of 12th October, 1973.

        I notice that you are thinking of appointing a Technician for Visual Aids. It is extremely unlikely that we would be able to find a woman able to cope with this, and it would seem that your only chance of finding a Technician who could deal with Visual Aids would be to advertise for a full-time man on a fairly high grade such as Technical 3.

        A full-time Technical 3 appointment would consume 18 points. Your remaining 7 points would entitle you to a Technical 2 post for 21 hours a week for 40 weeks per annum or a Technical 1 post for 24 hours a week for 40 weeks per annum.

        Perhaps you would like to consider whether we should rephrase your draft advertisement.

                        Yours sincerely,

                        Chief Education Officer

The term of September 1976 opened with eight new laboratories in the main building and a large prep room converted from room 22. This enabled the technicians to make many of the articles previously obtained from the manufacturers at a cost. When Cosmetics and Forensics was introduced for the pupils to whom the regular sciences did not appeal, they needed human hair to practise perming. This was obtained cheaply from a very sympathetic supplier but was found to be full of nits when it arrived!

Another problem was the nightmare of chewing gum on school uniform although they were amused when known regular chewers arrived in high dudgeon at the prep room door covered in gum!

The office staff is indispensable in any school. Mrs Rita Doyle, Mrs Jill Beard, Mrs Coupland, Mrs Stewart and Mrs Buchanan were secretaries in the 1970s and 80s. The librarians like Mrs Hazel Darbre always needed the help of teams of girls. As numbers increased and worksheets became the order of the day as well as examination papers we needed the expertise of the duplicating department with Keith Harcourt, Jill Reynolds, Pat Cousins and Jan Haspinal

When Jan Sage became the school headmistress, she heard of a special training scheme for the involvement of all the staff in the school from cleaners to senior teaching staff.

THIRTEEN   KEEPING THE SHOW ON THE ROAD

Its organisation in the school was the responsibility of Lorraine Kelleher who worked for two years before she was satisfied that the database that she produced clarified the staff's evaluation and entitlement to training with job opportunities. They were assessed over two days, being interviewed at random, and did very well.

Investing in People, Lorraine Kelleher and Chairman of the Governors, Tony Miles.

In addition to John Evans with his team of four site staff, the security of the site was enhanced in 2006 by the appointment of security guard, Barry Wyatt, who is seen 'everywhere.' John and his wife again showed their sustained interest in the school when they came to the surprise party organised by Chris Watmough at High Elms on 11 November 2007 to celebrate Mrs Herzmark's 80th birthday. Past secretaries, Thelma Mullinger and Brenda Riley were also there.

Today with a school of over 1,600 pupils, there is a large number of support staff among whom are 19 in the office and business, 5 technology technicians, 19 SEN staff, 3 librarians, 8 site staff and 5 Science technicians. Mrs Nevcan Kazim won the Salter's National Science Technician Award in November 2007, a magnificent achievement for an outstanding technician but Nev said she is extremely proud to be part of such a dedicated and highly motivated Science team. The other technicians are Mrs Susie Batt, Mrs Maria Brennan, Jim Lyons and Richard Southworth.

Nev, Richard and Maria are in the picture.

Sheila Muir

Audrey Handy

Margaret Wellington

Alison Prince

THE SHERWOOD HERO

Alison Prince

Jenny Evans

Yvonne Blyton

Ria Keen

Sonia Rees

FOURTEEN   GIFTED & TALENTED

Yvonne Antrobus writer and dramatist with work frequently on Radio 4.

Last November, 2006, I found myself sitting at a table (*see left*) while a polite queue shuffled past me with pictures of myself to sign. These pictures were almost unrecognizable from the person sitting at the table, and not just because I am some forty years older, but because the books and DVDs showed me as Dyoni Queen of the Thals and my face was green.   Little did I think when I went into Shepperton Studios for my two hours' makeup every morning that one day that image would become part of a cult? For the film was called *Dr Who and the Daleks* and I had been invited to a wonderful specialist shop called 10th Planet, situated in – wait for it – Barking.

But it is not only my green face that seems unrecognisable now.   For in those days I was a reluctant actress while today I am lucky enough to be doing what I always really wanted to do. I have become a writer.

Yvonne (far right) as Phoebe in Quality Street at school

It sounds ungrateful to be a reluctant actress when so many people would love to have had the chances I did.   But it's the truth.   I wanted to be a racing journalist, but at the time I took my A-levels women couldn't even hold a trainer's licence, so my mother persuaded me to try for RADA and I got in.   Then I was very lucky.   Amongst a lot of rubbish that most young actors have to do, I did five plays at the Royal Court Theatre including *Life Price* by Joe Orton. I was in over a hundred TV plays and films, including Ken Russell's *Debussy*, and Thomas Hardy's *The Withered Arm* playing opposite (well sort of) Billie Whitelaw. Later in my career I was in the first cast of *Noises Off* by Michael Frayn at the Savoy.   And the very last part I did was in a film *On Dangerous Ground* with Rob Lowe.

And now I must mention *The Effect of Gamma Rays on Man in the Moon Marigolds* at Hampstead.   Not really because I won the London Theatre Critics' Award for Best Supporting Actress, but because it was probably the only performance that I look back on with true satisfaction.   And because the part I played has some relevance to my school days.
I was thirty-two at the time and playing Sheila Hancock's fourteen-year-old daughter, Tilly. I was also very thin and yet without realising it I was playing a fat girl.

People met me afterwards and thought I had been wearing padding. I hadn't been. And I'm sure this was why I won the award. For the truth was that going back to being a teenager I became in some ways the girl I had felt myself to be then. when I was depressed and frankly fat. And that was why it was the best thing I ever did. But nobody knew that.

Meanwhile I had been writing. Three novels. I was married to a novelist, David Benedictus, who had had a best seller, *The Fourth of June,* about his time at Eton. I also had two children, Leo and Chloe. So, while there was some interest from agents/publishers the books kept being put into drawers while I got on with other things. Finally, when I was past fifty, and it wouldn't be long before the children left home, I decided that if I ever wanted to be a writer the only way I would do it was to give up acting so I had nothing else to fall back on. And in 1998 *True to Form* was published by Victor Gollancz, followed the next year by *Cut in the Ground.* Both crime books about horse racing, they were as near my original ambition as I could get.

Unfortunately the next book, *The Iron Stand,* crashed. Gollancz were taken over and ceased publishing anything but sci-fi. Also my books were psychological crime and racing readers prefer action by famous names in the sport, like Dick Francis and John Francome. By now my marriage was also pretty shaky so I had to earn my living and quick. Through my literary agent I got into the small and little known world of abridgement, editing John Simpson's *Strange Places Questionable People* for Macmillan Audiobooks. I have been abridging ever since and have learned so much from it. Well, when you are deconstructing writers such as William Trevor and Peter Carey, or analysing great swathes of Churchill's life as written by Roy Jenkins, you can't help but improve your critical powers, most particularly regarding your own work. I hope!

For I have also since moved into radio writing, mainly dramatisations of novels such as *Dr Jekyll and Mr Hyde*, although recently my first original play was broadcast. Called *Mixed Messages*, it was again psychological crime. And while I don't think it was entirely successful, again I did learn so much from writing it.

And that is what it is all about for me really, learning, perhaps because I started so late. Anyway, I have just sent my latest novel, *Change Blindness* (not about racing), off to my agent, and have just started on my next one, *The Charity Shop,* which I hope, as always, will be better. I often work a ninety hour week. Meanwhile I still see a lot of my children. Leo writes for the *Guardian* and is getting married this summer. Chloe was married two years ago and is a reader for BBC film. My ex-husband and I are good friends and we all meet up for high days and holidays. Retirement is simply not on my horizon although I look forward to being a Grandwoman, as my children say they'll tell theirs to call me. And, hey, I have this new unexpected career to fit in, as Queen Dyoni from *Dr Who.*

Nita (Bowes) Benn (formerly Clarke) is a prominent Labour figure, wife of the Hon Dr Stephen Michael Wedgwood Benn, heir apparent to the Viscountcy of Stansgate. Their daughter, Emily, was selected in November 2007 to represent East Worthing and Shoreham for the Labour party in the next general election.

Susan (Tonkin) Bonell OBE, Group Captain in the RAF, outranks her retired husband John who was a Lt Col in the Army. Susan was awarded the OBE in 2006 for her work reorganising the Mint where the entire Forces medals are struck. Sister **Alison** accompanied Susan to the Palace wearing a superb new hat acquired for the occasion as you see here.

FOURTEEN   GIFTED & TALENTED

Alison runs a pre-school at Coney Hall. Susan and Alison are daughters of the late **Nancy Tonkin** who was the Adremian secretary for many years and co-author with Eric Inman, also deceased, of the book 'Beckenham.' Nancy's valuable and extensive postcard collection of Beckenham is catalogued by husband, Bill Tonkin.

Born in Beckenham, **Patricia Carroll's** musical talent soon impressed her fellow pupils at the Beckenham County School for Girls. Her impetuous personality, beautiful individual interpretation of the work and technical skill merged to produce unforgettable vital performances with such meticulous attention to detail. If only Patricia's outstanding performances of those school days of ours could have been recorded! If you ask Patricia about them, she says she remembers them with enormous pleasure, particularly Nancy Wiseman and Sylvia Cutler on the staff who were so enthusiastic and encouraging. Patricia also played piano and violin sonatas and the violin in a string quartet.

She began playing at the age of five and at 10 years old she had already entertained British and American troops at many war time concerts. She won a scholarship to the Royal College of Music where in 1951 she won the Chappell medal for piano playing and was forecast as one of the leading young pianists in the world. The Directors of the London Symphony Orchestra heard her play Rachmaninov's Third Concerto in D minor at a college concert and asked her to play at the Royal Festival Hall in 1952 under George Stratton. Her interpretation was true to the music, rising to moments of greatness in the cadenza of the first movement and the finale. In 1962 she played the Grieg concerto at the first night of the Proms, conducted by Sir Malcolm Sargent and in 1965 Patricia was one of four solo pianists in a performance of 'Les Noces' by Stravinsky. She studied at Paris under an exchange scholarship and returned to perform frequently for the BBC. Another scholarship to Vienna heralded recitals travelling all over the country. She won an international competition in Germany and studied with Arturo Michelangeli in Italy.

In 1978 she was one of two pianists in the film 'Lillie' with Francesca Annis playing Lillie Langtry. 'Piano Parlour' was a programme of Victorian piano music for Radio 4, where she introduced and played pieces such as those familiar to home pianists as well as brilliant show pieces for travelling concert artists. Patricia was Professor of Piano at the Royal College of Music for many years and says that perhaps her most extraordinary experience as adjudicator was in Hong Kong in 2002 when she heard 1600 pianists in three weeks! After a lifetime of music, Patricia retired to study and recently graduated with a BA Hons in Humanities with History of Art. She married in 1959 and became Patricia Newman. Her three children, son and two daughters, have been successful in their various ways.

Patricia (Pat) Doreen Coombs was born on 27 August 1926, in Camberwell. It has to be said that she did not seem to enjoy herself at school and started work as a nursery nurse. She became a beloved British comedienne, well known for her work on television and radio. A 'foil' for top comedians including Dick Emery, Bob Monkhouse and Peggy Mount, she reached the height of her fame in the 1970s in a succession of long-running television series and as a 'celebrity' in numerous games shows. In the 1990s she joined the cast of East Enders (1985) as Brown Owl Marge Green and played Pru in Noel's House Party (1991).

FOURTEEN   GIFTED & TALENTED

In the mid 1990s she was diagnosed with the bone disease, osteoporosis, but continued to work until the end of her life, recording a final instalment of the radio series 'Like They've Never Been Gone' (with June Whitfield and Roy Hudd) in February 2002. A lovable lady, Pat Coombs, who never married, died at Denville Hall, the actor's retirement home, on 25 May 2002. She was 75 years old.

Gillian (Brown) DuCharme, headmistress of The Town School, New York, became the Head of Benenden School until 2000. The newly renovated duCharme Cloisters were opened by her in May 2005. Housing the impressive Art and Design Centre, new bright and airy classrooms have been added to create a beautiful but practical area. She serves on the governing bodies of the University of Greenwich, Wellington College, Berkshire and Marlborough House School, Kent.

Mary Dove and **Carole Emus** received first class honours degrees at Girton College, Cambridge in 1965, Mary in English and Carole in Pathology. Mary was awarded a Major State Scholarship to return to Cambridge and won both the Charity Reeves prize and Pfeiffer Studentship for research. Her book, Wycliffe's Bible, was recently described on TV. Carole was awarded the Gwendoline Crewdson prize from Girton and went on to finish her medical

training at King's College Hospital, London. Carole met her future husband at their first day at college and they married when they were at medical school. She practised for over four years but then they moved to Michigan with their two little boys and Carole devoted her time to her children instead. Their daughter Rebecca was born in Michigan and Carole also gained a Master of Public Health degree before they moved to Colorado where they have lived for 25 years.

L to R back, Nick, Sam, Laura, Rebecca, Brent, Abby, Anthony; front, Carole, Geoff, Abby

Elder son Nicholas followed his parents into medicine but his brother Anthony is a newsman. Rebecca is a social worker at the Pikes Peak Hospice in Colorado. All three are married and Carole has two grandchildren. She is now interested in law and works as a paralegal.

Karen (Snazell) Edwards lives in Bristol where she runs her own pottery business making individual garden ceramics; these include plaques, decorative pebbles, birds, troughs, planters and shapes like the 50cm high gourd in the picture.

Jenny Evans, singer and writer, attributes her successful musical career to the exciting projects devised by Brian Newsome for his classes at Langley Park. She also remembers acting the part of Olivia in the Twelfth Night production where the Barnes twins, Jill and Elizabeth played the twins in the cast. She was 'Joan' in Anouilh's 'The Lark' and played supporting roles in other productions. She was a junior in Burrell House when Nita Bowes was House Captain in 1970 and Nita struck a new note in the singing competition by choosing a Hare Krishna Mantra as a contemporary folk song instead of the routine acceptable classic. They came seventh!

FOURTEEN   GIFTED & TALENTED

Jenny lives with her husband who is also her manager in Germany although she visits her parents in Park Rd, Beckenham regularly. She is trying to find the time to finish a historical novel set in Munich from 1967 to 1970 and in England in 1974. The student unrest all over the world but particularly in Germany provides the background to a socio-political study of an English family. She is also part way through writing a detective novel.

Ellen Gandy had a really successful trip to Australia and Singapore in December 2006. She competed in the Queensland Age Group National Swimming Championships and collected eight Gold, one Silver and three Bronze medals. She broke the Australian All-comers record for 200m butterfly and went on to train in Brisbane with an Australian club. We expect her to figure in both the 2008 and 2012 Olympics. In spite of all the time spent training, she achieved 5 A* and 4 A grades in her GCSEs in 2007 and was back in Manchester in March 2008, representing GB, looking to take part in the 200m butterfly in Beijing.

Thelma Handy lives in Liverpool with her husband and three small sons and leads the Royal Liverpool Philharmonic Orchestra. An article in the Independent in 2004 described her performance of Bach's E major Violin Concerto as follows: *Thelma Handy, one of the RLPO's most valuable assets, not only led the orchestra with quiet authority but gave an intimate reading of the concerto. Even in a hall built to symphonic proportions, she made a distinct impression with her rounded tone and precise intonation.*

Jennifer (Coppard) Hargreaves, sports specialist Professor at the Roehampton Institute, London, won an award in North America for her sports sociology book, 'Sporting Females.' Her mother, **Alice Anstey**, was one of the original pupils at school in 1919.

Barbara (Pitt) Heseltine became a Deacon in July 1988 and was ordained an Anglican priest in 1994 on 21 May at Southwark Cathedral. She first presided at the Eucharist at the festival of Pentecost in her local parish church of St Mary BV, Addington and is now Assistant Non-stipendiary priest at St Feock, Truro. In the picture, she is enjoying a few minutes relaxation in Banstead.

Norma (Preston) Izard, England women's cricket coach, was well known as a cricketer at school, along with other sports. She had been a forceful games captain for Wedgwood when Carole Prichard was at school but Carole was surprised that the Norma her daughter, Caroline Barrs, spoke of as the England Women's cricket coach was the very same Norma Preston. Caroline was playing for England in the 1980s as opening bat and slow left arm bowler. **Heather Dewdney** was another England cricket player.

Ria (Sharon) Keen PhD, MFA, B.Phil, Cert.Ed, SNHS (Arom, Hyp), C.AVC says 'I'm a singing teacher with a PhD in contemporary vocals, a performer, arranger, hypnotherapist, aromatherapist and psychotherapist. I use the alternative health stuff to help performers with their problems, especially issues of confidence, audition nerves, memory, concentration, relaxation and stress relief.

FOURTEEN   GIFTED & TALENTED

I run a very busy private teaching practice here in sunny (ha!) Worcester, as well as lecturing at the Birmingham Theatre School, and being an Associate Professor at Calamus International University. Additionally, I'm lucky enough to still be performing - mostly in theatres these days, although I used to be a bit of a rock chick. Yikes! There's a tour coming up this autumn, of a show called 'Swing It On Broadway' - coming to a theatre near you. Life is busy, complicated and usually good fun. I'm luckier than most, as I get to do what I love and people seem to want to pay me for it. All good. So whether you know me as Ria, Dr. Keen, Renata von Trapp, Bernard or Ra-Ra, welcome'

Janet Lambert has been making charity cards since January 1990 & up to date she has raised £16,702 - not bad at £1 a card! £10,550 went to Leukaemia Research and the balance since 1999 has gone, and is still going, to Whipps Cross Hospital Rheumatology Fund. This helped to finance and now maintain a garden created by volunteers in a courtyard behind the rheumatology department, with raised beds to show that gardening is still possible even with limited movement. It was opened in 2003 by Jane Asher (President of Arthritis Care). Janet followed her rheumatologist to Whipps Cross Hospital when Bart's closed their rheumatology dept. Janet's other passionate hobbies are photography and family history research. Having had no time at all for hobbies (or anything else!) during her working years, she's loved every minute of some 20 years of retirement and is also a sort of unpaid social worker because lots of residents in her block of flats in Longfield, Kent seem to knock at the door for help and advice! Hers was the star letter in 'Family History Monthly' in November 2007. She wrote about Herbert's Dairy of Beckenham and Penge in an article called 'Cream of the Crop.' Her parents, Edwin and Hilda Lambert, were both employed by the dairy where they first met in the 1920s.

Beauty and Edwin Lambert   *Edwin and Hilda's marriage at St George's, Beckenham*

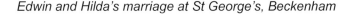

Janet remembers the two horses, Beauty and Kit that were stabled in the yard in Thesiger Rd where everyone worked a 7-day week.

FOURTEEN   GIFTED & TALENTED

Janet earned 15/- a week pocket money riding a tradesman's bicycle with two full crates of milk balanced at the front for customers who wanted their milk delivered early.

All the family would be occupied at Christmas completing the orders for cream that they poured by hand from jugs into waxed cartons of various sizes. Janet is now enjoying her prize of a free 12-month subscription to the Explorer package providing access to over 500 million exceptional family history records on www.findmypast.com.

The Langley Park School for Girls PSA

Kate Lawler
will open this year's
Christmas Fayre
Saturday 7th December
If you are interested in having a stall please contact the PSA via the school asap

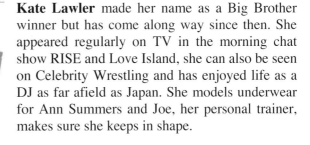

Kate Lawler made her name as a Big Brother winner but has come along way since then. She appeared regularly on TV in the morning chat show RISE and Love Island, she can also be seen on Celebrity Wrestling and has enjoyed life as a DJ as far afield as Japan. She models underwear for Ann Summers and Joe, her personal trainer, makes sure she keeps in shape.

Marion Mathews ran the Beauty pages in 'Woman' and launched the 'Health & Beauty Salon' magazine followed by 'Nail News.' She was head hunted after retirement to publish a new hair and beauty magazine in Dubai.

Elizabeth (Mynett) Adams says *'When I first decided to take up singing as a career I received tremendous support from the school – and not just from the music staff. I felt that some knowledge of German would be useful and both Miss Cutler and Dr Schöfer offered to give me lessons in their free time! I spent four happy years at the Royal Academy of Music in London before joining The D'Oyly Carte Opera Company – back to Gilbert and Sullivan but this time I wore dresses instead of military uniform! It was a great life for a young person, touring England (staying in theatrical digs) and America where we were entertained by many local fans and occasionally invited to smart receptions where we met celebrities such as Tom Lehrer and Sir John Barbirolli. In common with many others I met and married my husband in the company. Subsequently we both joined the English National Opera and after having a family I sang in the extra chorus at Covent Garden for ten years.'*

Natasha Newsham. (Design left) Graduating with a first class degree from Leeds University in Fashion Design Management, Natasha sourced new technologies and combined them to create a groundbreaking treatment for stain-free and crease-resistant clothes. There is no reduction in quality of the fabric which is not stiffened by the treatment. Natasha, who was at Langley from 1996-2003, says that the treatment is more environmentally friendly than any other and so appeals to a 'green' population.

Alison Prince is a well known author and illustrator but she says she hated school *'It was so boring. I spent most of the time dreaming up adventures, which never happened of course. That's how I came to write the stories about the school Mill Green where they really do happen.'*

Having attended the same lessons, I can read between the lines and see the origin of many of her ideas.

FOURTEEN   GIFTED & TALENTED

I can see her sitting uncomfortably on a stool while Miss Stephenson demonstrated the component parts of crude oil, thinking that if she really wanted to know she could look it up in a book. We all appreciated Alison's distinctive style of drawing and she was certainly a great success in the part of the Grocer in the 1944 production of 'The Knight of the Burning Pestle.'

It was said that 'the invasion of the platform by the sturdy Grocer and his wife was carried out with exhilarating vigour sustained by a prodigious supply of apples.'

As well as illustrating and writing, Alison has worked in television (remember Trumpton?) and at the zoo (serving teas at the Penguin Bar), sold newspapers, gilded picture frames, run a smallholding (getting up at dawn to milk the cows), driven a cattle truck, painted scenery and hitch-hiked across Europe. She is responsible for the drawings in 'Hello to Ponies' and 'Hello to Riding' and she wrote and illustrated 'The Good Pets Guide.' 'The Sherwood Hero' won the Guardian Children's Fiction Award and 'The Summerhouse' has been a recent success.

At present Alison lives on the Isle of Arran where she is a member of the local council. Her children are all over the world. Samantha, a writer, lives in the Cevennes in S W France. Ben and his Chinese Malaysian wife are currently in China. Andy, with Ruth and their two children, is a farrier and restorer of houses in Australia. Eldest son John manages a bus network in Edinburgh.

Mavis Gloria Spencer Read made her mark early as she was the first Jubilee baby born in Penge on Monday January 13 1935 for which her parents were given a pram. A year after joining the Beckenham Grammar School she had a play accepted by a BBC writing competition and went on win a road safety slogan competition. She took part in many school plays also as a member of the Beckenham Children's Theatre. By 1960 she was working as a doctor at the Charing Cross Hospital.

Although **Sonia Rees** kept her maiden name for her professional appearances, she was first married in the summer of 1961 at St Mark's Church, West Wickham with her two sisters, Anita and Wendy as bridesmaids.

Her bridegroom was Vincent O'Hagan of the Kentones whom she met when playing in the Clown Jewels with the Crazy Gang at the Victoria Palace. They did not have time for a honeymoon as Victor was due to appear on TV the next day and Sonia was off to Scotland for 'Stars in your Eyes,' a show starring Eartha Kitt. Sonia was in the original British company of the Sound of Music and took the leading role when Jean Bayless left.

FOURTEEN   GIFTED & TALENTED

Sonia Rees always knew she wanted to sing - but had no idea that her passion would lead her to the West End, starring in The Sound of Music as Maria. As a tiny girl, her primary school teachers could never persuade her to take an afternoon nap, so she used to sit on the teacher's desk and sing to the class!

She came from a musical family, singing and dancing with her two talented sisters Anita and Wendy, and their father John Rees, a leading light in the local operatic society. She fondly remembers Miss Wiseman, the teacher who recognised that she had such extraordinary potential - and it was Miss Wiseman who encouraged her and fostered her talents from the beginning. Miss Wiseman encouraged her to take part in many competitions, poetry readings and productions - and Sonia remembers singing in the choir, and performing in productions of The Gondoliers at school. Once under contract with Jack Hylton, she starred in pantomime with Arthur Askey, toured with the Fol de Rols and thrilled her Welsh family with a season of Land of Song on television singing with Ivor Emmanuel. She was back in London for the run of 'Oh My Papa!' at the Garrick Theatre with Peter O'Toole and Rachel Roberts, two shows with the Crazy Gang at the Victoria Palace and opened the first Royal Command Performance to be televised in 1961, singing 'Clown Jewels' from the show of the same name. She is best known, however, for her vibrant performance as Maria, in The Sound of Music, which ran for six years at the Palace Theatre. She still lives in Beckenham with her husband Peter Cook. She has three children, Mark, Merion and Shan, six grandsons and one granddaughter - and she still sings all the time!

Margaret (Wellington) Restrick was the fastest woman over 100 and 400 yards in the swimming pool in GB when she swam in the 1948 Olympics held in London. Of her many medals, there were three silvers and one bronze in 1950 at the Empire Games in New Zealand and she can still swim 100 lengths at the Crystal Palace 50 m pool in just over two hours. See her picture on page 156. Her swimming style was once analysed in the Pathé Pictorial. Margaret was in the same year at school as **Yvonne (Blyton) Elkington,** *the niece of Enid Blyton.* They gained their school certificate with matriculation exemption during the war in 1942. They were both in the school cricket team with wicket keeper **Joyce (Robinson) Nicholson** who has contributed two sets of their school examination papers to the Adremian archives, one set for when they were in the first form aged 11 in 1938 and the second set from their fourth form days in 1941. We have included the first form English paper but decided not to embarrass the readers with any others! Flautist **Ruth (Sawyers) Holden** was also in the same year at school and her son Arthur is one of the librarians in the Local Studies Department of Bromley library. Ruth's granddaughter, Kezia Holden, is similarly musically gifted, now studying music at Southampton. Ruth was also a formidable bat and thundering bowler in the cricket team. A wonderful archive in the school's records is the original sheet of confidential results from their School Certificate Examination of 1942. The high mark obtained by Yvonne Blyton in her French Oral helps explain why she chose to leave school to improve her languages at the Bromley Commercial School. From there in 1943, she moved on to humanitarian work with the joint organisation of the British Red Cross and the Order of St John of Jerusalem, seeking lost relatives through the centre in Geneva. Another contemporary was **Barbara Peake MBE** whose award was given for her service to the British Council.

Pat (Finn) Roberts, recent Mayor of Downham Market. Pat started at St George's Hospital, Hyde Park Corner, training as a Registered Nurse, 1960-1963, followed by midwifery training at Beckenham Maternity hospital 1965. (Did she deliver your baby?) Then she served as lieutenant and captain in Queen Alexandra's Royal Army Nursing Corps, serving in Hannover, W. Germany and on to Berlin in the cold war period and Hong Kong. She married Peter, RAF navigator in 1968 and they had one son and one daughter. She recommended nursing when the children started school and the family returned to England where she trained as a District Nurse 1984-85 at Ipswich College and managed community nurses with Cambridge Health Authority 1985-1994.

FOURTEEN   GIFTED & TALENTED

Following retirement she was elected Town Councillor in 2000 and Mayor for 2004/5. She remains a Town Councillor, Trustee for West Norfolk MIND, member of local Royal British Legion and organises the Remembrance Parades. Among her clubs are Heritage, Family History, Twinning with Civray, South of Poitiers in France, and Bridge. We have included several pictures with Pat, but we like the snail judging competition the best!

Claire Shaffer won a ten-week tour of South Africa as a result of coming second in the World Youth Forum Essay Competition held in the USA. The Council was very impressed by her essay on 'The World we want.' Her destination was Johannesburg where she was the guest of the Helpmekaar-Melsieskool. Claire's chief impression was of the immense size of a country where a 40 mile trip there and back before lunch was just a 'trip next door.' Highlights of the trip were a cable car ride to the top of Table Mountain, a journey down a gold mine and an excursion into the Kruger National Park. Claire gave numerous talks about our English Schools to audiences of South African children that made her feel that she wanted to invite them back for a return visit but it was too expensive. In 1960, the air trip had cost £300 but to go by sea took 4 weeks.

Helen Starr, ballerina, trained at the Royal Academy of Dancing and the Royal Ballet with whom she toured the world as soloist and ballet mistress in 36 countries over 5 continents. She is the assistant artistic director of the Louisville Ballet for which she performed as the principal dancer for twenty years, continuing now in cameo roles.

Linda (Hardy) Young. We asked her friend, 'Is Linda talented?' This is her answer. *'Most definitely so, although she was discouraged from pursuing a career in creative and design skills because Miss Henshaw did NOT approve of a career as a fashion designer. Sadly, Linda, like so many others comprising the non-university group at the grammar school in the early to mid-1950s, was channelled into a secretarial course at (the now defunct) Springhill College at Bromley North. She went on to serve as the trusted Executive Assistant to various powerful CEOs in the USA and in London and her fashion design talents remained largely unrecognized except by her many friends and acquaintances.*

I clearly recall, as a teenager, how Linda would look at the newspaper pictures of the annual Paris Fashion Collections and then cut the material to make an outfit from memory, using her terrific design sense to adapt the dress to her own physique and incorporate her own fashion notions. She was always beautifully dressed.

You might, however, be interested to know that Linda has put her talents to a wonderfully philanthropic use, making literally hundreds of beautiful quilts over the past several years, which she donates to the parents of babes in the neonatal ward at the Atlanta (Georgia) Children's Hospital and in which they are wrapped once they are strong enough to go home. Not surprisingly, these special quilts are treasured by the parents, especially by those whose babies do not survive.'

Form I ENGLISH 1 hr. 20 mins.

Summer Term, 1938

Answer Question I and four other questions, choosing at least one from each of the Sections A, B and C.

FOURTEEN   GIFTED & TALENTED

1. Make a list of four nouns, three verbs, two adjectives, one adverb, one pronoun, three prepositions and one conjunction from the following passage:-

Martha had scoured the boarded floor carefully to a white cleanness, and it was adorned with a brilliant piece of oilcloth on which customers were to stand before the table-counter.
The wholesome smell of plaster and whitewash pervaded the apartment. In the middle of the room stood a table laden with sweets.

Analyse the last two sentences into subject and predicate, dividing the latter into verb, object and extension of the verb.

SECTION A

2. "A Midsummer Night's Dream"

   (a) Why were the following people in the wood:- Bottom and his friends; Theseus and
        Hippolyta; Demetrius?
and (b) name all the pairs who were married at the end of the play.

3. "Gulliver's Travels"

What was Gulliver's most interesting adventure among the ………………………………?

SECTION B

4. "Hiawatha"

Write in full the story of how the maize was given to the Red Indians.

5. "The Heroes of Asgard"

Either (a) What happened to Asgard after Iduna left, and how did she escape from the giant Thiassi?
Or   (b) Describe the three tests of Thor in Giant-land and say what each really was.

6. "Christmas Carol"

Either (a) What did the Spirit of Christmas Past show Scrooge at his old school?
Or (b) How did Scrooge celebrate Christmas after his adventures with the three spirits?

SECTION C

7. "Goblin Market"

How did Lizzie save Laura after she had eaten the goblin fruit?

8. "The Ancient Mariner"

   (a) Why was the Ancient Mariner under a curse and when was it lifted?
and (b) Describe the coming of the spectre-ship.

9. "Atalanta's Race"

Imagine that you are Atalanta, and tell the story of your race with Milanion.

FIFTEEN   EVERYONE WANTS TO GO ON THE STAGE

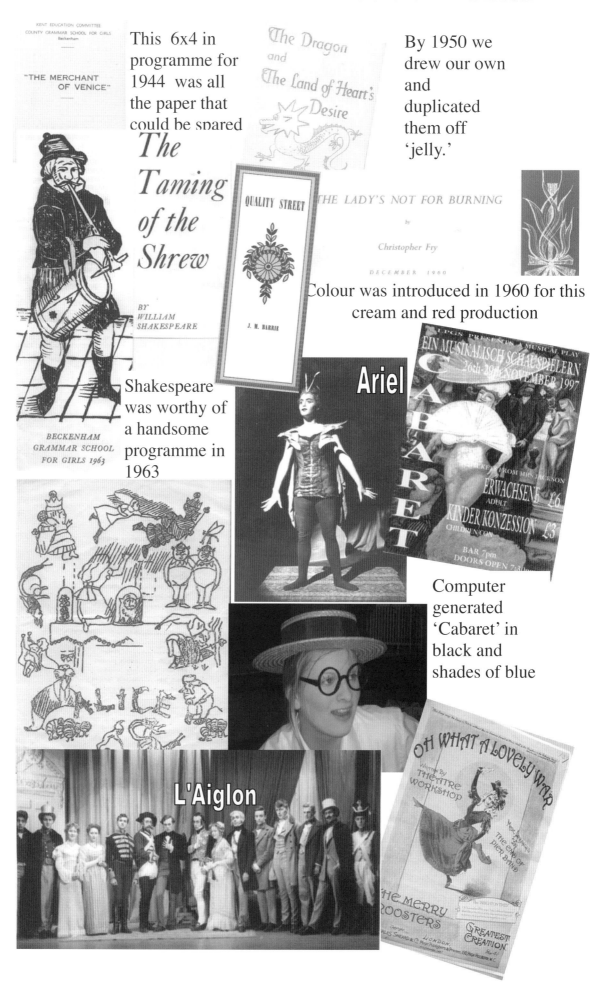

This 6x4 in programme for 1944 was all the paper that could be spared

By 1950 we drew our own and duplicated them off 'jelly.'

Colour was introduced in 1960 for this cream and red production

Shakespeare was worthy of a handsome programme in 1963

Computer generated 'Cabaret' in black and shades of blue

FIFTEEN   EVERYONE WANTS TO GO ON THE STAGE

Well, maybe not everyone, but a great many girls (and boys) have appeared in school drama productions over the years. Some even went on to fame, like Sonia Rees who appeared in 'The Sound of Music' in the 1960s, Yvonne Antrobus who has appeared on stage, TV and radio, Ria (Sharon) Keen and Jenny Evans.

Of course, not everyone can be famous, but those who took part certainly enjoyed their moments in the limelight, just as do the pupils in the present day school. The first school year in 1920 finished with play readings from 'Alfred and the Cakes' and scenes from 'Pride and Prejudice' by IIa (year 6) and the UIV (year 9). There were play readings at various times of the year, but from December 1922 the Christmas entertainment became the year's main showing to parents and friends. That year 'A Kiss for Cinderella' raised some £13 for the Beckenham Cottage Hospital. Excerpts from two, three or more plays became established, as at Christmas 1930 when 'The Mill on the Floss', 'Swineherd', 'Maker of Dreams,' 'The Merchant of Venice' and 'Alice through the Looking Glass' were included.

In 1934 Miss Rose helped by Miss Matthews and Mr & Mrs Luxford who did the sets, produced a magnificent 'Toad of Toad Hall' which raised £44 for the X Fund and various charities. This was followed by Walter de la Mare's 'Crossings' in 1935, Sir James Barrie's 'A Kiss for Cinderella' in 1936 and Richard Sheridan's 'The Rivals' in 1937.

'Twelfth Night' the play chosen by Miss Rose for Christmas 1938 was the last normal production for several years. It was acted in true Elizabethan style with little scenery and demanded much from the cast whose costumes were commendable.

The promised Christmas play for 1939, 'The Knight of the Burning Pestle,' was produced for the pleasure of the school only as, during the term, the girls were scattered all over the place because the school lacked air raid shelters. There was no play at all in 1940 as the blitz prevented after school activities entirely.

Miss Rose's choice for 1941 was 'She Stoops to Conquer,' which displayed spirited acting and amazingly elaborate costumes as suited the period. Music provided by the orchestra played a big part in the success of 'Toad of Toad Hall' in 1942 when nearly all members of the cast were under fourteen. The girls who played the parts of Ratty, Mole, Badger and Toad deserved high praise but Alfred the horse was the star of the show. Sadly, the girl who played Ratty, contracted meningitis and died before the last showing of the play.

The choice of a Nativity play written in verse for the Autumn term of 1943 was something of a surprise but the costumes were most effective, the choir sang carols appropriately, the characters entered their parts with enthusiasm and everyone appreciated the hard work of Miss Rose, Mrs Grunspan and Miss Wiseman.

Miss Rose and Mrs Grunspan braved the threat of flying bombs at Christmas 1944 to produce 'The Knight of the Burning Pestle' and the whole cast was congratulated on the creditable performance. Many costumes were recognised as old favourites and Miss Wiseman coached the girls for their songs.

A A Milne's 'Make Believe' was Mrs Grunspan's choice for Christmas 1945 as a play to suit all those young in years and spirit. The play was supposedly written by the nine Hubbard children on Christmas Eve. In the first act, Evelyn Eminton played the part of the princess who chose the handsome woodcutter instead of one of three royal suitors. Act two followed the fortunes of children Jill and Oliver who escaped to a tropical island. The last act told how Mr and Mrs Hubbard, played to perfection by Ann Eminton and Mary Goodison, met the story book friends and ended with all the characters dancing round Father Christmas.

FIFTEEN   EVERYONE WANTS TO GO ON THE STAGE

Miss Pelling's scenery was ambitious and actually included the children sailing into the lagoon on a raft. The three performances raised over £100 for the School Fund and for Beckenham Hospital.

School for Scandal L to R Ann Eminton, Christine Bridge, Alison Prince, Fay Wrench, Janet McDonald, Mary Goodison, Lorna Sanders, Ena Thorrington.

'School for Scandal' was a complete change from the children's play of the preceding year. It called for polished dialogue and skill of characterisation especially for the male parts of the lovable but irritable Sir Peter Teazle, the hearty Sir Oliver and the handsome Charles. The property cupboard had to be turned out and even old curtains used to make costumes as coupons were unobtainable this being December 1946. Blackout curtains discarded from WW II were stitched together for the backcloth and the Art Club produced rows of books and a whole gallery of 'Old Masters' to set the scene. Even more ambitious was 'Murder in the Cathedral' produced by Miss Taylor in 1947 with the help of Mrs Grunspan, Miss Kobrak and Alison Prince designing the costumes. Miss Pelling and the Art Club used their considerable skill to create banners, armour and the Cathedral setting. Essentially the study of Thomas, a proud man striving to resist the four Tempters, Christine Bridge's performance as Thomas was outstanding.

Miss Taylor's 'The Merchant of Venice' with the masterly performance of Shylock by Ruth Jordan in 1948 was followed by Mrs Grunspan's production of 'The Ivory Door' in December 1949 during her final year at school. Mr Nash built a magnificent gateway and Miss Pelling's workers painted old tablecloths to relieve the neutral backcloth for the palace scenes while the contents of the property cupboard were remodelled to make a world of flowing robes with extravagant sleeves and crazy slippers.

Two Irish plays at Christmas 1950 were 'The Land of Heart's Desire' and 'The Dragon.' One of the two eerie fairy songs was composed by Miss Wiseman. The production of 'Major Barbara' by the Boys' School involved our actresses in 1951.

" THE MERCHANT OF VENICE "

CAST

Duke of Venice - - - -		J. Hurford
Prince of Morocco ⎱ suitors to		M. Magee
Prince of Arragon ⎰ Portia		E. Edwards
Antonio, a merchant of Venice .		C. Bridge
Bassanio, his friend - - -		S. Wilson
Gratiano ⎱ friends to		R. Morgan
Salarino ⎰ Antonio and		B. Bruce
Salanio ⎰ Bassanio		J. Wood
Lorenzo, in love with Jessica - -		D. Baker
Shylock, a rich Jew - - -		R. Jordan
Tubal, a Jew, his friend - - -		P. Jones
Launcelot Gobbo, servant to Shylock -		S. Handy
Old Gobbo, father to Launcelot -		H. Ricketts
Leonardo, servant to Bassanio - -		P. Evans
Balthazar, servant to Portia - -		B. Muncey
Portia, a rich heiress - - -		P. Mitchell
Nerissa, her waiting-maid - -		E. Hewison
Jessica, daughter to Shylock - -		B. Powell

Scene: Partly at Venice, and partly at Belmont,
the seat of Portia

In 1952 the Autumn Term was spent on the production of 'Tobias and the Angel' by Miss Taylor even though the great London smog of that November nearly destroyed all their efforts. The demon, Asmoday, gained a special round of applause when she crept in wearing a wonderfully gruesome mask created by Miss Pelling.

Jennifer Crier's sincere simplicity in playing St Joan in 1953 was most moving at times and special mention was made of Celia Antrobus's portrayal of the difficult Cauchon. Again Miss Pelling's skill went into the settings of castles, cathedrals, tents and riverbanks as always, with the cheerful assistance of the caretakers, Mr Nash and Mr Jewell.

Sadly December 1954's production of 'She Stoops to Conquer' was the last to benefit from the expertise of Miss Pelling. Only those who have worked with her know how unselfishly and cheerfully she worked for us. The two young girls, Kate Hardcastle and Constance Neville, were pleasantly contrasted in the acting of Yvonne Antrobus and Pat Logan. Yvonne went on to become a writer and actress for the BBC and Pat returned to school as a teacher in the English department, now Mrs Williams.

Jennifer Crier as Ariel in 'The Tempest'

In 1955 Shakespeare's 'The Tempest' was an unusual and certainly ambitious play for a girls' school. The cast, which included a dignified Jill Saunders as Prospero, cunning Antonio played by Ruth Huxstep, Jennifier Crier's graceful Ariel and the cringing Caliban, Wendy Lloyd, acted with aplomb and the island was magical. It was set with fantastic vegetation, conceived by Miss Savage and executed by the VI form, and peopled by grotesque spirits who were trained in their dances by Miss Maynard to music arranged by Miss Wiseman. Miss Newland and Miss Savage designed the costumes, which were made by 'all sorts of people.' Junior pupils made the fruit for the banquet and seniors controlled the mechanism to snatch it away. Third formers designed amazing masks and Sixth formers created lightning and thunder. This was, in every sense, a School Play.

FIFTEEN   EVERYONE WANTS TO GO ON THE STAGE

Miss Taylor had a job on her hands in 1956's offering of 'Quality Street.' Before serious rehearsals could begin she went to great lengths to instil in her cast a sense of gentility and delicacy of these characters of the early nineteenth century. It was an extremely successful production with a high standard of presentation and acting. Lesley Perkins opened the run playing Valentine, and was succeeded by Gillian Brown giving a most convincing portrayal of the same character. Yvonne Antrobus contrasted their manly acting with a very feminine Miss Phoebe, who had to age ten years between acts. A note in the School Magazine refers to Londex Ltd 'who transported the period furniture during the petrol shortage.' This shortage was as a result of the Suez Crisis, an important event in British History that has had lasting effects.

The last play to be staged at Lennard Road was Christopher Fry's 'The Boy with a Cart' in 1957. It is about the faith of a Cornish shepherd boy, played with feeling and sincerity by Wendy Farndale. He follows the call of God to travel across the South of England before finding fulfilment in building a church. The play is moving with a beautiful script, to which the large cast was committed. The Prologue was created especially for the occasion by Miss Maynard. Four dances representing the Seasons were performed by first formers and interspersed by Madeleine Pope's Bible readings. Juliet Griffiths as Tawm, provided some light relief, with Madeleine Pope and Sheila Stocks playing his daughter and son-in-law. Juliet fell a victim to the epidemic of Asian 'flu' rampant at that time, and Sheila Morrow took her part at very short notice on the final evening.

As the School moved in the Christmas holidays of 1958–1959 there was no school play that year: the staff and pupils were industriously involved in packing up. In December 1959, Miss Taylor's Twelfth Night was the first play to be performed in the new hall of the school at Langley. The play calls for a large cast and so gave the opportunity for many girls to be involved. The inspired comedy of Margaret Withers as Sir Toby Belch was much enjoyed and Jane Dewey gave a delightful performance of the cowardly Sir Andrew Aguecheek. As for the twins, Viola was played by Wendy Farndale and her brother Sebastian by Sheila Stuart. Make-up and Costume worked hard to produce the necessary resemblance between the twins.

Mrs Rosenburg's 1960's 'The Lady's Not For Burning' again benefited from the outstanding Jane Dewey who played the leading performance of the Lady Jennet. Humour was provided by Margaret Withers playing Hebble Tyson, the Mayor, with Mary Dove as Tappercoom, the Town Justice but a high standard of acting by the whole cast carried the play along enjoyably. Thomas was played by Barbara Pitt (shown here on the first night) and Claire Shaffer. Helen Mynett and Elaine Fox remember the crowded conditions backstage. Miss Hawkins had selected Vaughan-Williams' 'Variations on a Theme of Thomas Tallis' as the theme music. The gramophone was placed on a desk under which the two girls sat. At appropriate moments they would emerge to put on the record, and hope the needle went on at the right place. It was an inexact science!

The skill and unending patience of producer Miss Daniels resulted in the outstanding 'She Stoops to Conquer' in December 1961.

FIFTEEN   EVERYONE WANTS TO GO ON THE STAGE

It was distinguished by most enjoyable performances from the many listed as 'servants and fellows.' They ranged from the rustic naiveté of Hardcastle's servant Diggory played by Christine Paul, the exuberant Tony Lumpkin of Margaret Withers and Susan Jenkins' debauched landlord of 'The Three Pigeons.'

The setting and costumes were a delight to the eye and special thanks were due to Mr Jewell, who constructed the heavy 'oaken' staircase.

The entire cast of 'The Prodigious Snob' includes all the backstage helpers

'The Prodigious Snob' of 1962, is a lively translation of Moliere's comedy 'Le Bourgeois Gentilhomme' in which M. Jourdain tries to rise in society by means of his wealth, not realising how others take advantage of him. It needed a large number of dress designers to provide the costumes for all the cast and many instrumentalists to record the music.

'The Taming of the Shrew' was Mrs Langley's choice for 1963. It is a play within a play and as such it presents many difficulties in production. Petruchio was amusingly and powerfully played by Stephanie Hesketh with Jill Bruck giving a suitably spiteful performance as the shrew. The principals were ably supported by the rest of the cast who all gave life and character to their parts. Miss Thompson designed and painted the set, Mr Jewell constructed the realistic staircase and Miss Atkins made the beautiful dresses for the ladies.

December 1964's 'Double Image' started with the light-hearted, one-act play 'A Phoenix too Frequent,' and was followed by 'The Trojan Woman,' a tragedy directed by Mrs Langley and Miss Morris. The problem of burning Troy was overcome by dramatic lighting but on the first night too much smoke was made and the Chorus retreated coughing! Letters of appreciation to Miss Chreseson said: 'I thought the girls (and the producer!) gave quite a remarkable performance. Some of them seemed so mature it was difficult to think of them as actually schoolgirls!' and another, 'I thought Euripides classic play was splendidly done, in acting, scenery and in sound and lighting effects.....As a comedy Christopher Fry's play has many very funny quips and situations........I thought your girls very courageous in attempting what seemed an impossible task and doing so extremely well.'

November 1965 saw three very fine performances of William Congreve's 'Way of the World' yet another of Mrs Langley's choices. The complicated plot took the cast a long time to understand but their high standard of acting made it all clear to the audiences.

FIFTEEN   EVERYONE WANTS TO GO ON THE STAGE

Atmosphere was given by the attractive scenery achieved by Miss Storr and the costumes made by Mrs Crowston to Mrs Langley's design. The principals, Gillian Pleant and Susan Dickinson were ably supported by Viki McAdam's villainous Fainfall and Ann Deacon's equally villainous Mrs Marwood and the numerous minor characters added fun to the play.

Way of the World, L to R Ann Deacon, ??, ??, Celia Greenwood, ??, Francis Hoare, Helen Friskney, ??, ??, ??, Susan Owen

Ann Deacon, now Garner, runs a successful theatre company in Bath called 'Next Stage.' Helen Friskney playing 'Foible' remembers how the unflappable and humorous Mrs Langley took her aside on the first night with a slight flicker of her eyelid to tell her that the headmistress had asked for the line 'Mr Mirabell seduced me' to be changed to 'Mr Mirabell *persuaded* me.'

The polished production of Schiller's 'Mary Stuart' by Mrs Langley and Mrs Hook in November 1966 was remarkable in that so many girls were able to take part both on stage and behind the scenes. The rivalry between Elizabeth I and Mary, Queen of Scots, was acted passionately by Celia Greenwood and Helen Friskney and the costumes were truly remarkable. It was the height of the 'swinging sixties' and the cast had to master the art of walking with dignity in long dresses instead of flitting along corridors in rolled-up-at-the-waist school mini-skirts. Celia went on to study drama at R.A.D.A (letter in 1966 file – possibly now Director of WAC Performing Arts and Media College – Hampstead Town Hall -Harringey). Helen Friskney, now Corkin, still relishes dabbling in amateur dramatics and is grateful for the chance school gave her to take part in proper productions with lovely costumes, real make-up, music and lighting effects.

The school play of 1967 was 'The Knight of the Burning Pestle' produced by Mrs Hook with Mrs Langley as usual mustering up her troops to produce professionally made costumes. It was a great challenge to attempt to create the atmosphere of the Globe Theatre in Shakespearian times.

FIFTEEN   EVERYONE WANTS TO GO ON THE STAGE

Full cast of 'Mary Stuart'. L to R back row Heather Long,??, ??, Christine Aynsley, Celia Greenwwod, Helen Friskney, Anne Deacon, Francis Hoare, Susan Owen, Margaret Dawson. Front ??, ??, ??, Victoria Collins, Anne Scade, ??, Gail Palmer, ??, ??, Rosemary Bruck.

This is a farcical comedy where a grocer and his wife force themselves onto the stage to be censors of the action, as the grocer considers the play 'The London Merchant' casts aspersions on his profession. The two constantly interfere with the play and insist on introducing a new character, a knight who will uphold the honour of the grocery business. There emerges a 'play within a play.' The crisis occurs when the interference at last gets completely out of hand, at about the same time as the two subplots reach their climax. This is a play that has been a joy both to act in and to see, and it is not difficult to see why it has been so appealing to producers. In this year Elizabeth Standen and Gillian Marshall played the Grocer and his wife, and Ralph, their employee, the Knight. The scenery remained on stage throughout but by placing simple but effective props on the stage, the site of each scene rapidly changed. Ralph, played by a five foot high girl, needed a suit of armour but the theatrical supplier had just hired out 500 suits for a film so our knight errant ended up with a large, cumbersome suit of armour minus an arm and a leg. The cast probably enjoyed the play more than the bemused audience!

As a change in 1968 from the run of eighteenth century and Elizabethan plays, Mrs Langley helped by Mrs Hook directed the Nativity scenes from the 'Wakefield Mystery Play Cycle.' Rosemary Bruck played a serene Virgin Mary and Elizabeth Pote a terrifying Herod, especially where he tried to manipulate the Three Kings for his own purposes. Light relief was given by the shepherds on the hills with Barbara Lording and Gail Palmer showing a talent for comic acting.

Mrs Langley's production of 'Twelfth Night' performed in January 1971 was distinguished by the identical twins Elizabeth and Jill Barnes who played Viola and Sebastian. The audience really thought that both parts were being played by one person until the girls appeared on stage together. A fine performance was given by Jenny Evans as the Countess Olivia. As you can find elsewhere in the book, Jenny continued her talent for entertaining, becoming a well known singer in Germany to this day. She remembers with pride the beautiful black and white taffeta dress made for her by Mrs Langley.

175

FIFTEEN   EVERYONE WANTS TO GO ON THE STAGE

These reports come from the school magazines and as such omit many of the actresses who made the plays so successful. Since there were no more magazines after this time, we may have omitted some subsequent productions, but times were changing. The old style of production by gifted members of staff was being supplanted by the girls themselves. The two Langley schools, like their predecessors had always worked together and the future was to bring them closer together with joint lessons and productions, including drama and music.

For a decade, the girls livened us up after Christmas dinner with a L6 pantomime starting in 1968 with Cinderella presented by Jacqueline Grace and Nita Bowes. This particular end of term afternoon we greatly enjoyed singing the chorus of 'Lily the Pink' over and over again.

There was a 'pop' group in the 1960s in Britain called 'Scaffold' whose main claim to fame was that one of them was Paul McCartney's brother and one was the Liverpool poet Roger McGough. However, they had a long-running number one hit with what most people took to be a children's song called 'Lily the Pink'. Its verses went on for ever but here's the chorus.
> We'll drink a drink a drink
> To Lily the Pink the Pink the Pink
> The saviour of the human race
> For she invented medicinal compound
> Most efficacious in every case.

In the early 1970s Rebecca Abbott produced 'Peter Pan' with Jane Dawson playing a riotous fairy. By the 1980s the pantomimes had ceased but they had a great send off with a production by Sharon Keen of 'Grease' in 1979 that involved members of staff (Peter Rowland, Richard Macauley and David Blake) who borrowed the leathers of the cast's boyfriends.

Fiona Croft dances with Peter Rowland in 'Grease'

FIFTEEN   EVERYONE WANTS TO GO ON THE STAGE

Peter Rowland's 'Sweet Charity' was the production with a mixed cast for March 1977 with direction from Carol McLeod and Richard Macauley and assistance from many other members of staff including Mr Sampson, Head of Drama at Kelsey Park. Richard also directed 'Alice Through the Looking Glass' in 1978 where Cheryl Webster played Alice and Mrs Barbara Smith of the Biology department made the masks for the cast.

Keith Harcourt from the Resources Dept produced 'The Crucible' in 1979/80, again a mixed cast with the Boys' School, assisted by Peter Rowland, Barbara Smith, Greta Bayley and Pat Williams who was by now accustomed to the role of 'costumes.' For the 1980 production of 'She Stoops to Conquer' in March 1980 almost twenty staff assisted the directors Sue Harding, Carol McLeod, Pam Bristow and Peter Rowland. Soon afterwards in May 1980, Miss Jayne Richards produced 'Dark of the Moon' at the Boys' school with 14 year old Kathy Jowitt, playing a convincing heroine.

It was Mrs Langley who talked Fiona MacDonald (née Shore) into reviving the tradition of staging G&S. Fiona and music teacher Jane Vandenbrink brought back 'Trial by Jury' in 1977/78, followed by an informal concert where Fiona's husband sang. Fiona and Jane

performed the Rossini 'Cat Duet' while the audience was milling around eating lavish refreshments. Their 'HMS Pinafore' of 1979 where Head of Spanish, Geoff Buckley, played Sir Joseph Porter, was also eventful in that the part of Ralph Rackstraw was to be taken by a sixth former from the boys' school. However he went down with appendicitis. Fiona found an old university friend, Peter Allanson, to play the part but he was a baritone and Jane transposed his aria into a key he could manage----- quite an undertaking!

Josephine (Tracey Williams) and Ralph (Peter Allanson)

The production of The 'Murder of Maria Marten' in 1980 saw Sharon Keen assisting the director Richard Macauley. Sharon was not only a regular member of the cast of the productions of this time but also extending her influence as a director. She is now known as Ria Keen, professional entertainer.

THE MURDER OF
MARIA MARTEN
OF
THE RED BARN

FIFTEEN   EVERYONE WANTS TO GO ON THE STAGE

CAST

Euripides	-	Nigel Burt
Mnesilochus	-	Andrew Stone
Preunos	-	Clive Turner
Ajax	-	Paul Smith
Polybustos	-	Matt Kemp
Agathon	-	Jon Pitt
Kliestenes	-	David Alder
Staemon	-	Guy Smith
Asphyxia	-	Gill Manning
Kakaphonica	-	Sharon Keen
Paprika	-	Drucilla Dyson
Phriske	-	Elaine Kelly
Praisenese	-	Claire Farrow
Krike	-	Angela Justham
Erotica	-	Gill Ingram
Phisephusia	-	Juliet Ramsey
Peone	-	Sara Watkins

The joint sixth form of the Langley Boys' and Girls' Schools led to the introduction of subjects like AO Drama and the production of 'Roots' over three evenings in the Drama studio at Christmas 1978 by Richard Macauley (Girls) and Richard Gray (Boys). L6 Drama Group D produced and directed 'Thesmophoriazusae' where the women of Athens vent their fury on Euripides, a poet who persisted in degrading them.

Richard Macauley introduced the idea of a review with mime, song and dance at the end of the summer term in 1979 and the tall, dark and handsome Physics master, Martin Larrington, performed the function of compere to perfection. Accident prone stage hands, Michelle and Tricky, were especially popular with the audience.

1980 saw the continuing resurrection of G&S with the spontaneous production of Iolanthe. Everyone rallied round, Jane Vandenbrink took on the music, Mrs Langley organised costumes and lots of staff took part. They rehearsed between the end of exams and the end of term and had terrific fun (probably more than the audiences did) girls and staff all 'mucking in' together. Miss Watmough as a fairy in Iolanthe is an image that always brings a smile!

In 1981, Fiona found that Iolanthe led on to the more ambitious enterprise of staging 'Noyes Fludde' by Benjamin Britten - a whole school project involving a number of departments. Her husband sang Noah and Mrs Anne Handy (then Chair of Governors) sang Mrs Noah. Pupils took all the other parts, the whole of the first year being involved as animals in the ark, all having made their own masks in art lessons.

The production in 1982 was 'Hansel and Gretel'. 'Alice in Wonderland' was another play of the 1980s, also 'Amahl and the Night Visitors.' 'Fiddler on the Roof' was a rousing success in July 1984. In April 1992, A-level pupils of the Performing Arts group put on a double bill. The first was 'To,' Jim Cartwright's play about people in a pub. Then they played Jean-Paul Sartre's 'In Camera,' that concerns a group of individuals who must stay together through eternity.

In 1995 Brigid Doherty, Head of Performing Arts, began her contribution to the dramatic life of the school by designing and producing shows which have received great acclaim. The first production was 'Sweet Charity'. Miss Sage wrote:

'I am delighted the present school is about to launch its first major drama production. Ms Doherty's enthusiasm for this project has created a valuable opportunity for collaboration among the pupils from Years 10 – 13 as well as enabling individuals to demonstrate their performance skills. They have seized the opportunity eagerly and energetically. So too have members of the teaching staff. Drama and Music specialists have worked closely and keenly together, whilst others have taken on a variety of production responsibilities. This is a huge undertaking, demanding much from many people – and giving so much to the life of the school'

FIFTEEN   EVERYONE WANTS TO GO ON THE STAGE

It was indeed a huge undertaking with a cast of 50, some playing more than one part, a band of 20 and a large number of backstage and production workers. This continued the former pattern of large, colourful productions involving an impressive number of people and rehearsals taking place at weekends and in the holidays. This has always been the case throughout the life of the school and we owe a debt to the generosity of the staff and caretakers for giving up their time in this way. From 1995 to 2008 the productions have included 'Sweet Charity', 'The Visit', 'Cabaret', 'The Grimm Tales', 'Guys and Dolls', 'Chalk Circle,' 'Once in a Lifetime,' 'Oh What a Lovely War,' 'Daisy Pulls it Off', 'Calamity Jane', 'The Wizard of Oz,' 'Ramayana,' 'A Year and a Day' and 'Capetown.'

'The Chalk Circle' is about the plight of refugees. A servant girl, Grusha, fleeing with baby Michael who is heir to the throne, is one such refugee seeking security and a place to call home. She leaves behind her fiancé, Simon, a soldier of the Palace Guard, and risks everything to save the child. The story ends with the case brought before a corrupt judge who has to chose between Grusha's claim on Michael since she saved and reared him and the child's biological mother who only wants to claim her son to gain access to his dead father's money.

In 2002, over 75 people were involved in the play from the 1960s called 'Oh, What a Lovely War.' Although the play has a wide appeal with its catchy songs a serious message is conveyed. In the cast were Naomi Tamblyn and Suzy Payne from year 13 and musician Wendy Spear from the sound team enjoyed solving the problems of achieving the right balance.

<u>Rebecca Cryan and Oh what a Lovely War Dec 2002</u>

From the moment the audience walked through the foyer, they were transported to an early twentieth century seaside resort. Flags were draped from every available surface. In the hall a pier had been constructed with signs like 'Sniper Alley' and 'Arras 10km' decorating the walls. The performance began with the music from the ever popular Langley musicians, renamed 'The End of Pier Band.'

The performance itself was spectacular as the actors proved themselves to be incredibly skilled with regards to accent and dialect with Emma Daughtry astounding the audience with her wide range, encompassing Irish, South London, French and Scottish. Congratulations must also go to Vicki Moore for the breathtaking choreography. Another solo from Claire Kenning proved as popular as ever. A particularly funny scene included Nida Vohra's amusing linguistic mix-up with the French commissariat, thanks to the six members of the cast from the Boys' School, who provided emotional impact and comic relief. The play managed to combine the tragedy of WWI with an entertaining performance without losing impact and a good time was had by all.

FIFTEEN EVERYONE WANTS TO GO ON THE STAGE

In Daisy Pulls it Off, the Adremians supplied pictures of past pupils of the old box-pleated tunics and girdles of the 1920s and 30s for the costume department to copy but they seemed to think that the 1960s boaters were old enough!.

For 'Calamity Jane' in 2004, the school hall was transformed into 'The Golden Garter Saloon' beginning in the entrance hall. Calamity, played by Vikki Brown, is the rootin', tootin', tomboy heroine who drives the stagecoach and enjoys a love/hate relationship with Wild Bill Hickock (Simon Drayson). When the expected actress turns out to be a man because the cowboys can't tell the difference between Francis and Frances, it's up to Calamity to bring back the famous Adelaide Adams from Chicago to save the day. The acting was superb, especially from Dave Parry (Francis/Frances) and Vicky Brown's voice was amazing as she was in virtually every song like 'The Black Hills of Dakota', 'Careless with the Truth' and 'Whip-crack-away.' Line dancing in the interval completed the Wild West theme.

In 'The Wizard of Oz' there were ten Dorothys and four wicked witches at times speaking and moving as one, which enhanced the spirit of the story.

In February 2007, as part of the National Theatre Connections Festival, the drama department presented 'A Year and a Day,' a new play by Christine Reid. The National Theatre's enthusiastic review led to an invitation to appear at the Hampstead Theatre on 16 April. Comments included 'fantastic show' and 'the performance was outstanding' which was highly rewarding for the 55 pupils involved.

Having obtained Leading Edge Funding, the Drama department was able to build on its work with the Women Unite Organisation in South Africa started when 40 students went to Cape Town in 2005 to work with professional performers and students from the Langa township. This culminated in a performance at the amphitheatre on the Victoria and Alfred Waterfront. Since then they have been raising money for the organisation, eg Cabaret Evening. One of the women from Cape Town, Thandi, came over for a week of song, dance and drumming to year 10 pupils from Cator Park, Selhurst Boys and Langley Girls. This raised £1,000 to go towards an Arts/Culture Centre in Langa.

Sarah Powell of 12B writes of the emotional rollercoaster of Cape Town 2005

Before going on the trip I don't think anybody anticipated the type of work we would do and we were surprised how well we progressed. Not only did we create 'Can dances', played the marimba and sang traditional African songs but went on a number of excursions and theatre trips.

There was the famous cable car ride up Table Mountain, a trip to Cape Point to see the wildlife like the jackass penguins, baboons and ostrich and a visit to Robben Island where an ex-political prisoner took us for a tour and told us of his experiences. We found his courage in sharing his past very moving. Another emotional experience was when we went to the local township of Langa especially when watching the dancing of the primary school children. The realisation that only very few children were given an education made us appreciate how lucky we are to have everything on offer. Their standard of living was shocking compared with ours and yet they all seemed so happy.

When it was time to leave I felt sadness and guilt for the way they live and yet found myself questioning whether the way we live ourselves makes us truly happy. It was the most amazing experience I have ever encountered and is something I will never forget.

Members of the drama and citizenship groups paid another visit to Cape Town in 2008.

At the end of 2007, a large cast mimed 'Arabian Nights' to various narrators with the story lines. One particularly good effect was created to produce Sinbad the sailor's ship as you can see in the picture below.

Iolanthe 1951,

Patricia Carroll

Princess Ida

In memory of
Miss Wiseman
House Mistress
of
Goodhart House
1948-1963

Iolanthe 1959

Gondoliers 1949

Gondoliers 1968

Fascinating Rhythms

Brigid Doherty

SIXTEEN   OUR MUSIC OVER THE DECADES

Music, when soft voices die, vibrates the memory...

A poem by Shelley set to music by Charles Wood- a song sung many times by many choirs over many years. Our school has always had a reputation for music; it has always been an important part of the curriculum. Reading through many school magazines and records there are many references to the musical activities at the school, whether they were internal, such as inter-house competitions, in-house concerts, operas or plays or other special occasions, or external at festivals, charitable functions or indeed, overseas broadcasting

In the past, the Autumn Term was time for Speech Day, the Beckenham Festival, a school play, pantomime, or other entertainment, Remembrance Day and Carol Services. In the Spring Term there was often a school concert involving choirs, orchestras and soloists, and then in the Summer Term, when examinations were over, there were many rehearsals at all times of day in preparation for what, in my time at the school was the highlight of the year, an operetta by Gilbert & Sullivan; the first was performed in 1941.

In 1942 the choir performed 'Hiawatha's Wedding Feast' by Samuel Coleridge Taylor, described as with *colourful costumes, rhythmic movements and delightful singing*. This was followed by an entertaining operetta, 'It might have happened to you', written by the Music Mistress, Miss Wiseman, as an excellent foil to the serious music of Hiawatha. The doodlebugs stopped the performance of the planned 'Pirates of Penzance' in the summer of 1944, but thereafter G&S continued for every year until 1968; more of that later. The choir always did well at the Beckenham festival, starting in the 1930s with elocution and solo items. In 1950, although the senior choir was the only entrant in its class, the Adjudicator awarded it 98 marks for *the most beautiful singing he had ever heard*!

At Remembrance Day, the choir would lead the service at the Beckenham War Memorial. Before Christmas, the choir led the carols at the Rotary Club's Goodwill Christmas tree and Carol Services were also held at Holy Trinity Church, Lennard Road, and later at St. John's Church, Eden Park.

Mention must also be made of Clubland, run by the Revd J. Butterworth, a boys' and girls' club in the Camberwell Road, where over a number of years a choir would go to sing at an evening service. There was a special event in 1961 when a new chapel was opened, and in the presence of many celebrities, the Girls' School choir sang some anthems.

The choirs met regularly- sometimes there were as many as three groups (Junior, Middle and Senior). Singing exercises helped the sopranos to achieve good, clear top notes and there were others to encourage the altos in the lower regions. In the days of regular school assembly, not only was a hymn sung, but also a psalm set to Gregorian chant; the chant had to be practised by the choir to make sure that it was correct so that they gave a good lead to the rest of the school.

Part songs were a main feature of rehearsals in preparation for festivals, speech days, and concerts, but there were also occasions when the choir would join with other schools and sing choral works by the classical composers such as Haydn, Mozart, and later more modern composers such as Britten, Kodaly and Orff. Inter-form and inter-house music competitions, singing set songs judged by an outside adjudicator, were fun because lessons were cancelled for the day! In 1968 the singing competition became a music competition. Each House gave half an hour of instrumental, choral and, in more ambitious cases, orchestral entertainment and those Houses 'less abundant in talent,' excelled in the variety and organisation of their efforts.

SIXTEEN   OUR MUSIC OVER THE DECADES

The first time an orchestra is mentioned in the magazines is in 1924, when the Toy Symphony was performed. In 1926 there was a school concert in aid of the Music Fund with entrance fee one penny, which raised £1 0s 4d. (Remember £1 = 240 old pence). Over the years the orchestra had its ups and downs with too many strings, not enough woodwind and rarely much brass but in 1962 potential instrumentalists were asked to turn their talents

to the mastery of a stringed instrument to help avert the tragedy of our orchestra becoming a military band, we desperately needed strings to balance seven or eight clarinets, four flutes, two oboes, a bassoon and a French horn! The main point was that hopefully, all of the performers were enjoying themselves playing together; they were doing their best and were in the hands of a competent conductor, who had put much time and thought into the choice of music, matching their capabilities. In 1964 the orchestra acquired a distinguished pair of copper-shelled kettle drums; these were bought along with a number of other instruments, from a fund in memory of Miss Wiseman, Head of Music for twenty five years.

There were occasions when artistes performed at the school. As early as 1923, there is mention of a pianoforte recital by Miss Desiree McEwan of the Tobias Mathay School (a technique favoured by the Royal Academy of Music). In 1947 a very excited sixth former climbed on to the platform to turn the pages for the pianist Ronald Smith, who was playing with the violinist Colin Sauer! In 1967 the Dennis East Chamber Orchestra visited the school---- an event arranged by the Music Adviser of the newly formed London Borough of Bromley.

SIXTEEN   OUR MUSIC OVER THE DECADES

Of those who made music a career, some hit the highlights in the musical world. Patricia Carroll in the 1950s gained fame as a concert pianist and performed at the Wigmore Hall, the Festival Hall and at the Promenade concerts in the Albert Hall. Christine Kobrak won a place to Oxford with her voice as her instrument and Sonia Rees became well known on the stage in roles such as Maria in 'The Sound of Music' in 1965. Here we see her on the left in the school performance of 'The Gondoliers' in 1955 playing Gianetta to Ann Caws' Marco while Tessa and Guiseppe were played by Maureen Moon and Pat Logan.

The Handy family is well known locally. Audrey (piano) and Shirley (cello) attended the school and two former pupils, Elise Beeton (viola) and Ann Eminton (piano), married into the family. In the next generation Thelma, Kate and Corinne Sergeant came to the school. Thelma now leads the Royal Liverpool Philharmonic orchestra and has retained the name Handy although married with three small sons.

Peter Handy, Rosemary Johnson, Elise Beeton, Shirley Handy

Miss Nancy Wiseman was a wonderful teacher from 1938 to 1963; sadly she died of cancer at the early age of fifty two. Her vitality and enthusiasm were inspirational to us all.

Miss Mavis Hawkins, who was her deputy, kept the school's musical traditions going splendidly until she left in 1968.

EASTER CONCERT

LANGLEY PARK GIRLS SCHOOL

Her successor was Mr. Brian Newsome - a 'modern' man who introduced the girls to music of more recent times, including works by 'avant garde' composers of whom he was one. He once said that his music was difficult to play on the pianoforte - so difficult that he could not play it!! He held workshops, encouraging the girls to improvise; this was put to the test in some of the orchestral performances.

In 1971 not only did the programme include 'Finlandia' by Sibelius, and Copland's 'Billy the Kid', but also the first public performance, by a group of instrumentalists, of Patrick Stamford's Nocturne; the composer was present on this unique occasion. Among others, Pam Cracknell (née Worthley) remembers the great experience of Brian's and Mrs Hook's production of Dido & Aeneas; the second-soprano music has stayed with her ever since.

The Girls' School orchestra often joined with the Boys' School to form a bigger orchestra with a fuller range of instruments. In the 1970s there were a number of occasions when more modern works were performed- Kodaly, Britten, Orff, Janacek, and on one occasion an 'avant garde' work by Bernard Rands -'Per Estempio' - a new experience when the instrumentalists were 'composing' part of the work for themselves.

Mrs Molnar tried hard to request a new piano in December 1969 to replace the Bluthner Grand in the hall as its tone had totally gone but she was unsuccessful and the school still has to make do with the original.

African Jigsaw

In 1990, the Fairfield Hall was booked for the choral cantata, 'African Jigsaw,' accompanied by the school band with Maria Busen-Smith.; there are seven narrations in the musical which add to the stories told by the songs. Written in 1986, it was first performed in the Barbican Concert Hall in London and so it was an ambitious project to be undertaken by the school. Its success guaranteed a repeat booking in 1992 for Ocean World - the magical ocean world of the humpback whale.

SIXTEEN   OUR MUSIC OVER THE DECADES

There was a series of 24 songs with seven narrations and the Beckenham School's orchestra and bands playing a variety of pieces. Miss Sage made the following comment in the 'Encore' programme for 2007: *'Shortly before I took up the headship here, I was invited to a performance of a musical piece called "Ocean World" which the school staged at the Fairfield Halls. I didn't know what to expect, but the performance took my breath away. It was staggeringly good and so moving in places I was almost in tears.'*

L to R Helen Tibbett, Elizabeth Harris and Gemma Birch in 'Ocean World' in 1992

Fifteen years later, in February 2007, the present school once again used the Fairfield Halls for their wonderful production of 'Encore' by the head of Music, John Hargreaves. The Jazz orchestra was fresh from a fantastic tour of Poland and the Langley Park Concert Band was a welcome collaboration with Langley Park School for Boys at a time when both the Langley Schools have their own mixed sixth forms. The concert included the whole of year 8 singing a medley from Andrew Lloyd Webber's 'Cats' and Rodgers & Hammerstein's 'You'll Never Walk Alone.' Dance included 'All that Jazz' from year 10 and 'Coppelia' by the A level group. There were aerobic and gymnastic displays as well as many items with soloists, notably singer, Clare Phillips.

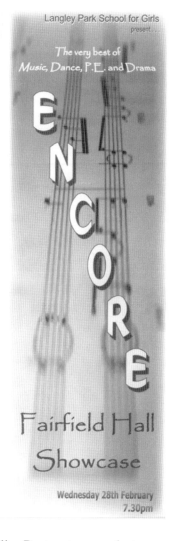

Langley Park School for Girls
present...

The very best of
Music, Dance, P.E. and Drama

ENCORE

Fairfield Hall
Showcase

Wednesday 28th February
7.30pm

Comic Opera by G&S

Nancy Wiseman had not been a member of staff for long before she showed her talent for producing comic opera. She arranged all of the parts to suit girls' voices (having gained permission from the D'Oyly Carte Opera Company), training them to sing beautiful arias and/or to get their tongues round the patter songs. Miss Wiseman not only taught but also sang and acted all the parts, showing the girls exactly how she wished them to be performed. Finally at all the performances, she was the accompanist- an outstanding achievement. Her enthusiasm was infectious and many girls owe a great debt of gratitude to her for giving them the confidence and opportunity to perform in public.

So many names spring to mind when recalling these exciting and demanding times- Kathleen Rands, Marjorie Russell, Audrey Handy, Pat King, Monica Weeks, Daphne Perkins, Ann Eminton, Elise Beeton to name but a few.

SIXTEEN   OUR MUSIC OVER THE DECADES

On 29 July 1941, the choir presented 'The Mikado' to the school even though Miss Wiseman was away at the time. Miss Barnard, Miss Dibb and Miss Scopes (later Mrs Grunspan) put the finishing touches to Miss Wiseman's training; ingenuity provided the costumes. In July 1943, 'The Gondoliers' was Miss Wiseman's choice for the choir and 'The Mikado' again for 1945. On both occasions the cast was dressed splendidly in spite of clothes rationing. The next summer, 'Trial by Jury' was presented with a prologue of G&S songs.

Alison Prince was an old gentleman listening with his granddaughter, played by S. Wilson; Ann Eminton's 'Tit Willow' was a particular favourite. The seemingly inexhaustible property box stretched to include realistic Victorian costumes with a little help from the parents and Miss Pelling.

By 1947, Miss Pelling with her Art department helped by Miss Taylor took the scenery in hand. Miss Wiseman was able to produce 'The Pirates of Penzance' to the very high

standard that we came to expect for evermore. The crowning glory of the piece was the policemen headed by a stout red-face sergeant leading trembling heroes with knocking knees and turned-out toes; never were policemen so loth to meet colourful pirates at close quarters.

The choir excelled itself for 1948's 'HMS Pinafore' and the next year was the turn of 'The Gondoliers' again. Miss Wiseman chose 'The Mikado' again for the summer of 1950 when the audience particularly admired the 'wonderful make-up' the work of Miss Taylor, Mrs Grunspan, Miss Kobrak and Miss Pelling. Shirley Handy's Koko and Evelyn Eminton's pompous Pooh Bah deserved special mention.

'Princess Ida' was the G&S presented in July 1951 with Jean Mantle playing the title role. Her powerful voice had excellent tone and was complemented by Glenys Creighton as the dashing hero.

SIXTEEN   OUR MUSIC OVER THE DECADES

The three sons of Gama played by Valerie Cundy, Jill Andrews and Elizabeth Olby never failed to amuse the audience with their clanking armour. Mrs Ida Poole assisted the other faithful members of staff with make-up and Miss Wiseman had once more produced a wonderful evening's entertainment.

Miss Child dressed the fairies for 'Iolanthe' of 1952 in silk and muslin and the Lords looked truly noble in their hired regalia. Mavis Read was the Lord Chancellor, Janet Kitchen was Lord Tolloller, Shirley Griffiths was Lord Mountararat, Shirley Willis a charming Iolanthe, Jean Mantle made a delightful Ward of Chancery and Eileen Beale her Arcadian shepherd lover and Jane Luckman was the awe inspiring Fairy Queen to all but the irrepressible Valerie Ryan playing Sergeant Willis. The effective backcloths had been painted by Miss Pelling and Adrienne Dart.

Here we see Valerie Ryan and Celia Antrobus taking a female role, unusually for her.

The less well known 'The Sorcerer' was performed in July 1953 after only two days use of the stage; its lighting was installed just in time. Mavis Read was the wonderfully grotesque sorcerer to Jane Luckman's benevolent vicar and the colourful chorus enjoyed pretending to be drugged. Miss Child and Miss Newland saw to the costumes and of course Miss Pelling and her helpers managed the scenery and backstage.

The production of 'HMS Pinafore' in 1954 was another to add to Miss Wiseman's long list of successes. The costumes seemed even better than usual, especially the little hats by Miss Child, and the new stage curtains enhanced Miss Pelling's excellent scenery.

L to R Elizabeth Mynett, Yvonne Antrobus, Ann Perry in HMS Pinafore of 1958 (see next page)

SIXTEEN   OUR MUSIC OVER THE DECADES

Miss Pelling's backcloth of Venice for 'The Gondoliers' in 1955 was the last that she painted for us because she was moving to the Suffolk coast and Miss Child and her helpers spent so much time and energy on the costumes

1956 saw the return of 'The Mikado' by special request of the choir and the following year Miss Wiseman was in charge of her one and only production of 'Patience' although Miss Hawkins oversaw another performance in 1965.

Patience satirizes the 'aesthetic craze' of the 1870s and 1880s, when the output of poets, composers, painters and designers of all kinds was prolific, but perhaps empty and self-indulgent. This artistic movement was so popular, and also so easy to ridicule as a meaningless fad, that it made Patience a big hit. The costumes for the chorus of the 35th Dragoon Guards were hired and the cast had trouble finding the right sized boots but on the night the military precision of their marching onto the stage brought immediate applause!

For 1958 it was another performance of 'HMS Pinafore' and the last in the old school building. A strong line-up of soloists resulted in a spirited and enjoyable show with Elizabeth Mynett as Captain Corcoran. She went on to sing with the D'Oyly Carte Opera Company, and when asked at her audition what solo parts she had sung as an amateur, Captain Corcoran was not the answer they were expecting!

The first production of any kind in the new school was 'Iolanthe' in 1959. The Peers looked wonderful in their hired costumes, and the 'dainty little fairies' tripped around the stage to the bewilderment of some of their families! Elizabeth Mynett, this year singing a female role, was the Fairy Queen with Juliet Griffiths, as the Lord Chancellor.

In 1960 it was Gillian Brown's turn to play the Sorcerer with Delia Smith and Jane Brown as Lady Sangzure and Sir Marmaduke Pointdextre. Anne Collings made a sweetly blighted Constance alternately in love with the vicar played by Mary Smith and Elizabeth Pote's ancient notary. Eleanor Horobin made an exquisite lovely Aline and Audrey White a miraculously masculine Alexis of the Grenadier Guards. The chorus gained an encore for its rendering of the rustic romance.

L to R Juliet Griffiths, Barbara Pitt, Carolyn Wood, Claire Shaffer, Jill Bury. Iolanthe 1959

Gondoliers of 1961

1961's G&S operetta was the ever popular 'Gondoliers' with the cast able to act as well as to sing admirably. The quartet 'In a contemplative fashion' by Jean Davies and Margaret Try as Marco and Guiseppe and Janet Rose and Mary Smith as Gianetta and Tessa gained an encore on two of the three nights as did the gavotte by Jill Cruwys and Barbara Pitt as the Duke and Duchess of Plaza-Toro. The scenery was designed and staged by Miss Thompson and Mrs Cohen.

Princess Ida in 1962

We were not to know that Miss Wiseman's customary energy and enthusiasm that she put into 1962's 'Princess Ida' was to be her last The soloists were both good actresses and strong singers and so many staff helped to make this G&S a resounding success.

SIXTEEN   OUR MUSIC OVER THE DECADES

Miss Thompson and Joan Pardon worked on the set, Mrs Atkins and Mrs Langley produced the costumes and props from war tunics and hatchets to academic robes and medieval hats.

There was no G&S in 1963 as Miss Wiseman died in February 1963 when we realised that so much we take for granted is a gift from teachers who sink their own interests into those of their pupils. Instead Miss Hawkins and Miss Cooper produced Bizet's 'Carmen' from a combination of the choirs and orchestras of our school and of the Boys' augmented by friends and past pupils.

'The Mikado' of 1964 was the first G&S for Miss Hawkins and Mrs Langley and for the first time a small orchestra enhanced the musical quality of the performance. The costumes were made by the school using 'Tie and Dye' and lino printed patterns on the kimonos. Owing to the lapse of copyright, topical references were made to politicians Wilson, Home and Grimmond.

There were four more G&S productions from the team of Miss Hawkins and Mrs Langley, 'Patience' in 1965, 'HMS Pinafore' in 1966, the little known 'The Grand Duke' in 1967. A letter written to the Beckenham Advertiser in August 1967 described the mayor's state of helpless mirth at the performance, which he thought deserved a Gold Medal.

Taking only eight days to rehearse, 'The Gondoliers' was the last of the long series of G&S presented from 1941 to 1968. Then Miss Hawkins left us for Cambridge and we entered the period of more serious modern music under Mr Newsome and various entertainments produced spontaneously by girls, boys and staff alike.

The cast of the Gondoliers with Miss Hawkins and Mrs Langley in the centre

Fascinating Rhythms

The Performers

Session Band Dulwich Village People Dave & Jeff (comperes) Erica Slater & Jenny Batt	Back with the Lads	The Lads ....again....	The Lads....yet again....
First Rhythm	**Second Rhythm**	**Third Rhythm**	**Fourth Rhythm**
Birdland The Big Band	Fever Kylee Wright	Chatanooga The Langley Sisters	Cute Big Band plus Vicki & Jo
Back on the Sofa with Joan & Margery Emma & Kirsty	American Dream The Absurdists	The Couple Sue & Dave	Stormy Weather Claire Kenning
'Gladiolus Rag' Jerry	Don't it make your brown eyes blue Elise Fisher	Grease The T-Birds & The Pink Ladies	Scousers The Boys
Jazz Dance Vicki Moore	The Rolf Tribute	Here's That rainy Day Catherine	Fernando Beyond Bjorn Again
Blue Remembered Hills The Thespians	Scott Joplin String Ensemble	Bouncers The Men	Woman Know your Limits Victorian Values Theatre Co
Blue Moon Wendy & Mary	Fatitude Emma Brynon	Anything Goes Jenny Fullick	The Lads Final Chapter
Walk on By Amy Walters	D.I.V.O.R.C.E. The Tammys	Big Spender The Big Band & Kylee	New York New York The Big Band Plus Lizzie Williams
	Wonderwall Wendy, Mary, Julia & Jo		

These musical evenings started in 1996 and have continued year by year. They take the form of the hall set out with tables for refreshments for the audience to listen informally to music from the combined orchestras of the two Langley Park Schools since 2000. The above programme comes from 2001 when the proceeds went to promote the Terrence Higgins Trust and Aids research. In other years money has gone to supporting girls suffering from HIV in a township in South Africa.

Brigid Doherty sings with (L to R) Aimee and Jessica Imms, Lara Toomey and Charlie Jennings-Sewell.

These evenings of Fascinating Rhythms are the idea of Brigid Doherty with the help of so many of the school: Year 13 performing Arts, all who help with stage management and refreshments, the resources staff, the caretakers, those who help with setting up the hall, all those involved on the staff and the audience for continuing to support the endeavours to raise money for Aids research.

L to R, Jenny Wooster, Jessica Kenny, Samantha Bernardis, Melanie Bowman.

It is heartening to see that over the life of the school music has continued to play such an important part. Many students learn to play an instrument and are involved in the department ensembles which perform in the termly concerts: Junior Band, Senior Band, Junior Orchestra, Senior Orchestra, Jazz Orchestra, Big Band, Choir, Year 11 vocal group, Year 7 Chamber Choir, Guitar group, Percussion group, String Quartet, Sax ensemble, Year 7 mass choir, Year 8 mass choir.

The school Jazz Orchestra and one of the many choirs distinguished themselves at the Bromley Schools Prom at the Fairfield Hall early in 2008, radiating an easy professional confidence. An annual music tour now takes place in February: Prague 2003, Austria 2004, Black Forest 2005, Belgium Xmas 2005, Poland 2007, Leipzig 2008. Many of the students are also involved in BYMT bands, choirs and orchestras, from the training bands to the flagship ensembles: BY Concert Band & BY Chamber Orchestra. Currently, Hannah Masson-Smyth is leader of the cello section of the Bromley Youth Symphony Orchestra.

As this book approached publication, auditions for the company of 'Les Miserables School Edition' had taken place, surpassing all expectations in terms of sheer talent and performance. The company consisted of 36 girls and 28 boys from LPGS, LPBS and Ravenswood, with joint production by LPGS and the West Wickham Operatic Society. It was a massive project staged in the school courtyard from 8–12 July 2008 with a full orchestra of 20+ players from LPGS.

Gravesend Cricket
Cup

Rounders, anybody?

SEVENTEEN   GAMES WE USED TO PLAY

While you will read of many who would do anything to avoid standing out on a cold hockey or lacrosse field, there were those who felt that was the main reason for going to school at all and continued to support the Old Girls long after they had left school. Certainly for the school's first thirty years, the annual game to wrest the cricket cup from Gravesend County School was the chief event on the school calendar.

Cricket team 1948, winners of the Gravesend Cup. L to R back row ??, Eva Dineen, ??, Norma Preston, Marjorie Akehurst, ??. Front row Sylvia Jane, Jenifer Jennings, Elise Beeton, Evelyn Andrews, Pamela Mitchell.

Joint matches with the Staff were always warmly anticipated and were used as occasions to make collections for charity.

1956 Staff v U6 netball teams. Back row Sally Thompson, Miss Symonds, Miss Richards, Miss Savage, Dilys Powell. Middle row Miss Ord, Miss Newland, Miss Swan, Miss Maynard. Front row Norma McLeod, Greta Richardson, Gill Forster, Jacqueline Cherry, Janet Lambert

SEVENTEEN   GAMES WE USED TO PLAY

Squash by Lorna Sanders 1941-1948

'Let us,' said my room-mate, 'go and play squash.' So we did. To realise the full significance of that statement, you must understand that neither of us had so much as seen a squash racquet, let alone played, before. I ascertained the route to the courts and on a cold, foggy night we struggled up a muddy, bumpy cart track, fell over a tree stump, staggered through a ditch and arrived at last at a long, low building resembling an uninhabited cow shed.

Once inside we were greeted by a strong smell of cold, damp whitewash and the sound of a tin tray being battered by a football. We climbed into a narrow gallery and were greeted by two masters of the art playing vigorously beneath us. The lines on the walls were not optical illusions calculated to misguide the novice, they explained, but were the court boundaries. The tremendous bangs occurred when the small black ball, a little larger than a golf ball, hit the tin edging of the front wall. We nodded knowledgeably but wondered about the scoring.

After half an hour, in which we learnt that eyes all round the head and two pairs of ambidextrous hands are an asset to a squash player, we descended to ground level, borrowed a racquet each and entered the court with some trepidation and a ball. The first thing to learn is that squash is not tennis as the strokes are all short wrist flicks. The second is that players do not intentionally hit their opponents. With these maxims in mind, we played (if such a word applied here) but fatigue soon set in.

Wallowing down the hill between kitchen gardens and cucumber frames at 10.15pm we wondered if squash would be an antidote to the enormous starch content of Hall food and whether we should take up squash seriously. Then on the other hand, just think how our tennis would suffer, the games are so different. It would be better to stick to tennis where we had a little skill already. Squash should be left to lithe, slender beings who saw the ball before they hit it and could run about the court with all the elegance of a gazelle. We firmly agreed that for us tennis was enough.

This morning I bought a squash racquet.

A game no longer played--lacrosse

Florence Penseney, Sheila Garrod and two PE teachers, Miss Elizabeth Williams and Miss Mary Edwards at the school pavilion in about 1940 when Sheila was Head Girl and Florence a Prefect and winner of the cricket bat award.

It must be agreed that lacrosse is not a game for everyone, especially as we played it. We thought we could cradle, catch, throw, run for the ball on a pitch that had no boundaries but it took a visit to a county game played by Miss Edwards for us to realise our complete ineptitude.

The Lacrosse team 1944; L to R; back row Thelma Flack, Jennifer Jennings, Audrey Handy, Pat King, Betty Morrison, Barbara Stanyon: front row Aline Barber, Elise Beeton, Jean Hopkins, Barbara Kirkland, Pat Ridler, Anne Barber.

L to R, back row, Rosemary Bentley, Jennifer Russell, Susan Pickering, Margaret Eastcott; middle row, Elizabeth Wilkinson, Linda Neal, Meriel Jones, Philippa Kyle, Margaret Attwood; front row, Carolyn Wood, Sheila Stocks, Elizabeth Mynett, Christine Aylott, Anne Thom. 1958

SEVENTEEN   GAMES WE USED TO PLAY

Some of our favourite games for morning break and lunch hour were hopscotch, film stars and bad eggs. We would also hit a tennis ball against the back wall of the hall or practise netball shooting. Rounders was popular in the first two years before we started cricket. We had our own version in the summer on the field at the back of the school where a soft ball and a tennis racket were ideal to send enormous hits to anyone who felt like joining in.

Hopscotch dates back to the Roman occupation in Britain when it was thought to improve the agility and footwork of the Roman soldiers in full kit. Children copied them, the word meaning 'a scratched line,' originally taken from the French 'escocher' meaning 'to cut.' This is exactly how the first formers at Cyphers played the game, scratching the squares into the cinders. If the ready painted games in the school playground were all occupied, we would certainly chalk out our own. The best kind of stone was a piece of slate or otherwise we used a small purse. When morning lessons finished and you had second sitting lunch there was a stampede to get one of the hop-scotch places for you and your friends. These were greatly enjoyed and we were surprised to see them still marked out when we visited the old school building a few years ago. The number of feet that have trodden the hop-scotch area over the years must be phenomenal.

Another game enjoyed at lunch time was throwing a ball to a friend, who would stand on the far side of the play ground. We would throw the ball to each other trying to get the ball as high in the air as possible and catch it without it touching the ground. Throwing the cricket ball was one of the requirements for the Athlete's badge in the Guides.

The café at the old Beckenham swimming baths was a favourite meeting place and after school swimming for life saving and diving was well attended. Yes, there were spring and diving boards in both the first and second class pools from where we hurtled ourselves into barely five feet of water. You only needed to scrape your nose once on the bottom to make sure that you didn't do it again!

EIGHTEEN   TEXTILES COMES OF AGE

Our needlework of the 1940s and 1950s was an apron made from scraps of material

The wardrobe of the 1970s

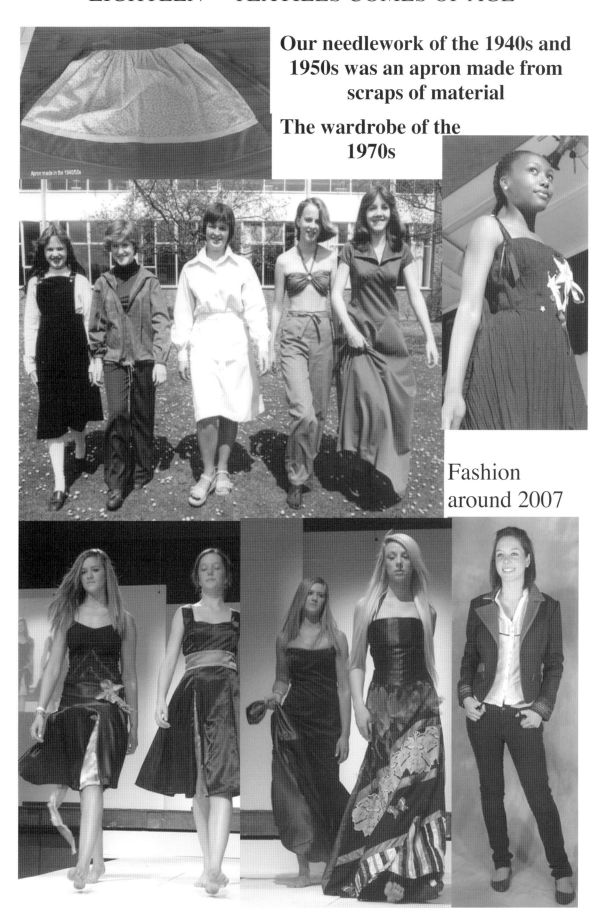

Fashion around 2007

EIGHTEEN   TEXTILES COMES OF AGE

In the 1940s and 50s our needlework did not progress much further than making aprons and impossible-to-wear cotton drawers with bias binding edges. In 1938, the first form was expected to do a practical needlework exam, taking 1 hour 20 minutes. They were asked to join two pieces of material with a run and fell seam leaving an opening that had to be faced and neatened with a wrap. As the subsequent pictures show, the subject by the 1970s thoroughly deserved the new title of 'Textiles'. Three fashion shows were given by textile students at Debenhams in Bromley and at the school. The students visited Debenhams and chose patterns, then were taken round the fabric department to select materials. The themes were wedding, holiday and day wear for summer and winter. The hair and make-up for the girls was done by Debenhams before the events.

In 1987 Joyce Helt and Erica Hancock invited a group of 26 boys and girls from the local Balgowan primary school to a highly successful 'hat design' day. They also had links with Oak Lodge, Marian Vian, Orchard and Clare House schools. Below are L to R Lesley Austen, Alison Boutle and Sue Helt.

From 1986 to 1990, real life opera added spice to the work of Langley and Ravensbourne after two visits to the Royal Opera House. The first was for a lecture on costume, set and property design and the second was to explain their designs with samples, and to see the opera, Eugene Onegin. Although they did not seem too impressed at the time, the details stayed in their minds and they set themselves to design a set or a costume. Liza Darvill was inspired by the opera and decided to make a beautiful silky bolster for the bedroom scene where Tatiana sings. The apricot acetate material cost her £30. Corinne Harper dressed a six inch doll in peasant costume with the intention of making a dress for herself later. Jane Pullen of the Royal Opera House wardrobe department was most gratified at the results. They went on to work with other theatres subsequently.

EIGHTEEN   TEXTILES COMES OF AGE

Another visit to the Royal Opera House gave students the opportunity to be given a brief and themes for designs and they later returned to show their work. In October 1990, members of the Royal Opera House gave a demonstration to the fifth year textile and art groups as part of a joint project. The girls followed the work of the dancers as they prepared for the ballet 'Prince of the Pagodas.' They examined make-up, costumes and dance steps to present a display on the aspects of the production of a ballet.

Joyce Helt ran a craft club at the school and the girls made Christmas decorations from beads which Joyce had brought back from America.

In Feb 2000, Natalie Davidson 10LH ran her 'Clothes Show Live.' She said

'The most enjoyable part was the actual fashion show because the clothes were stunning and of wide variety, in different themes and with very strong colours. The dance routines were exciting and showed off the clothes. I also found the variety of designs very inspiring for me to design my own garments. It showed and made me realise that I can be bold and different and put a variety of colours together without them looking awful. The clothes were also modern even the ones in the seventies style because they are all back in fashion now. What surprised me most was how men in skirts or kilts in leather or tartan were fashionable now.'

In April 2003, technician, Pauline Green, was invited to the Design and Technology Show in Birmingham to demonstrate how CAD/CAM computer aided design can be used for Textiles GCSE using a package called PhotoShop. In July, Eleanor Blackwell showed a cotton fashion skirt with dyed and digitally printed panels, Charlotte Kennedy a rayon 'Charity' ball dress with a message 'Buy nothing until you buy Vogue,' and Rebecca Nebel a silk and cotton corseted bustle dress with digitally printed bow.

In July 2006, as part of the Leading Edge Project, a one day textile workshop for year 8 was run with three partner schools and the Croydon school, Edenham, involving many boys. The object was to design a logo for an eco-friendly design company at the Chelsea Flower Show and to finish the day each with the design 'heat transfer' printed on a T shirt.

Head of textiles, Helena Jedlinska, says *'Today, students work hard to produce their examination products at GCSE and A level in Textiles Technology. The vast majority of students who select textiles at GCSE and A level choose a fashion route to express their ideas, imagination and skills so we had a catwalk show. We finally selected ninety garments for the students to see their products on a moving model, not just a tailor's dummy or in a fixed pose for a photograph. We created projects for Years 8 and 9, both based on recycling and Year 10 produced hip yoked circular skirts incorporating design influences from their studies.*

The clothes of course could not be presented without models. Adverts were posted and slowly we gathered a reliable team of enthusiastic, talented and increasingly confident models who were willing to give up their time at weekends and after school for rehearsals. In fact, the models have been talked about as much as the clothes. We included students of all different shapes and sizes to reflect the reality of dressing the human figure and a typical customer. We have been very lucky to have the support of Pauline Green, a textile-trained technician, who joined us in 1995.'

The visit to Barcelona at Easter 2006 included a 'Salvador Dali Day' and a day at La Caixa, a reclaimed textile factory housing contemporary art and the work of Diana Arbus.

EIGHTEEN   TEXTILES COMES OF AGE

Designer Ted Houghton visited the school to interest his year 12 audience of textile students in knitted textures. His aim was to allow everyone the chance to machine knit and to learn to hand knit and to crochet. He spoke of his trade visits to Italy for inspiration and trend forecasting. His clients include Topshop and he lectures at Middlesex University.

Alexandra Gardener and Charlotte Rutherford left Year 13 in 2007 to take up places at Central Martins, England's most prestigious design college.

Rachel Costa is studying at its equivalent, Parsons Design College in New York.

Hockey team 1950

Boys' & Girls'
Prefects' Badges

NINETEEN   THE ADREMIANS

'In the hands of the Old Girls more than those of anyone else lies the honour of the school and I am confident you will not fail us' Miss Fox 1934

Long before the name Adremians was coined, Miss Fox's Old Girls played an important part in her life. She was always asking for news as to their progress and they even had a blazer of their own. In 1930 it was obtainable at Ardec in Beckenham High St for 31/ 6d inclusive of badge. The school magazines detailed their marriages and births of their children with space allowed for pictures of their offspring. When quite an old lady, she judged a baby competition for her past pupils. She had a tale to tell the meeting in 1934. A friend gave the school museum a pair of bison horns and a Mexican cowboy's whip and the rumour spread that Miss Fox had been a big game hunter before she came to Beckenham!

Pages in the early magazines were devoted to Old Girls' progress in the world of work and an impressive variety of employment was revealed. Among the clerks, typists, secretaries and telephonists was a governess in Egypt teaching English in an Arabic Girls' College and a model in a wholesale gown and coat showroom in the West End. There were many nurses, midwives and shop girls but they would be as a florist at Selfridges, working for Marshall & Snelgrove, Debenhams and Lafayette's the Court Photographers. There were teachers at local schools like Marian Vian and Alexandra and at other schools all over the country, including our Nancy Wiseman who started her teaching career at Grange Girls' High School, Bradford before returning to Beckenham. Still Miss Fox wished that more girls would stay on into the sixth form, a desire fulfilled by her successor, Miss Henshaw, who could not have been a more apt replacement as the new Head.

In the late 1940s, the Adremians ran netball and hockey teams and Thelma Pedgrift (née Flack) organised a lacrosse team based at St Christopher's School in Bromley Rd.

The following report appeared in the Beckenham Journal of Sat 15 April Easter 1950 of a hockey match against the Dutch team, Wageningen Ladies.
Grammar School Old Girls v Wageningen Ladies
The final game of the ladies hockey was played in a bitingly cold wind on Monday morning at the ground in Lennard Rd. The Dutch Ladies were the better side in combination but the Old Girls possessed a very fast left winger (Sylvia Jane) who made several constructive attacks and the inside forwards found luck with them. At half-time, the visitors were ahead 2-1 but Beckenham soon drew level and added two more. Miss Veen on the Dutch left wing then organised some valuable forward movements and amid growing excitement the visitors scored twice more to share the honours, a very fitting result at 4-4.

It was at the very next committee meeting that the Old Girls resolved to find themselves a name. Adremians was the inspiration coined by the secretary Betty Bleay from the school motto Ad Rem: Mox Nox. Adremians v Wageningen would have sounded so much better!

Since we assumed our new name, there have been relatively few secretaries in charge and with today's Jill (Bury) Jones 1952-1959, affairs run as smoothly as ever. When asked what she liked about school, Jill had to think long and hard but then came up with 'friends' some friendships surviving to this day. Then she remembered the lovely times that we had rehearsing G&S between and after the exams, especially when the costumes arrived in huge hampers and we rushed to the hall to see what they were like. The whole thing was such huge fun with Miss Wiseman at the head of it all. Rushing home to see Wimbledon on TV if not busy playing herself and oddly not being made a prefect stayed in her memory. Was it because she was not wearing her house shoes when in the senior school or had she made an enemy in high places? We shall never know but we could not have a better secretary!

NINETEEN   THE ADREMIANS

She will have been secretary for 25 years by the time this book is published although she feels it will be time for a younger member to take over.

Brenda (Wixey) Brent has been the longest serving committee member as she has stayed helping for over half a century including ten years as the secretary.

Secretaries of the Adremian Association

The first secretary was in 1922 when the 'Old Girls' Association' began. She was Madeline Arnold. Then the list goes as follows:

1925   Vera Greenman
1928   Agnes Aitken
1929   Agnes Stubbs
1930   Kathleen Wiseman (Nancy Wiseman's sister)
1931   Marion Bryars
1935   Joan Prevett
1938   Joan Hyland

During wartime, things get a bit sketchy, but we have the names of Margaret (Jesshope) who resigned in 1944-5, and Glenna Benbow took over from her.

1946   Marjorie Sanders
1947   Betty Bleay
1952   Lorna White
1954   Violet Purser (and Brenda Brent became Assistant Secretary)
1955   Diana Scott
1958   Brenda Brent
1968   Barbara Thomas
1975   Nancy Tonkin
1983/4 Jill Jones

In the 1920s, the subscription was 2s. 6d per year, which was quite a large amount. We have

been contacted by several nonagenarians who started school in its first few years: the late Margaret Alice (Peggy Robertson) Harris lived at Saltdean and was referred to us by Ann Waugh a close neighbour, Betty (Lewis) Nickalls, Eileen (Andrews) Brook, Olive (Beadle) Hamer and Audrey (Forrester) Leaver.

Nancy Wiseman is seated on the ground front left.

NINETEEN   THE ADREMIANS

Betty Nickalls remembers Nancy Wiseman very well as they were best friends with the same love of music and PE. Betty was a tomboy, playing boys' parts in Shakespearean drama, but  she says that Nancy was a real tearaway. They both played netball, hockey, lacrosse, tennis and cricket, rolling down their stockings and turning up their sleeves to be instantly ready for action. PE mistress Miss Loxdale taught Betty to spin bowl at cricket.

Born in 1911, Betty (Lewis) Nickalls started as a scholarship girl in 1922 as she left Oakfield Primary School in Anerley. For a few days, Betty walked all the way from the Crystal Palace with two prefects until her mother had to attend Betty's medical. She was so shocked at the distance, that she prevailed upon Betty's father to give his daughter the fare for the tram to the Pawleyne Arms. When Betty was a prefect herself, one of her duties was to check that girls on the tram were wearing their hats and gloves.

Living a good distance away, Betty always had her lunch at school. They were quite expensive at 9d each but there were two puddings. They were so popular that tables had to be set up on the corridors as well as the dining hall until the extensions were built. Some days they were all very quiet because they were only allowed to speak French. They took turns to be waitress and there was one unfortunate day when Betty's friend spilt the gravy boat into a teacher's lap.

As it has been throughout its history, the school was very musical and Betty much enjoyed the choir. The music mistress, Miss Fincham, played them classical music on the wind up gramophone. It is hard to credit today that most homes were without wireless at this time and black and white TV was at least twenty years into the future.

Betty left school after six years to work for an insurance company although she would have liked to have studied history at college. She lost her job in the slump and then was employed by Imperial Airways (now British Airways) at Croydon Airport. She married in 1939 and her husband became an Anglican clergyman but her two brothers were killed in WWII. We owe our thanks to Helen and Elizabeth Mynett who visited Betty in Bristol to share her memories of the Beckenham County School for Girls.

The Adremians Science Prize, dedicated to Miss Henshaw in 1963, was to be given to the most promising scientist of the year and the amount of two guineas was given. This usually meant the girl with the best results for A level Biology, Chemistry and Physics but the requirement was widened in 1982 to include Mathematics as one of the three subjects. At times prizes were not awarded at all and so our list is incomplete but the prize is now £50.

Olive Rippengal donated funds for an annual travel scholarship in 1991 when Mrs Herzmark was the headmistress. She helped some 15 girls visit abroad by donating about £200 each. It was last awarded in 2002 to Elizabeth Oliver and Claire Ransford who went to Romania with a group from Christ Church (Beckenham) Youth Club to help at an orphanage which had just opened where they saw a very different way of life. They also had the opportunity to spend a few days in the Romanian mountains and in Hungary.

NINETEEN   THE ADREMIANS

Olive went to Elizabeth's home to see their photographs and to talk over their experiences, but Olive became increasingly distressed by the loss of life in such tragedies as 9/11 and she discontinued the scholarship.

Winners of the Adremians Science Prize

1963/4	S. Ashby
1965	No prize
1966/7	Christine Adams
1967/8	Susan James
1968/9	Jane Sayers & Katherine Williamson
1969	Susan Challen
1970	Susan Stone
1971	Susan Haws
1972	Mary Higgins
1973	Pamela Mann
1974	Deborah Clarke (trained Manchester Uni in Dentistry)
1975	Rebecca Abbott (see p 62)
1976	Wendy Bowell
1977/78	Jane Pomeroy
1979	Jane McGlasson
1980	No prize
1981	Elaine Gibbs
1982	Sally Carson
1983	No prize
1984	Jill Robson
1985-6	No prize
1987	Jenny Hirst
1988	Rachel Clark
1989	Susanna King
1990	No prize
1991	Sarah Russell (see p 93)
1992-98	No prize
1998	Elena Costa
1999	Nicola Pounder
2000	Not awarded – discussions taking place re prizes
2001	Ditto
2002	Jacqueline Beadle
2003	Stephanie Hunt
2004	No prize
2005	Sarah Coombs
2006	Sophie Irwin (see p 93)
2007	Elizabeth Hird

Deborah Clarke chose 'To Kill a Mocking Bird' for her Adremians prize which her daughter is now reading for her A Level English. (see p 68)

Sarah Russell studied Mining Geology and now lives and works in Salt Lake City, Utah for a mining company.

Sophie at the leavers' ball

Many groups of past pupils have kept together over the years, in particular Janet Lambert's friends and the Exeter evacuees although increasingly we are finding celebrations of 25 and 50 years occurring at the Eden Park Hotel and the annual lunch in September. Janet writes as follows:

Fifty years ago during the Whitsun half term of 1957, six friends in the UVI caught the early morning workman's train to Brighton for the day. They sat playing cards on the beach waiting for the bakers to open to buy lunch – no supermarkets in those days! Little did they realise that this would be the start of regular gatherings that would enlarge with classmates through the ensuing years. Now they are somewhat greyer and hopefully wiser but still in touch. Happy days of retirement replaced coffee mornings by ladies who lunch. They have chatted, swapped news and photographs and never been short of conversation. Despite living miles apart, the original six met up for a special 50-year reunion in July 2007.

NINETEEN   THE ADREMIANS

Di King flew from Toronto, Jane Caley drove from Dorset, Liz Honey travelled from S Wales, Ann Jolliffe from Chislehurst and Angela Rodwell from Sidcup. They met Jan from Longfield for a celebratory day at Eltham Palace. Later they joined others for a delicious supper by courtesy of Elizabeth Mynett at her home. This says a lot for friendships first made at the Beckenham Grammar School for Girls in the 1950s.

A day at Brighton in 1957. L to R Janet Lambert, Ann (Joliffe) Barnard, Diana King, Angela (Rodwell) Everett, Jane Caley. Photo taken by Liz Luck (née Honey), inset.

Janet Lambert has not only raised in excess of £15,000 by making cards to sell for charity but has also researched her family history which was published in the Family History magazine for December 2007.

Eltham Palace reunion after 50 years. L to R Janet Lambert, Ann (Joliffe) Barnard, Liz (Honey) Luck, Diana King, Angela (Rodwell) Everett, Jane Caley.

Reunion of Exeter evacuees in 2007 L to R June (Ridout) Burrows, Sheila (Bates) Meakins, Pamela Daymond, Jean (Cocking) de Jong, Wendy (Jones) Field, Ina (Foster) Jenner, Freda Long, Marjorie (Sear) Davy, Dorothy (Lawrence) Appleyard.

The Adremian dinners between 1951 and 1966

The attendance at the annual Friday night dinners was remarkable at this time especially for the number of staff who joined in and the sixth formers who acted as waitresses.

Head girls serve Governor Alderman Gully and Miss Henshaw in 1954

One such occasion was in November 1956 when a former teacher, Miss Broadhurst, was the guest of honour. Having retired to Edinburgh three years earlier, she had travelled down especially for the function with her memories of the school since she joined it in 1929. This was when even the upper sixth wore box-pleated tunics with thick black stockings and the staff had to wear regulation long sleeved dresses although sleeveless dresses were the fashion. She recalled the many cats that had been associated with the school like Sooty and the marmalade cat, Patrick, also remembered by Mrs Grunspan. Then there was Billy whose mind never rose above food.

NINETEEN   THE ADREMIANS

Arranged by Diana Scott, the menu for the occasion would seem simple today with soup, lamb chops with roast potatoes and cauliflower and finishing with trifle but it was a delight to all present to have a meal cooked by the kitchen staff and served by the senior girls. A former Head Girl, Jeanette Saunders, introduced Miss Broadhurst and another Head Girl, our chairman, Monica (Weeks) Duncan replied to the toast to the Adremians.

Toasts

The School
Ald. J. H. Atkins J.P.
Reply
Hazel Carter
The Guest of Honour
Jeanette Saunders
Reply
Miss E. M. Broadhurst
The Association
Mrs. M. F. Martin Ph.D. B.Sc
Reply
Mrs. Monica Duncan

The Adremians' dinner of 1956. L to R Norma McLeod, Jeanette Saunders, Sheila Andrews, Jackie Scott, Gillian Brown, ??

The staff present included Miss Henshaw, Miss Preston, Miss Barnard, Miss King, Miss Stephenson, Miss Grice, Miss Hatfield and Miss Rabson

Reunion at EPH March 1996. L to R Back row Christine Kobrak, Alison Liney, Julie Duffin, Deborah Hughes, Susan Appleyard, Deborah Clarke, Geri Dudley, Helen Baker, Caroline Terry, Janet Knell, Gillian Cornthwaite. Front row Sally Ratcliffe, Adrienne Earl, Yvonne Jex, Vanessa Miller, Rosalind Jackson, Jennifer Logan.

NINETEEN   THE ADREMIANS

L to R Susan (Evans) Morgan, Mandy Walsh, Gwyneth (Gibbon) Try, Bronwen (Lewis) Howells, at the Adremians lunch 2006

Reunion in 2007 at Windsor Castle, L to R back row, Mary Russell, Christine Popp, Delia Smith, Barbara Pitt; front row, Roslyn Parvin, Jane Brown, Susan Compton.

Visit to Kew, L to R, Gill Moore-Martin, Ruth Hixson, Sheila MacKenzie, Christina Rex, Maureen Jordan, Mary Hardcastle, Ann Bartlett, Merrill Drzymala, Janet Woods, Anne Simmonds, Pat Williams, Edith Worthington, Joyce King, Pat O'Brien, Jennifer Elgar.

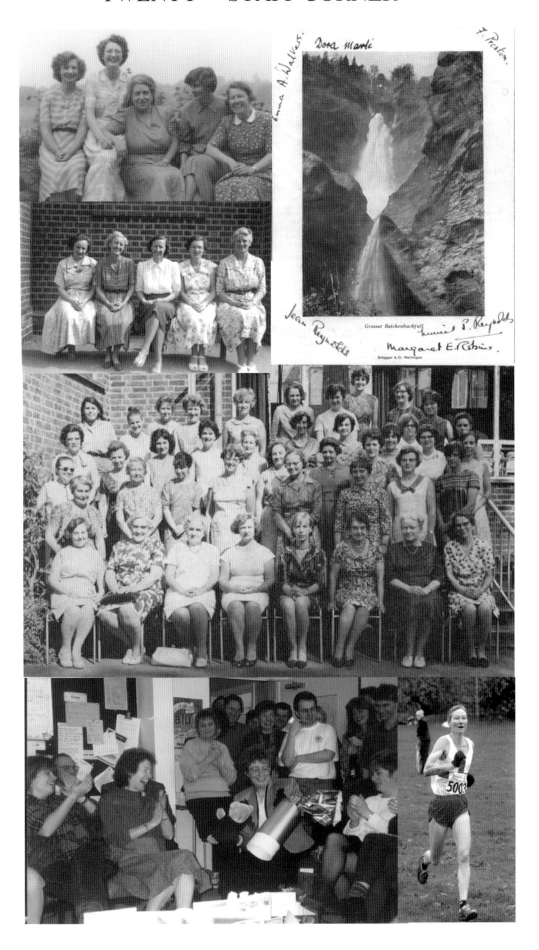

TWENTY   STAFF CORNER

A message from Miss Rene Hatfield with her memories

I am now aged 92 in the summer of 2007 and have very fond memories of the very well behaved girls at your school. I took prayers once a week and remember one particular cycle trip out with the girls which ended in a very nice tea. I went on to become Headmistress of Ilminster Grammar School for ten years from 1959 until its closure, when I was appointed Deputy Head of the new Wadham Comprehensive, Crewkerne until I retired in 1976.

During my retirement, I was very much involved in the village of Barrington, in particular the village church. I continued my passion for history, researching and writing about the Ilminster Grammar School. I spent time in Canada on an exchange with a Canadian teacher and among other places visited Russia twice. I wish you every success with the book and look forward to receiving a copy in due course.

Miss Wiseman, deputy headmistress

The school was greatly privileged to have known Nancy Wiseman as a pupil and as a teacher. Her sense of fun, her enthusiasm, fairness and high standards of service made life exciting for her and for us. She gave happiness and revealed the richness of life to generations of girls, many of whom are leading richer lives because they came under her influence.

As a memorial to Miss Wiseman, the £326 collected was used to provide a rostrum and some instruments for the orchestra but she created her own memorial in the memories of all of us who knew her and still think of her with gratitude and affection.

Miss Wiseman, who became Deputy Headmistress in 1959, was a pupil at the school from 1921-1929. Of outstanding ability, she was awarded a State Scholarship but decided against a university career to study at the Royal Academy of Music where she qualified as LRAM and GRSM in 1932. After teaching at Bradford for six years she returned to her old school where for nearly twenty four years she gave selfless and devoted service.

No-one ever asked her help in vain, whether to provide a trio of Elizabethan strings for 'The Merchant of Venice,' a zither accompaniment to a Jewish wedding in 'Tobias and the Angel' or the leadership of a party to climb a Swiss mountain. Her secret was that she *enjoyed* everything so much. Her own zest for living and appreciation of life meant that in her company we forgot fatigue and could see the humour in even the most uncomfortable circumstances. Just as she sat patiently in the dark and heat playing the music for the Gilbert & Sullivan opera each year for the choir's pleasure, so she anonymously wrote the satirical, witty lyrics sung by the staff at the end of her Spring concerts, organised the off-stage effects for Miss Pelling's puppet shows and quietly made all the arrangements for the trip to Switzerland every other year. Former pupils recall their most lasting impression of Miss Wiseman was her tremendous energy and enthusiasm. Even the staidest of hymns was played at a brisk tempo and her National Anthem was an example to us all.

Miss Wiseman joined in all our competitions and parties, appearing at one heavily disguised as a burglar, complete with mask and a bag of loot. Her uninhibited performance at rehearsals was always enjoyed as she coached us for the dance of the cannibals or collapsed with helpless laughter at the sight of the beautiful Tiger Lily puppet, now a grotesque creature with one leg dangling from the shoulder. At Christmas we tramped for miles singing carols with her, usually finishing at her house, voiceless but still able to eat hot potatoes. She was an outstanding member of the staff netball team and the most feared by the school goal keeper when we played the staff at hockey.

Those of us who left to study music have never ceased to appreciate the tremendous grounding she gave us in harmony and counterpoint. One distant memory is of sitting in the school shelters in the days of the flying bombs having to pitch our own notes to sing rounds and cantatas. She drove us hard but was always fair. She never imposed her own musical leanings on us. Even now, it is impossible to play, sing or just listen without sooner or later thinking of her. How fortunate we were to have known her!

A Tribute to Dorothy O'Dell at her funeral January 1998 by Diana Scott,

In 1943, I started at the Beckenham County School for Girls in Lennard Rd. As my tutor group occupied room 14, Miss O'Dell in room 13 was one of the first teachers I knew. It was a small school in those days, about 400 pupils in all and Miss O'Dell took us all for Religious Knowledge. She was an exceptional teacher. Her enthusiasm was apparent and rubbed off on to all her pupils. She brought the bible to life; she spoke of Amos and Hosea as if they were her personal friends. We followed St Paul's journeys as exciting adventure tales using a large map on the wall.

You were never in any doubt that Miss O'Dell was a devout Christian although in no way did she try to influence us. She did however influence us by her example and I'm sure that many of her pupils have her to thank for their first steps in the Christian way of life.

In those days, such phrases as 'pastoral care' and 'careers teachers' were unheard of but it did not mean that they did not exist. Miss O'Dell was a person to whom many turned for help and guidance. She was a wise and tolerant person to whom even the more rebellious (and yes there were a few rebels even then) would turn, knowing that they would get a fair hearing and sensible advice. I can remember my parents commenting after a parents' evening how impressed they were with her far-sightedness and in-depth knowledge of her pupils. It was during my time at school that the first Christian Union was started with Miss O'Dell at the helm. At Old Girls' Meetings, which she never missed even when far from well, she was always surrounded by ex-pupils and amazingly she remembered them all.

We owe Dorothy O'Dell a great debt as a teacher and a friend. She will not be forgotten by any of us.

And at Muriel Uglow's memorial service November 2007

My first memory of Muriel Uglow is when she came to teach at Beckenham Grammar School in about 1947 when I was a pupil. She was employed to teach history, but it soon became apparent to her that she was far more interested in RE and accordingly, after attending a year's training, she came back to the Grammar School in about 1950 to join Miss O'Dell and they became the RE department for the next 25 years. Muriel had great biblical knowledge and many pupils have her to thank for gaining good A level results. Jill Jones has been in contact with some of these old girls and has received emails expressing their appreciation of Muriel's teaching. I quote from one of these messages, '*I remember Miss Uglow with affection and gratitude. She was always kind and patient and taught me so much about the New Testament and Church history*'.

Muriel was a reticent person and it is only during the last few years that I heard about her early life. She was an only child and, because her father had been employed by the Navy, she went to school in many places, among which were Malta and Gibraltar. She did not enjoy her early years at school and felt very much an outsider, and it wasn't until she went to school in Scotland, Glasgow I think, that she really reached her potential. Apparently she had a marvellous history teacher who saw how able Muriel was and persuaded her father, her mother having recently died, to sit the Oxford University entrance exam.

 The result was that Muriel got a scholarship to Oxford in the 1930s. Not many women achieved such an honour at that time. Muriel always had a great love of Scotland – her early years of teaching were spent in a school in Ayr – and she and Dorothy had many happy holidays there.

At this church in 1991 our then Minister, Ken Walker, decided to start a Christian Doctrine Diploma class which necessitated study in depth of many aspects of Christianity. I among others joined this class and Ken and Muriel ran it. Muriel was my tutor and, although I gained the diploma after five years of study, I really think that Muriel deserved the diploma more than I did. I certainly would not have gained it without her. In that diploma class was a previous Grammar School pupil of Muriel's – **Julie Aylward** – and this class started her on a course of study and as many of you know, she is now a Baptist minister.

Muriel and Dorothy O'Dell were great friends and they shared a home together for many years. It was a great sorrow to Muriel when Dorothy developed Alzheimer's disease, but she was adamant that Dorothy should not go into a home and Muriel nursed her for many years until Dorothy died in January 1998. The great sadness was that Muriel herself began to suffer in the same way and the decision had to be taken in 2004 that she should go into a nursing home. In this home, although she was well cared for, she felt great sadness at not being of use to anyone any more.

I should like to mention here a great friend who supported Muriel constantly over many years. She took Muriel to hospital visits, cared for her everyday needs, brought her to church every Sunday until recently (a round trip which took about an hour) and was a constant visitor. I am of course referring to Wendy Runcie and I know how Muriel relied on her and was so grateful to her. Those of us who visited Muriel regularly got very fond of her and, despite her confusion and memory loss, she would always greet us with so much affection and she never lost her sense of humour. I shall miss her.   *Diana Scott.*

Barbara (Pitt) Heseltine reminds us that projects came our way in the past and particularly remembers 'Travels with St Paul' set by Miss Uglow. She also made the 'Scroll of Isaiah' from old organ stops for the handles and burnt edges to the paper to make it look old. Another time Barbara was set to learn I Corinthians 11, 24-26 because she had chosen not to do the question in the exam. That was useful later!

To Miss Cutler by the staff when she died in service in 1965

Although Miss Cutler had been in indifferent health for some considerable time, it came as a great shock when we heard of her death in hospital after one weekend. We were unprepared for such a blow as she rarely mentioned her health and was expecting to retire in the summer to live with her sister in the country.

Miss Cutler came to us in the unsettled years of the war and for more than twenty two years she did her best to ease the transition of the juniors from small primary schools to a large grammar school. This was particularly so during the few years after the war when, as numbers grew rapidly, the first years were exiled across the park to Cyphers' Sports Club. Later she became the Head of Burrell House. This was in the days when to become a House Head was an honour that did not carry a monetary award.

She was a gifted linguist and a devoted teacher of German who believed in the power of tongues to break down international barriers. Her racy sense of humour and unexpected chuckle could enliven dull moments. A musician of no mean ability, she played first violin in the school orchestra, greatly enjoying all our musical activities.

TWENTY   STAFF CORNER

Memories of Mrs Joan Grunspan

My connection with the school goes back to the early days of the war and lasted ten years, so I have many memories. Episodes connected with Miss Fox stand out. Some of you may remember what it was like to be one of her girls, but I think by now I am probably the last survivor of her staff. Like all memories, mine are personally biased and mine come in little stories.

My home was in North London. I had been teaching in the West Country; it was just after the Battle of Britain and I was desperate to be back nearer to the centre of things. Teaching jobs in London were hard to come by, so when I heard there was a vacancy for an English teacher in Beckenham I was determined the job was for me, even though I had been warned that the headmistress was exacting. 'Miss Fox's eye missed nothing'. These words made such an impression on me that when, on my way to the interview I found that I had left my gas mask behind, I convinced myself the job was already lost. At that time everybody had to take a gas mask wherever they went and I was sure such negligence could not be overlooked.

As I walked down leafy but slightly bomb battered Lennard Road and saw what a handsome building the school was, and found inside it was bright with pictures, books and flowers, I felt depressed. It would have been such a pleasant place to work. Though the interview seemed to have gone quite well and I was shown around the school, I had no hope. At the back I saw that windows had been blown out and heard how a bomb had fallen on the air-raid trenches alongside. I remember this in great detail and can still hear the pride in Miss Fox's voice as she told me how it was her fire-watching squad who were the first on the scene and how they helped put out incendiaries and how next day the school was open as usual. What a pity, I thought, to have spoiled my chances of becoming part of such a team. Then I was amazed to find the job was mine! *(There was actually a week between the two incidents of the bomb on the trenches and the incendiaries on the school.)*

Looking back, I can see that to Miss Fox at this time I must have appeared as an answer to prayer. She was devout and the school was her mission. She had built it up from small beginnings and every year found something more to add to its amenities. She had been thinking it would be good for her girls to have a Girl Guide Company and what her eagle eye had fastened on was not the gap where my gas mask should have been but a few lines in one of my testimonials saying I had been an enthusiastic Guide when I was at school. Here then was the potential captain! As for the school's more pressing needs I fitted them, too. Miss Rose had questioned me about my work and was satisfied. She herself had seen that I would be a sturdy addition to the firewatchers she organised and so give relief to the older, frailer members of staff. Moreover, Miss Rabson, who had been devotedly looking after the evacuation party, needed a break and I had declared myself more than willing to look after the evacuees during the holiday.

Those few weeks in Exeter were almost a holiday. The bomb had yet to fall there and it was a lovely place to be. The girls remaining were all well settled with their local families. I had little to do but check individually that there were no problems and give each girl a personal message from Miss Fox. It did not take me long to discover that they all looked on her as a sort of godmother they could count on if all else failed. Back in Beckenham, I found it was like this with all her girls. Later I was to learn that Miss Fox included in her protective benevolence each one of us whom she accepted as part of her school.

The process of becoming accepted was not easy for her staff. Ironically, my clashes with Miss Fox were nearly all connected with those extra wartime duties to protect the building that had so impressed me at the interview. I found I was not only expected to live near the school in case public transport failed, but to stay there 'on call' for set periods.

TWENTY   STAFF CORNER

This was even during the holidays, and I saw my name appearing on the fire watching rota rather too often for the weekend shifts.

I did not mind the duties themselves. They gave us a chance to get to know colleagues and it was fun practising with the stirrup pumps and bucket. Once the alert sounded we took our duties seriously, keeping vigil till the 'all clear' gave everyone permission to sleep. Every provision was made for our welfare; we had comfortable beds, a bath, breakfast and I believe there was something for supper too.

Today it is generally recognised what a lot the country owed to the school cooks. Ours were among the best. At times of greatest shortage they produced a nourishing meal and usually school dinners were excellent and nearly everybody stayed. The school could then be accommodated in the hall in two sittings with the senior staff 'on high' on the platform and the rest of us below at the head of tables of eight. Our instructions were to promote good table manners and polite conversation (difficult) and to see that no food was wasted and all got fair shares, which was easy. There was always someone hungry enough to eat up the vegetables and I found no problem serving the usual dinners. Stew was easy to ladle out fairly and I could divide puddings and pies equally into eight, but I can't forget the day we were served roast lamb and <u>nine</u> minute pieces appeared on the serving dish. As I passed the plates down the table, all eyes were fixed on the remaining extra morsel and I had almost reached my own plate before I could think what do to with it.

After lunch a comfortable staff room awaited us but we were likely to be called up for extra tasks if we went there, and some of us found it hard to get through the day without a cigarette. A small group of us used to take ourselves off to a bombed building nearby where we could relax and smoke at ease. Smoking was prohibited in any part of the school premises, although in those days it was accepted almost everywhere else. Smoking then was the norm and Miss Fox's ban we considered the most unreasonable of all her demands.

There were many school rules and the girls must have had their grievances, too, but I don't remember complaints – only a cheerful, friendly atmosphere and quiet orderliness. The school felt a secure haven in a troubled world. A neighbour's cat must have felt this too for he decided to move in with us. A big, ginger tabby, he might appear anywhere for he made himself at home with everybody. In the afternoons he liked a nap and could be seen outside the Headmistress's room where a cosy corner and a saucer of milk awaited him. As he wandered in and out of lessons I used to think he fancied himself as a sort of benevolent school inspector. I was picturing him like this one summer day (it must have been in 1943) when I was teaching a small group on the field and watched him coming over, full of his usual self-importance, as if to make sure that everything was in order. Suddenly the shriek of an air

raid siren startled us all. Instantly he deflated into a very scared cat as he bolted for cover. We followed fast enough but we, of course, observed the school no running rule!

TWENTY   STAFF CORNER

The shelters at that time were the reinforced cloakrooms where we were supposed to continue with our lessons but, crowded together, we found it difficult to concentrate. My pitch was next to Miss Grice. One of the indomitable 'old school', she carried on regardless. Like my class I found myself listening to fascinating history lessons. We were living through troubled times then and had to spend many of our days in and out of those shelters. For months it was Miss Rose who saw that life went on as normally as possible, for Miss Fox was away seriously ill. When she returned we could see that, although her spirit was the same, her health now was poor and her sight failing. Someone was asked to switch on a light that was already on and we all wondered how we would have responded. I felt there was dimness all round when Miss Fox retired. Happily, she enjoyed years of retirement and came back to visit us.

We were lucky to get Miss Henshaw as her successor for she tackled the many problems ahead of her with good humour and great efficiency. The intensified air attacks and doodlebugs had brought evacuation and peace brought its problems too. Everybody crowded back and so many girls wanted to join the school the building could not hold them. We expanded into sports pavilions nearby. I have memories of those days, too, but it is Miss Fox and that school in Lennard Road I think of when I think of Beckenham.

By the time the school had moved to Langley Park I too had moved on. I know good schools of today continue on both sites and that a chain of Adremians links Langley Park to the school I knew. I wish this venture back into the school's history every success, and to anyone left from these very old times who remembers me I send my greetings.

Fifty Years of memories by Miss Stephenson in 1979

LENNARD ROAD, BECKENHAM

On a lovely sunny day in May 1929 I got out of the train at New Beckenham and walked along Lennard Rd. I was delighted with the open fields and the absence of houses. When I reached my goal, Beckenham County School, I stood and stared as I murmured, 'What a lovely building, I hope that I get the job.' It seemed a very long journey from British Guiana which I had left in 1905, but I had at last reached my final home, Beckenham. I had already lived in Portsmouth where I was both pupil and then teacher in the same school. I had also taught for six years in a Liverpool Boarding School.

How very different Beckenham County School was, but I felt at home there from the very first day and this in spite of its very formidable but truly remarkable Headmistress, Miss Fox. What a coincidence that her name rhymed with the School Motto! Ad Rem; Mox Nox became Ad Rem; Mox Fox and indeed she was ever present. Nothing escaped her attention from the details of school uniform to Higher Education for Women. The teachers were compelled to wear hats and gloves on all occasions when out of school.

TWENTY   STAFF CORNER

My first years before war broke out were very peaceful. I cycled to and from school: few teachers in those days could afford a car. I started a Science Club and the seniors enjoyed being taken to the Science Museum and to various factories. Then came the war and things changed dramatically. There were day time air raids and fire watching at night.

The teachers were earning the princely sum of three shillings (15p) for a night of 12 hours on duty. Air raids in the day could be hair raising as we had the children to look after as well as the school building. One day when I was on dinner duty the playground was machine gunned and often we had to shepherd the girls to the shelters with their dinners plus knife and fork.

In 1944 Miss Henshaw came and so did the flying bombs but peace followed and with it new developments at school. Miss Henshaw introduced the seven day timetable. At first we found it so confusing but we soon realised that it gave a choice of subjects and we applauded her understanding of modern education. She initiated a House system which included Day 2 afternoons. All sorts of activities were introduced and we saw that it offered a valuable understanding of community life. It was in my House, Red House, that we started collecting and selling stamps. Soon the parents asked me to sell stamps at their Annual Bazaar. This proved a great success and continued to be so in the hands of the Adremians.

I still collect stamps but I don't cycle to school any more. I have become a devoted gardener AND I remember you all with great pleasure.

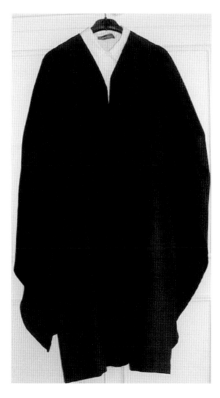

Miss Stephenson's gown

When Miss Stephenson retired, she passed her gown to Mrs Manning with the result that, because of their difference in height, the gown in the picture has been shortened by about ten inches! It is 80 years old.

In its shortened form, it was worn by several academics at various speech days when teachers were expected to wear gowns and by graduates receiving their degrees doing a turn at the Albert Hall in front of Princess Anne, then Chancellor of London University. It also served some time on the school stage.

However, it never again attracted the admiration as when worn by Miss Stephenson with her fur trimmed hood and mortar board perched at a cheeky angle on her silver hair.

Jane Georghiou (née Bennet) runs for England

After leaving the Science department at Langley, Jane Bennet moved to Germany for 8 years teaching in the Forces schools. There she had the opportunity to enjoy a range of outdoor activities including downhill skiing, ski mountaineering, mountain walking (including an ascent of Mont Blanc), trekking in Peru as well as learning to windsurf and sail.

Since returning to England to teach in Farnham, she does a lot of cycling with her husband e.g. across the Alps or along the Pyrenees and one holiday in the foothills of the Himalayas in India. She has particularly concentrated on running, finishing 11 London marathons with a best time of 3.10.22 and being selected for several years for an age group England cross country team, taking a bronze individual medal in the Home International in 2007. Look for her picture on the first page of this chapter when she was representing England at cross-country in 2004. Many staff left to become heads of other schools. These include Mrs Elizabeth Blackburn, Miss Jackie Thomas and Miss Sue O'Neill who is still the Head of a Catford school. Look on the picture page to find her unwrapping a teddy as part of her farewell from Langley staff.

Sandra Brown (1961 to 1964) wrote: *I had three very full and enjoyable years at Langley, teaching all aspects of the P.E. curriculum, including hockey, lacrosse, netball, cricket, tennis, gymnastics and swimming. I was very fortunate to have some amazingly talented games players such as Jill Cruwys, Sara (Clayton) Rowe and Heather (Hole) Dewdney, all of whom became international sportswomen although I was very sad to hear of Jill's premature death.*

I was fortunate to be selected to play cricket for England in three Test matches in 1963, and was given wonderful support by Miss Henshaw and the girls. However, my swimming credentials were poor, and I recall the captain, Mary Piper, virtually running the swimming training for me! I found the 7-day timetable an interesting concept and I soon took to the system as it gave greater variety than usual.

Miss Henshaw was a firm, but very fair Head. She was particularly benevolent in allowing Heather Dewdney and Barbara Burden to accompany Marg Jude (another member of the P.E. staff) and me to Southampton to wave us off as we set sail for Australia, where I have lived for almost 44 years. I continued my teaching career for another 11 years before changing careers to study and work in the Horticultural industry. I am now happily retired, and live opposite the famous Bradman Oval in Bowral, NSW, where I tend the gardens and score on a regular basis.

Nigel Sharma's Physics Class talks about the sundial to be donated by the Adremians 2009

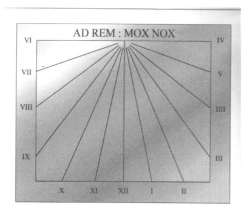

In the appended list of teaching staff, we hope you can find your teachers mentioned but apologise to those we have inadvertently omitted. Much of the compilation was carried out by Jean Parrott of the Adremian Committee. Records were not kept in the 1970s and 1980s and we have relied on our memories to complete the list.

Title	Surname	Forename	Approx Date-from	Date-to	Subject
Ms	Abbots	Zara	2002		
Miss	Ajah	Stella	2007		RE
	Akoh-Arrey	A.	1994	1996	
Mr	Alam	Jamil	2006		ICT
Miss	Allen		1969		
Dr	Allt	Win	1981	1994	Biology/Computing
	Alves	Benvinda	1999	2003	
Mr	Amos	Malcolm	2004		Head of Chemistry
Ms	Anciaux	Agnes	1992	1999	French
Ms	Anderson	Brenda	1982	2004	Art /Pottery
Dr	Anderson	Douglas			Physics
Miss	Andrews	Dorothy	1935	1945	Latin
Mrs	Angelo	B	1980s		
Ms	Antoniou	Eftehia	2001		Art
Miss	Archer	Brenda	1955	1958	Science
Ms	Aspa	Katie	1997	2001	
Mrs	Atkins	Flora	1958	1969	Dom.Sc.
Miss	Atkinson	Ursula	1932	1951	Dom.Sc
Miss	Babbs	Kathleen	1931	1942	Geography
Mrs	Badcock	Tracey	2004		Personal tutor
Ms	Bain	Jennifer	1997	2000	Technology
Ms	Ballantine	Jane	2001	2004	
Miss	Barnard	Winifred	1931	1958	French
Mrs	Barnard	Joy	1959	1982	Geography
Mr	Barnett	Steve	1997	2006	
Ms	Barrett	Gill	1980s		English
Mrs	Barrett (née Blake)*	Phyllis N.	1958	1980s	Latin
Mrs	Bartel	Christine	2003		Learning support
Ms	Batchelor	Maureen	1999	2004	
Miss	Bates	Judith	1959	1969	Fre/Latin
Mrs	Bates	Janet	1980s		Maths
Mrs	Batten	Monique	1970s		French
Miss	Bayley	Marjorie	1929	1930	English
Mrs	Bayley	Greta	1960	1990	French
Miss	Baylis	Joy	1933	1936	Biology/Maths
Miss	Beale	Elaine	1956	1958	Science
Miss	Beamish	Dorothy	1920	1924	Lwr Sch Subs
Mrs	Beasley	Daphne	1970s		Art/Pottery
Ms	Beaudry	Katharine	1993		Languages
Miss	Beck	Rachel	1929	1932	German
Miss	Beck*	Valerie J.	1959	1964	Ger/Span
Mrs	Bell	Janet	1980s		Science
Miss	Bell* (Cox)	Sybil F.	1947	1953	Music
Miss	Benison	E	1980s		
Miss	Benson	Emily	1919	1921	PE
Ms	Bettridge	N	1980s		
Mrs	Beynon		1969	1972	
Mr	Bhinda	Madhu	2000		English
Miss	Binks	Lesley	1971		French
Miss	Binning	M	1980s		
Miss	Birch	Margaret	1967	1979	Geography
Mrs	Bird	M	1980s		
Miss	Bishop	Emily	1920	1922	Hist/Eng
Mrs	Bishop (Maloney)	Maureen	1969	1973	Eng/Spanish
Mr	Black	David	1998	1999	Music
Mrs	Blackburn	Elisabeth	1974	1982	History/Deputy Head
Miss	Blackman	May.	1935	1937	History
Miss	Blackwood	Jean	1955	1959	French/Ger
Ms	Blair	Andrea	2004		Learning support
Mr	Blake	David	1977	1985	Head joint 6/Dir studies
Mrs	Blakeway	Christine	2006		EAL
Miss	Blundell	Barbara	1957	1985	Maths
Mr	Bodochi	Marius	2005	2007	Maths
Ms	Bohan	Maria	1990	2002	Chemistry
Mrs	Bolton	Maggie	1980s	1980s	History
Ms	Bond	Maria	1995	2002	
Mrs	Bond	Shona	1970s		Physics
Miss	Bone (Roberts)	Elizabeth	1928	1932	Sc/Maths
Mrs	Boothman	Valerie	1970s		Maths
Ms	Bowden	Samantha	2000	2007	Textiles
Miss	Bowler	Eileen	1956	1960	Geography
Mrs	Bradford		1960s		English
Ms	Brady	Harriet	1998	2001	Maths
Mrs	Bremner		1969		
Ms	Bridge	Louise	1994	1998	
Mrs	Briggs	Margaret	1975	1979	Maths
Ms	Briggs	Margaret	1993	1998	Maths
Mrs	Bristow	Pamela	1963	1969	Geography
Mr	Brittan	Anthony	2006		Science
Miss	Broadhurst	Ethel	1929	1954	French

TWENTY   STAFF CORNER

Title	Surname	Forename	Approx Date-from	Date-to	Subject
Mrs	Brooks	Lisa	2003		PE
Mrs	Brookwick	I	1980s		Food Technology
Miss	Broomhead	Olive	1949	1954	PE
Miss	Brown	Sandra	1961	1964	PE
Mrs	Brown	Alison	1988	2002	Maths
Mrs	Brown	Jackie	1980s	1980s	Physics
Ms	Brown	Janet			
Ms	Brown	Jennifer	2003		Maths
Mr	Brown	D	1980s		
Mr	Brown	Ian	2004	2005	
Miss	Bryan	Ursula	1937	1939	PE
Miss	Bryant	Jacqueline	1958	1959	Latin
Ms	Buckland	Jane	1988		English
Mrs	Buckley	Alison	1975	1978	French
Mr	Buckley	Geoff	1977	1982	Spanish/Head Languages
Miss	Bull	Gill	1970s		PE
Ms	Bunn	Helen	2000	2002	RE
Mrs	Bunting	Marianne	1969	1997	German
Ms	Bunting	Carol	1989	2000	Food Technology
Mrs	Burn	Pam	1980s	1980s	Biology
Miss	Burrows	M.A.	1960	1963	History
Miss	Burrows	Barbara	1961	1963	Geography
Mr	Burton	A	1980s		
Miss	Burton	Ena	1946	1969	Science
Mrs	Bury	Jennifer	1990	1998	Special Needs
Ms	Busen-Smith	Maria	1980s		Music
Miss	Butcher	Edith	1925	1928	Geography
Ms	Butler	Joanna	2002	2003	Drama
Mr	Butler	Michael	2002	2004	English
Mr	Byrne	Aran	2001		Modern Languages
Miss	Byron	Irene	1956	1980	Chemistry
Ms	Cadman	Rachel	2000	2002	Drama
Miss	Caley*	Jane	1960	1962	Piano
Miss	Caley*	Jane	1963	1969	Music
Mr	Cameron	D	2007		DT
Miss	Cappuccio	Stefanie	2008		Textiles
Miss	Carley	Brigid	2007		RE
	Carrington	Diana	1980s		
Miss	Carson	Jean	1979		Biology/Ass Headteacher learning
Ms	Carter	Anne	2002	2003	
Miss	Chambers (Blakeney)	Evelyn	1932	1935	PE
Ms	Chaplin	Yvette	2000	2002	Science
Miss	Chappell	Eunice	1948	1949	
Ms	Chetwood	Iva	2002	2003	Chemistry
Miss	Child	C.A.	1952	1958	Dom.Sc
Mr	Chilton-Higgins	Edward	2002		SEN
Miss	Chreseson	Joan	1963	1967	Headmistress
Mr	Christie	Kevin	1997		Biology
Mr	Christophy	Demetric	2004	2007	Media Studies/English
Mrs	Clapham	Anne G.	1960	1962	English
Miss	Clark			1969	
Mr	Clements	Mike	1980s		History
Mrs	Clifford		1960s		Maths
Mrs	Codling	J	1980s		
Ms	Cody	Danica	1996	2000	English
Miss	Cohen	Lana	1960/61		Art
Miss	Cole	Rosemary	1927	1929	Lwr Sch
Mr	Coleman	David	1996		Head Technology Faculty
Miss	Collar	Dorothy	1941	1942	French/German
Miss	Collier	Winifred	1921	1922	Maths
Miss	Collins	N.R.	1963		
Mrs	Collins(Shaw)	Helen	1980s		Biology
Ms	Colloff	Tracey	1994		English/Head of Faculty
Miss	Colyer	Editha	1928	1932	PE & Jnrs
Mrs	Compton(Moore)	Linda	1960	1973/4?	French
Mr.	Conan-Davies	David	2000		DT
Miss	Conroy(Lowe)	Yvonne	1958	1960	Mathematics
Ms	Conway	Rachel	2006	2007	
Miss	Cook		1972		Science
Miss	Cooke	Hazel	1919	1923	Ndwk etc
Miss	Cooper	Margaret	1952		Piano
Miss	Coote	Alice	1936	1943	Maths
Ms	Cordner	Patricia	1994	2002	
Mrs	Costaras	Grace	2007		Mandarin
Mrs	Coulson	Lorna	1996		Science
Miss	Cowley	Mildred	1937	1940	English
Miss	Cowley	M.J.	1940	1941	
Mrs	Cox (née Leech)	Joan	1943	1945	PE
Mrs	Crawford	Sandra	2006		Science
Mrs	Crawley	Patricia	1963	1964	PE

Title	Surname	Forename	Approx Date-from	Date-to	Subject
Ms	Crean	Rebecca	2003	2006	
Mr	Crosley	Robin	1994		Graphic products
Mrs	Cross	Gillian	2007		English
Ms	Crossing	Janette	2006	2007	
Mrs	Crossing	Gillian	2007		English
Mrs	Crowston	J.	1964		Domestic Science
	Cryer	Therle	1970s		
Ms	Cumming	Elizabeth	2001	2005	PE
Ms	Cummings	Ann	1997		
Miss	Cummins	Beryl	1959		
Ms	Curran	Julie	1997	1998	
Miss	Cuss	Muriel	1951	1952	Art/Ndwk
Miss	Cutler	Irene	1942	1965	German
Mr	Cutler	David	1989	1995	Drama
Mrs	Dale	Phyllis	1942	1943	Geography
Mrs	Daniel	Caroline	2007		Music
Mrs	Daniel	J	1970s		
Miss	Daniels	Mary	1958	1963	Eng/Speech Train'g
Mr	Darbourne	Richard	1995		Eng/Dep Head Curriculum
Miss	Darling	Margaret	1923	1927	Maths & Drama
Mr	Davey	Martin	2006		Ass Head Community/History
Mrs	Davey*	Johann		1979	Canteen supervisor
Ms	Davies	Diana	1990	2001	Art
Mrs	Davies(Norvell)		1960s	1960s	PE
Miss	Davis	Julie	1994	1999	
Mrs	Davis	Doreen	1972	1974	Chemistry
Miss	Dawson	Maud	1941	1942	Latin
Ms	Day	Tamsin	2006		Languages
Miss	D'Cruz	Pamela	2003		Head of RE
Miss	Dean	Joyce	1938	1944	Art
Mrs	Dean	Ann	1960	1970	Maths
Miss	Dehal	Herjit	1997		Languages
Mr	Desai	Ajay	2008		Assistant Head teacher/Science
Mrs	Devonald	P	1980s		
Miss	Dewdney*	Heather		mid 70's	PE
Miss	Dibb(s)?	Barbara	1936	1941	Languages
Miss	Dickerson	S	1980s		
Mrs	Dixon	Audrey	1962	1963	PE
Ms	Doherty	Brigid	1995		Performing Arts
Miss	Doherty	Tracey	2003		Geography
Mr	Doran	Nicholas	1994	2001	Maths
Ms	Douglas	Catherine	2000	2001	English
Mrs	Dowsett	Monica	1946	1951	Maths/Geogr.
	Doyle	Kit	1999	2002	IT
Ms	Doyle	Kit (Rita)	2002		
Mrs	Duffy	Elaine	1990	1994	Languages
Mrs	Duggan		1970		
Mrs	Duncan née Weeks)*	Monica	1959	1978	Music
Ms	Dunn	Jill	1991	1995	Science
Ms	Dunseith	Teresa	1996	2000	English
Ms	Dunstall	Tussi	1990	2001	Art
Ms	Durkin	Barbara	1996	2000	
Ms	Dury	Sue	1992	2002	Sociology
Miss	Earle	Jane	1919	1923	Maths
Ms	East	Sally	2004	2006	
Miss	Edwards	Mary	1938	1943	PE
Miss	Eisner	Lucy-Anne	1980s		
Mr	Ellen	Christopher	2007		Travel & Tourism
Mrs	Ellerton		1970		
Ms	Elmes	Sara	1991	1995	RE
Mrs	Endersby	E.	1958	1959	Science
Miss	Evans	Esther	1932	1933	English
Miss	Evans	Nikki	1980s		Chemistry
Mr	Evans	Tristan	2006		English
Mrs	Ewen		1967	1969	Biology
Ms	Eynon	Lynda	1996	1997	
Ms	Fahidi	Nicola	1995	1997	
Miss	Farnham	Ann	1976	1991	Maths
Mrs	Fassam	Gemma	2006		Psychology
Miss	Fawcitt	Stella	1931	1935	Latin
Miss	Ffinch(Stewart-Smith)	Kathleen	1928	1932	Piano/violin
Miss	Fincken	Irene	1920	1926	Singing etc
Mr	Fisher	Dean	1994	1996	
Ms	Fitzgerald	Kate	2004		
Ms	Florey	Leela	2002		Maths
Miss	Flower	Catherine	1920	1921	Mathematics
Ms	Forgione	Julie	1999	2001	Art & Design
	Forrell	Gaby	1994	1995	
Miss	Foster	Peggy	1970s		Head RE
Mrs	Fowles	Fiona	1980s		Geography

TWENTY   STAFF CORNER

Title	Surname	Forename	Approx Date from	Date to	Subject
Miss	Fox	Edith	1919	1943	First Headmistress
Mr	Fox Joyce	Edward	2004		Head of Art
Miss	Fraser	J.	1952	1955	Science
Mrs	Freeman	Marian	1980		Deputy Head
Miss	Freeman	Rebecca	2007		Maths
Miss	French	Adele	1929	1931	French
Ms	Furlong	Jayne	2002	2004	English
Miss	Galbert	Sandrine	2002		French/German
Miss	Gatehouse	Janet	2006		Science
Miss	Gay	Joan	1955	1957	Fr/Sp
Mrs	Geary	Audrey	1944	1947	Languages
Miss	Gedye	Margaret	1923	1924	Maths/Physics
Mrs	Gee	Dora	1959	1965	Geography
Miss	George	L'Tanya	2006		IT
Mrs	Georghiou (Bennett)	Jane	1975	1979	Biology
Miss	Gib	Faith	1925	1928	PE
Miss	Gibson	Angela			French
Mr	Go	Nils	2006		Media & Film Studies
Miss	Gobbett	Helen	1921	1926	Science
Mr	Gonzalez	Urbano	1979		Spanish/ French
Mrs	Gooch	Sandrine	2002		Business Studies
Miss	Goodchild	Undine	1955	1956	Science
Mrs	Goodenough	Christine		70's	PE
Ms	Gorvett	Jane	2001		Art
Miss	Graham	Eleonor	1929	1932	Lwr Sch
Miss	Grandjean	Grace	1924	1929	French
Miss	Green	Dorothy	1932	1934	Latin
Mr	Green	Bill	1994	1999	
Mr	Green	Bill	2000	2001	
Miss	Grice	Mary	1923	1948	History
Ms	Griffin	Hilda	2002	2004	
Mrs	Grunspan (née Scopes)	Joan	1943	1952	English
Ms	Gunning	Rebecca	2002	2006	Drama
Miss	Hague	Joan	1964	1975	Maths
Miss	Hall		1969	1972	
Ms	Hall	L.	1977	2006	
Mrs	Hallas			1960's	PE
Mr	Halse	Steve	1981	2006	English
Mr	Hamilton	Patrick	1995	2000	Science
Miss	Hamlett	Nerys	2006		PE
Miss	Hammond	Muriel	1948	1950	RI
Mrs	Hancock	Erica	1970s		Embroidery
Mrs	Handy (née Beeton)*	Elise	1952	1953/4?	Violin
Mrs	Hannabus	Susan	1968		English
Ms	Hanson	Donna	1997	2001	
Miss	Happs (Haffs?)	Gwendoline	1929	1931	Geog/Eng
Miss	Harcourt	Marjorie	1936	1938	?
Mr	Harcourt	Keith	1977	1985	Head resources/Graphics
Ms	Hargrave	Rachel	1996	2001	PE
Mr	Hargreaves	John	2000		Head of Music
Ms	Hargreaves	Jane	2004	2005	
Miss	Harris	Dora	1934	1935	Maths
Miss	Harris	Patricia	1968		Flute
	Harrison	J.	1994	1996	
Ms	Haskins	Judith	1989	1995	Art/Design
Mrs	Haspinall	Jan			Resources
Miss	Hatfield	Rene	1948	1959	History
Miss	Hawkins	Dorothy	1953	1968	Music
Mrs	Hawkins	Louise	1999		Head of PE
Ms	Hay	Valerie	1990	1996	
Mrs	Hayday	P	1980s		
Ms	Hearn	Lisa	2003		
Miss	Heath	Margaret	1956	1958	Geography
Mrs	Helt	Joyce	1969	1990	Needlework
Miss	Henry	Theresa	1974?		History
Miss	Henry	Theresa		early 70's	History
Miss	Henshaw	Kathleen	1944	1963	Headmistress
Miss	Henson	Margaret	1950	1954	History
Mrs	Henson	Margaret		1954	History?
Mrs	Herzmark	B Judy	1979	1992	Maths/Headmistress
Mrs	Hewett	B.		1953	
Mrs	Hiett	Gillian	1977	1980	Biology
Miss	Hinchcliffe	Jan.	1985	2001	Latin
Ms	Hine	Lesley	2000		Head of Maths Faculty
Ms	Hirst	Amy	2005		PE
Mr	Hiscock	Derek	1990		Science?
Miss	Hodgson		1972		
Miss	Hogben	Margaret	1931	1932	Maths/Classics
Mr	Holland		1998		Maths
Mrs	Holland	Joan	1981	1992	Sociology/English

Title	Surname	Forename	Approx Date from	Date to	Subject
Mrs	Hollands	P	1980s		
Miss	Hollister	Ethel	1933	1935	Maths
Mr.	Home-Cook	George	2004	2006	
Mrs	Hook		1960s	1969	English/elocution
Ms	Horan	Tracey	1996	2002	
Mr	Horbury	Simon	1998	1999	Science
Mrs	Hornsey	Maureen	1959	1962	French
Mrs	Hornsey	Maureen	1976	1995	French
Mrs	Howells		1969		
Mrs	Howlett	Delphine	1960/70s	late 1970s	Economics/Geog.
Mrs	Hughes	Sarah	2003		Personal learning & support
Miss	Hunter	Fiona	1980s		Science
Mrs	Hulm	Angela	2003	2004	Vocational
Mrs	Hurford	Chris	1980s		Maths
Miss	Hutchinson	Miriam	1932	1936	RI?
Miss	Hutt	Margaret	1926	1929	French
Mr	Hyslop	Derek	1991	2006	Science
Ms	Ijsselstein	Cathy	1996	1998	
Miss	Inge	Margaret	1922	1925	PE
Miss	Ironside	Margaret	1929	1933	Maths
Miss	Jackson	Iris	1943	1946	Geography
Ms	Jackson	Amanda	1992	1998	English/Drama/Media
Mrs	Jacob	Lidia	1968		Dom.Science
Mrs	Jacob	Myrtle	1968	1980	English
Mrs	Jacob	Lidia	1982	1986	Food Technology
Mr	Janes	Barry	1993		Product design
Miss	Jarrett	Marion	1934	1943	Latin
Mr	Jarvis	John	1970	1977	English
Mrs	Jarvis	Joan	1970	1977	
Ms	Jedlinska	Helena	1999		Textiles
Miss	Jehan	Hilda	1929	1932	Physics/Maths
Mr	Jenkinson	Edward	1997	1999	Maths
Miss	John	Enid	1963	1964	History
Miss	Johnson	Mavis	1920	1922	PE
Miss	Johnson			1969	English
Mrs	Johnson	Sally	1991	2004	Art
Miss	Jones	Phyllis	1932	1936	Physics/Maths
Mrs	Jones	Lilian	1987	1997	History
Ms	Jones	Margaret	1993		Art
Mr	Jones	Kevin	1999		Head Humanities/History
Ms	Joslin	Gillian	1980s		Maths
	Jouhal	Iqbal	2005		Assistant Head for 6th
Ms	Jovanovic-	Natasha	1999	2004	
Mrs	Karaman	Ishil	1998		Business Studies
Mrs	Kaye	Elizabeth	1948	1957	Maths
Mr	Kazim	Raza	1996	1999	Maths
Mrs	Kelleher	Lorraine	1982	2000	English
Miss	Kelly	Kim	2006		ICT
Miss	Kelly	Jean	1980s		Child Devpmt
Mrs	Kent	Nicola	2002		Science
Miss	Kenyon	Aimee	2007		PE
Mr	Kershaw	Paul	1998		Head of Geography
Ms	Kibble	Sally	1995	1999	
Miss	King	Margaret	1936	1967	Science
Mrs	King	Monica	1990		Biology
Miss	Kingston	Patricia	1943	1946	PE
Mrs	Kiss	J	1970s		Maths?
Mrs	Knox	P	1970s		
Miss	Kobrak	Eva	1946	1951	Art/Nwk
Ms	Kranat	Jayne	2001	2004	Maths
Mr	Lacraz			80's	Maths
Mrs	Langley	Josephine	1961	1979	Craft/Nwk Sp.Tr.
Ms	Latham	Rebecca	1993	1994	
Ms	Latham	Rachel	1996	1996?	
Mlle	Lavigne-Kidney	Isabelle	1990	1994	French/ Spanish
Dr	Lawlor-Price	Susan	2003		Science
Ms	Laws	Angela	1993	1994	
Mrs	Lawson		1970	1972	
Mrs	Leake	Angela	1995		Maths
Mr	Leap	Richard	1995	1997	
Ms	Leap	Charlotte	1995	1997	
Mr	Leary	John	2006		Head of Drama
Mr	Lennon	Peter	2002		Maths
Mr	Lewington	David	1968	1980	History
Miss	Lewis	Judy		60's-1971	French
Miss	Liddle	Margaret	1931	1935	French
Miss	Lindsay	Joanna	1934	1935	Various
Mr	Lindsey-Noble	Simon	2001		Modern Languages
Ms	Llewellyn	Katie	2001	2006	English & Media Studies
Ms	Lloyd	Janette	1995	1996	

Title	Surname	Forename	Approx Date from	Date to	Subject
Mr	London	John	1970	1996	English
Miss	Long	Violet	1958	1962	French
Miss	Long	Frances	1981		PE/Learning support Faculty Head
Mr.	Lord	Ben	1994	1996	Science
Mr	Lord	Ben	2001	2005	Science
Mrs	Lowe	J.D.A.	1962	1966?	Maths
Miss	Loxdale	Florence	1922	1936	PE
Mrs	Lubkor		1969		
Miss	Lumb	Winifred	1924	1929	Hist/Maths
Mrs	Lumb (Thompson)*	Diana G.	1956	1964	Art/Ndwk
Ms	Lyes	Patricia	1980	1997	Biology
Mrs	Lyes	Patricia	1998	1999	Biology & Computing
Ms	Lyne	Elisabet	1991	1999	Music
Miss	Mabbott	Ethel	1937	1940	English
Mr	Macauley	Richard	1970s		Drama
Ms	Maclay-Mayers	Jeanne	2002	2003	English
Mr	Macnamara	John	1993	1998	
Mr	Major	Jordi	2007		Food Technology
Mrs	Manley			1971	
Miss	Mann	Marjery	1936	1937	English
Miss	Manning	Wendy	1971		PE
Mrs	Manning(Ridler)*	Patricia	1951/1960	1990	Biology
Miss	Mansergh	Deborah	1957	1959	Fr/Sp
Ms	Manville	Georgina	2004		History
Mr	Marsh	Jolyon	1999	2000	Maths
Miss	Marshall	Irene	1947	1956	Geography
Mr	Marshall	John	1994	1994	
Ms	Martin	Sandra	1970s	70's	PE
Ms	Martin-Kaye	Joanna	1995	1996	
Miss	Martyn	Beryl	1927	1928	Botany/Maths
Ms	Marvin	Sally	1995	2002	
Mrs	Massen		1969	1970	Biology
Mrs	Masson	Simrat	2002		Maths
Miss	Matthews	Dora	1919	1938	Art
Miss	Matthews	Emily	1919	1925	Geography
Mrs	Matthews	Elizabeth	1963		Physics
Mrs	Mayers	Maureen	1971		Biology/Science
Miss	Maynard	June.	1953	1961	PE
Mr	McFarlane	Marlon	2006	2007	Science
Mr	McGrath	John	1991		Head Business Courses
Ms	McLeod	Carole	1974	1980	English/Sociology
Mr	McManus	Sean	1979	late 1980s	Geography
Mrs	McPhail	Annie	1947	1960	English
Miss	Mead (Phillips)	Valerie C.	1962	1969	Physics/Maths
Miss	Melvin	Lauren	2005		Science
Ms	Mercer	Susan	2002	2003	Maths
Miss	Meredith	Gwenda	1969	1974	Art
Mrs	Meux		1950	1960	
Mr	Michell	Edward	2004	2006	
Mrs	Milburn	Beryl	1959	1969	Latin
Mrs	Miller	L	1980s		
Mrs	Mines	Moya	1970s		Head Art
Miss	Minty	Winifred	1955	1958	Maths
Mrs	Mollison	Maureen	2001		Maths
Ms	Molloy	Y	1980s		
Mrs	Molnar	Pauline	1967	1973	Headmistress
Mrs	Moncada	D	1980s		
Mrs	Moody	Pauline	1978	1981	German
Miss	Moore	Margaret	1949	1952	PE
Miss	Moore		1968		
Mrs	Morgan	Sheila	1970s		Domestic Science
Miss	Morris	Margaret	1963		Drama
Mr	Morris	David	1996	2000	Maths
Ms	Motson	Katherine	2000	2006	PE
Mrs	Mulford	A	1980s		
Mr	Mulhern		1998		Fr and Sp
Ms	Mullen	Lisa	1997	2000	PE
Mrs	Mullinger	Thelma	1980s		
Mrs	Munro (Smith)	Barbara	1970	1983	Biology
Mrs	Murphy	Michelle	2007		Technology
Ms	Mussen	Zoe	1998	2001	French/German
Ms	Mustard	Barbara	1975	1995	Maths
Mrs.	Nash	M.S.	1952	1953	PE
Miss	Neale	Jamie	2007		PE
Miss	Newland	Mary	1952	1960	Art/Ndwk
Miss	Newland	Mary		50's	Art
Miss	Newman	Lilian	1919	1927	Latin/Hist'y
Ms	Newman	Janet	1985	1996	Latin/English
Mrs	Newman	Sharon	1977	1981	Classics
Mr	Newsome	Brian	1968	1980s	Music

TWENTY   STAFF CORNER

Title	Surname	Forename	Approx Date from	Date to	Subject
Miss	Nicholls	Jane	1985		Geog/Deputy Head
Miss	Nickson	Christine	1933	1936	History
Ms	Norris	Pauline	1990	1995	Secretarial Studies
Miss	Oaks	Margaret	1920	1926	French/Eng
Ms	O'Byrne	Olive	1992	2006	History/Careers
Miss	Odell	Marion	1943		Geography
Miss	O'Dell	Dorothy	1938	1976	RI
Mrs	O'Donnell	Sally	2001		ICT
Ms	O'Neill	Sue	1987	Dec-94	History/Deputy Head
Miss	Ord	Helen	1954	1960	History
Mrs	Ormson	Anne	1998		Special Needs
Ms	Orr	Norma	1996	2001	Geography
Mr.	Owen	Stephen	2004	2005	
Mrs	Page	Eleanor	1961	1968	English
Miss	Paget	Mabel	1919	1925	Sec.Work
Mlle	Palluel	Marie-Therese	1972	1976	French
Mrs	Palmer	J	1970s		
Mr	Palmer	Simon	1970s		Chemistry
Miss	Pargiter	Dorothy	1923	1924	Eng/Latin
Miss	Parnham	Judith	1957	1959	Eng/His/Lat
Miss	Parrett	Marie	2005		Travel & Tourism
Miss	Parsons*	Margaret	1953	1956	Geography
Miss	Partridge	Janet	1919	1929	R.I.
Miss	Partridge	Joy	1947	1953	Geography
Mr	Pascoe	Guy	2003	2005	
Mrs	Payne	Brenda		1970's	Art
Ms	Peduzzi	Frances	1992	1997	German
Miss	Pelling	Nancie	1944	1955	Art
Miss	Perry	Ruth	2007		Art
Miss	Phelan	Hazel	2008		Special Needs
Mrs	Phillips	Valerie		late 60/70's	Science
Mr	Pickard	Alexander	2000		English
Mr	Plumeridge	Nicholas	2004	2007	
Mr	Pocas	Gil	1999		Languages
Mrs	Pockney	Rose	1980s	1980/90s	History
Miss	Poole	M.	1964		History
Ms	Porter	Grace	1994	2002	
Mrs	Potter	Alison	1980s		Maths
Miss	Potts	Helen	1924	1929	Physics
Ms	Prendergast	Sue	2004	2007	
Miss	Preston	Florence	1934	1958/9?	Maths
Mr	Price-Walker	Timothy	1994	1997	
Mr	Procter	Kevin	2002		Sociology
Mr	Proud			80's	Art
Miss	Pye-Smith	Gertrude	1959	1967	Science
Mrs	Quincey	Stephanie	1970	1972	Chemistry
Mrs	Quinlan			80's	
Mr	Quinn	Neil	2000		Head of ICT
Miss	Rabson	Margaret	1940	1974	French
Mrs	Rand	Joan	1966	1979	Physics
Mrs	Rapson	Ann	1961	1962	Physics
Miss	Raymond	Eve	1962	1963	English
Mrs	Reay(née Scriven)	Kerry	2002		Head Psychology/Sociology
Mr	Reece	Michael	1994	1995	
Ms	Reece	Sharon	2000	2002	Maths
Ms	Repper	Susan	1998	2003	Special Needs
Ms	Revington	Susan	1996	2002	
Mrs	Reynolds	Jill	1980s		Resources
Miss	Reynolds*	Jean W.	1946	1948	Geography
Mrs	Riley	Brenda	1980s		
Mr	Riley	Tim	1997		Politics
Mrs	Roberts	Norma	1963	1969	English
Mrs	Roberts	N.R.	1965	1969	
Mrs	Roberts	Ava	2001		PE
Miss	Robins	Margaret	1943	1955	Science
Miss	Robinson	Nancy	1924	1926	Lwr School
Miss	Robinson	Ann	1959	1961	Maths
Miss	Robinson		1968		Latin?
Miss	Robinson		1972		Latin ?
Ms	Robinson	Rachael	1994	1996	
Miss	Rogers	Mary	1936	1937	
Mrs	Rollinson	Ellaline	1948	1955	French
Mrs	Roper	Wendy	1976	1980	PE
Miss	Rose	Sybil	1924	1944	English
Mrs	Rosenberg	Sheila	1958	1964	English
Mr	Rowland	Peter		70s/80s	English
Miss	Rowland	K	2008		Media Studies/English
	Russell	Alex	1995	1998	
Miss	Sale	Marjorie	1930	1937	English
Miss	Salter	Betty	1952	1954	English

Title	Surname	Forename	Approx Date-from	Date-to	Subject
Mr	Sands	David	2003	2005	
Miss	Saunders	Heather	c1981	1986	Chemistry
Miss	Savage	Vera	1924	1928	Housecraft
Miss	Savage	Margaret	1955	1956	Art/Ndwk
Ms	Savva	Maria	1994	1996	
Mrs	Scales (Grimsey)	Gillian	1973	1978	Maths/Headmistress
	Scammall	Diana			
Ms	Scappaticci	Kate	1997	2001	French/Spanish
(Dr)	Schofer	Marie-Helene	1949	1969	Ger/Span
Miss	Scopes	Joan	1941	1943	English
Miss	Scott	Greta	1961	1990	French
Ms	Scutt	Lisa	1998	1999	History
Mrs	Searle	June.	1980s		Commerce
Mrs	Sennett	Alice	1980s	1990s	Geography
Mrs	Seseman	Eileen	1980s		Geography
Ms	Shadick	Janet	1985	1996	PE
Mr	Sharma	Nigel	2004		Science
Mrs	Shaw	Glenys	1980s		
Ms	Shaw	Helen	2004	2005	
Mrs	Shedden	J.C.	1959	1960	History
Mrs	Shelley (formerly Tweddle née Smith)	Catherine	1986		Music
Mrs	Shore	Fiona	1976	1980	RE
Miss	Shortridge	Yvonne	1993	1995	Food Technology
Miss	Skevington	Jill	1972		English
Miss	Slimmon		1965		
Mr	Small	Robert	1995		Science
Mrs	Smalldridge	Maureen	1996		Health & Social Care
Ms	Smart	Angela	1995	2000	
Mrs	Smart	Fiona	2003		English
Miss	Smith	Dorothy	1929	1939	Music
Mrs	Smith	Lorna	2002		Food Technology
Ms	Smith	Verity	2002	2003	
Mr	Smith	Niall	2004	2007	Assistant Head teacher
Mrs	Smith	Joan	1980s		Russian?
Mrs	Smith	Julia	2005		Dance & Sports Coord
Mrs	Smith	Glenys		70's	German
Mrs	Solbe	Joan	1970s	70's	English?
Mrs	Solomon	I	1980s		
Mrs	Sriram	Leena	2004		Science
Mrs	Stamper	Judith	1980s		Child Development
Mr	Standen	Barry	1995	1996	
Ms	Starr	Hayley	2003		
Miss	Starr	Hayley	2008		Drama
Mrs	Stephens	Rosemarie	2002		Sociology
Miss	Stephenson	Joyce	1929	1956	Science
Miss	Stewart		1967		
Miss	Stewart	Angela	2003		Science
Mrs	Stimson	J	1970s		
Miss	Stoker	Julie	2006		Languages
Ms	Stones	Nicola	2003		
Mrs	Stratford	Rosemary	1970s		Art/Pottery
Mr	Stratton	Christopher	2007		Law & Humanities
Miss	Strudwick	Elizabeth	1951	1953	Maths
Mrs	Sullivan	Melanie	2007		Business Admin/Exams
Ms	Sunman	Coral	1996		Head of faculty/German
Miss	Swan	Dorothy	1954	1959	PE
Miss	Swann		1967	1970	PE
Dr	Sykes	Jeremy	1986		Physics/Head of Faculty
Miss	Symonds	Rosemary	1954	1958	English
Mrs	Tagg	Phillippa	1994	2000	Geography
Mrs	Tailby	Joan		1980s	Geography
Miss	Tanton	Dorothy	1928	1933	Str/Piano/dancing/elocution
Miss	Taylor	Jessie	1945	1949	PE
Miss	Taylor	Barbara	1946	1970	English
Miss	Theasby	Susanne	1981	1986	Classics/Dance
Miss	Thomas	Lilian	1919	1921	Science
Miss	Thomas	Jean	1960	1962	History
Miss	Thomas	Rosemary	1962	67	History
Miss	Thomas	Jackie	1975	1978	History
Miss	Thompson	Norah	1936	1939	Botany
Miss	Thompson	Eunice	1945	1970	English
Miss	Thompson	Elaine	2001		Art & Design
Ms	Thomson	Patricia	1982	1996	Secretarial Studies
Mrs	Tidman			70's	Dom.Science
Mrs	Tiffin	Gillian	1959	1960	Science
Miss	Tomkinson	Margaret	1927	1929	Science
Miss	Towne	Muriel	1928	1934	Languages
Ms	Townsend	Sarah	2004		
Miss	Trickey	Elsie	1927	1935	Maths
Mrs	Trigg		1971		Geography

TWENTY   STAFF CORNER

Title	Surname	Forename	Approx Date-from	Date-to	Subject
Mrs	Trotter	Jacqueline	1960	1966	French
Ms	Tully	Susan	1989	2003	Maths
Mrs	Turnbull	Ann	1980s		
Miss	Turner	Muriel	1936	1938	Remedial/Games
Mrs	Turner	Dorothy	1970	1996	History/Latin
Ms	Turner	Laura	1993	2000	Design Technology
Ms	Turner(Tidswell)	Mary	1980s		
Mrs	Tutill	Jan.	1993	2006	
Miss	Uglow	Muriel	1947	1948	History/RI
Miss	Uglow	Muriel	1950	1977	RI
Ms	Van Huyssteen	Tania	2003	2005	
Ms	Van Laar	Louise	1997	2002	
Ms	Vandenbrink	Jane	1977	1980	Music
Miss	Vanes	Jean	1959	1967	Hist/Eng
Ms	Vauzelle-Falkner	Isabelle	2001	2004	Modern Languages
Mrs	Vic-Cole	M	1980s		
Miss	Wagnell	Constance	1930	1932	French
Mr	Waights	Nicholas	2003	2005	
Ms	Walls	Deborah	1991	1996	French/German
Dr	Wallwork	Iain	2004		Maths
Ms	Walsh	Charmian	1997		English
Miss	Walters	Emma	1945	1958	Latin
Mr	Walton	Richard	1994	1998	
Ms	Ward (formerly Seseman)	Eileen	1994		Geography
Miss	Wardman		1960s		PE
Miss	Warren	Marion	1919	1924	Eng/French
Miss	Watmough	Christine	1975	2003	PE
Miss	Watson	Sarah	2006		Maths
Miss	Watts	Rosemary	1966	1973	History
Miss	Webb	Marjorie	1938	1964	Maths
Ms	Webster	Jennifer	1983		
Miss	Wedmore	Nancy	1936	1938	Maths
Ms	Weeks	Katherine	1991	1996	English
Miss	Wenden	Christina	1921	1928	Violin etc
Ms	White	Celia	1995	1998	
	White	Lesley	2003	2006	
Mrs	Whitehead		1972	1974/5?	Maths
Miss	Wilkinson	Vanessa	2004		Art
Miss	Williams	Elizabeth	1939	1941	PE
Mrs	Williams	Julie	1974		Chemistry
Ms	Williams	Karen	1991	2000	PE
Mrs	Williams*	Patricia		60's	French
Mrs	Williamson	Mary	1947	1948	PE
Mrs	Williamson*	Eva	1962	1962	PE Aut.term only
Miss	Wilson	Beatrice	1936	1940	French
Miss	Wilson	Pauline	1959	1963	PE
Mrs	Wilson	Phyllis	1972	1994	RE
Mrs	Wilson	Phyllis	1997	1998	RE
Ms	Wilson	Lindsey	2001		
Ms	Wilson	Julia	2004		Sociology
Miss	Winn	Valerie	1961	1969	Maths
Mr	Winter	Philip	1998	2002	English & Media Studies
Mr	Wisden	Alistair	1995	2000	Music
Miss	Wiseman*	S.Nancy	1939	1963	Music
Miss	Wood	Doris	1926	1928	Music
Mrs	Woodhouse		1967		
Miss	Woolley	Sybil	1926	1927	Science & Maths
Mrs	Wotherspoon		1969	1970	Maths
Ms	Wylie	Marlene	1996	1999	
Miss	Yard	Catherine	2006		Drama
Mrs	Yates	B.		50's	English
	Yeates	Sam	2003	2004	
Miss	Yelland	Fay	1958	1959	Science
Ms	Yeoward	Virginia	1995	1999	

Please contact us if you can help complete any of the spaces in this table by writing to us or by emailing the school on its website. We apologise for any errors. There are over 700 of the teaching staff named here.

PROUD LANGLEY CALL YOUR SCHOOL GIRLS!

Proud Langley call your school girls!
And those who wore white socks,
Call Adremians, Ad Rem Mox Nox.
Call the names, and in the flames of memory
The girl within us will still 'Present' give reply
From Canadian, American, Sunny Oz and Beckenham.
Lab. technician, artist, those with the name of Dame .....
The girl is still within us who would flaunt
Her hair, bright eyes, and merry thoughts,
Homework, and tests, sports and jaunts.
We remember with delight, the staff and friends
Of school days. Long past? No, only yesterday .....
Wiseman, she of musical ways
Taylor producing Shakespeare plays.
Formidable Fox, followed by Henshaw. Now was that when

We walked, and walked to gain at end
This new school, our lovely Langley?
Let's make a book to share the treasures
Of sporting triumphs, trials and leisure.
For ninety years is our measure.
Give welcome, and to each her fame,

On every page a schoolgirl's name
Is written to remember. Remember then
The girl is still within us who was taught.
Blithe and bonny, merry thoughts.
Exams and fears, tears the years fade away .....
We remember with delight, the staff and friends
Of school days   long past? No! Just yesterday ....
Langley call your school girls!

Ruth (Jordan) Marchant,

So we hope you have enjoyed HATS OFF!

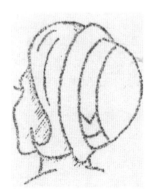

This creation is delightfully unsophisticated. Designed to crush any hair style, it can be worn at the back of the head, giving this cute 'about to slip off' look, or can perch on the top as a test of deportment.'

Sent by *Frances (Bates) Boyden from the 1966 magazine 'IT'*

AD REM: MOX NOX (loosely translated 'get to the point; time is short')

SUBSCRIBERS

Adam	Dorothy (nee Kidd)	1935-1940	Bromley, Kent
Adams	Elizabeth (nee Mynett)	1952-1959	Sidcup, Kent
Adams	Sandra (nee Nuthall)	1974-1981	Beckenham, Kent
Ansell	June	1939-1943	Bromley, Kent
Appleyard	Dorothy (nee Lawrence)	1939-1945	
Archer	Edna	1945-1951	
Ashman	Pat (nee King)	1938-1945	Tewin, Herts.
Axton	Sally (nee Fuke)	1951-1958	Southampton
Aylward	Helen (nee Smith)	1971-1976	Beckenham, Kent
Baird	Nina (nee Foxlee)	1946-1950	Warlingham, Surrey
Baker	Lois	1931-1937	Croydon, Surrey
Baker	Joan (nee Thorington)	1937-1942	West Wickham, Kent
Baldwin	Linda (nee Hardwick)	1970-1977	
Banfield	Janet (nee Knell)	1968-1974	
Barnard	Ann (nee Jolliffe)	1950-1957	Chislehurst, Kent
Bartlett	Ann	1948-1954	Hayes, Kent
Baugh	Susan (nee Ford)	1971-1978	Swanley, Kent
Bell	Constance (nee Curran)	1938-1943	Hadlow, Kent
Birchall	Joyce (nee Salter)	1942-1949	
Bottriell	Gloria (nee Carter)	1949-1954	Beckenham, Kent
Bourne	Margaret	1957-1964	Brighton, E. Sussex
Boyden	Frances (nee Bates)	1963-1970	Bromley, Kent
Boyden	Felicity (nee Edden)	1949-1956	Sevenoaks, Kent
Bradley	Shirley (nee Porrer)	1948-1955	Horsham, Sussex
Brand	Daphne (nee Perkins		
Bratt	Fiona (nee Croft)	1973-1980	Bromley, Kent
Bray	Helen (nee Vetch)	1952-1960	Bury St Edmunds, Suffolk
Brent	Brenda (nee Wixey)	1932-1938	Beckenham, Kent
Briggs	Margaret	1972-1979, Staff	
Broadbent	Helen (nee Baker)	1967-1974	Slough, Berks.
Bryant	Rosemary (nee Bentley)	1952-1958	Witley, Surrey
Buckle	Joy (nee Newell)	1940-1946	Uplyme, E. Devon
Bury	Catherine	1983-1990	
Bury	Elizabeth	1985-1992	
Bury	Cynthia	1953-1960	Beckenham, Kent
Butler	Janet (nee Wells)	1957-1964	Croydon, Surrey
Cahill	Sarah (nee Coombes)	1973-1980	West Wickham, Kent
Carter	Sue (nee Buffey)	1957-1964	Orpington, Kent
Chakraborty	Tanika	2003	
Chambers	Sharon (nee Freeman)	1962-1969	
Chandler	Fiona (nee Manson)	1966-1973	Berkeley, Glos.
Clarke	Maria (nee Kendrick)	1981-1988	Barbados
Clary	Rosemary (nee Stent)	1957-1964	Sevenoaks, Kent
Coeshott	Deborah (nee Clarke)	1968-1974	

SUBSCRIBERS

Cole	Barbara (nee Hall)	1946-1951	
Cook	Hilary (nee Whybrow)	1946-1952	Beckenham, Kent
Couchman	Rosalind (nee Almond)	1952-1960	Redditch, Worcs.
Cox	Audrey (nee Gilbert)	1936-1941	Sanderstead, Surrey
Creak	Jill (nee Player)	1949-1955	Beckenham, Kent
Cripps	Betty (nee Capon)	1931-1936	
Crumpler	Margaret (nee Ball)	1940-1945	Beckenham, Kent
Curtis	Pat (nee Howard)	1951-1957	Halstead, Kent
Daniels	Mary (nee Walker)	1974-1981	West Wickham, Kent
Davey	Lesley	1972-1979	Battersea, London
Davy	Marjorie (nee Sear)	1939-1944	Beckenham, Kent
Daymond	Pamela	1939-1944	Verwood, Dorset
Deans	Alice	2007-2012	Beckenham, Kent
DeVillars	Anne, Q.C.	1958-1965	Edmonton, Canada
Donaldson	Gill (nee Manning)	1973-1980	Wokingham, Berks.
Dowling	Angela (nee Knell)	1970-1972	
Driscoll	Valerie (nee Smith)	1946-1952	
Drzymala	Merrill (nee Salter)	1948-1954	Shortlands, Kent
Duncan	Monica (nee Weeks)	1942-1947 + Staff	Beckenham, Kent
Earthy	Denise	1939-1949	Shirley, Croydon
Elliston	Rosalie (nee Crimp)	1965-1972	Darlington, Co. Durham
Essery	Pamela (nee Waddell)	1941-1946	Hillsborough, N.Ireland
Etheridge	Jackie (nee Harben)	1966-1972	Forest Hill, London
Evans	Pamela	1944-1951	Shortlands, Kent
Everett	Angela (nee Rodwell)	1950-1957	Sidcup, Kent
Fabb	Jane (nee Webber)	1946-1952	Beckenham, Kent
Farrow	Claire	1973-1980	Bromley, Kent
Fenton	Mary (nee Dimmock)	1963-1970	
Fernandez	Ann (nee Dimmock)	1971-1978	
Firman	Anne (nee Bowles)	1945-1952	
Fish	Yvonne (nee Ames)	1943-1948	
Fleming	Brenda (nee Watson)	1958-1964	Crayford, Kent
Fraser Redman	Muriel (nee Dicker)	1945-1949	
Friend	Elizabeth (nee Wilkinson)	1952-1959	Hayes, Kent
Gaillac	Judith (nee Dickinson)	1954-1961	Montfermeil, France
Garters	Stella (nee Burr)	1951-1957	Hailsham, E. Sussex
Goodchild	Barbara (nee Lake)	1949-1955	
Gould	Mary (nee Endell)	1936-1942	Tamworth, Staffs.
Grant	Anne (nee Kilby)	1962-1967	West Wickham, Kent
Hall (Monteiro)	Margaret (nee Parkinson)	1964-1969	Kuala Lumpur, Malaysia
Hammond	Elizabeth (nee Thompson)	1959-1966	West Wickham, Kent
Hannam	Jennifer (nee Friend)	1943-1949	Bromley, Kent

SUBSCRIBERS

Hardcastle	Mary	1948-1955	
Hardisty	Claire (nee Sceats)	1950-1954	Wantage, Oxon.
Hardy	Joan (nee Russell)	1948-1955	Washington, D.C.
Harper	Margaret (nee Anning)	1944-1949	Shirley, Croydon
Hatfield	Rene	1948-1958	Langport, Somerset
Helt	Joyce (nee Long)	1945-52 Staff 1969-90	West Wickham, Kent
Herringshaw	Liz (nee Heeley)	1957-1964	Moreton-in-Marsh, Glos.
Heseltine	Barbara (nee Pitt)	1953-1961	Truro, Cornwall
Hetherington	Kate (nee Riddett)	1961-1968	
Hewitt	Eunice (nee Austen)	1944-1949	Dartford, Kent
Higgins	Ros (nee Powell)	1965-1970	Liphook, Hants
Highfield	Suzanne (nee Roe)	1952-1958	Tonbridge, Kent
Ho	Alison (nee Blackwood)	1975-1982	Hong Kong
Homewood	Jackie (nee Parfett)	1965-1972	Bickley, Bromley
Horsfield	Barbara (nee Loades)	1950-1956	Wythall, Worcs.
Hosking	Sheila (nee Thompson)	1939-1946	Poole, Dorset
Inzani	Jane (nee Joslin)	1968-1975	Whetstone, London
Irwin	Sophie	2004-2006	Thornton Heath, Surrey
Ivey	Laurie (nee Birmingham)	1932-1938	
James	Gillian (nee Buckman)	1954-1962	Dreghorn, Ayrshire, Scotland
Jenkinson	Mandy (nee Staples)	1964-1971	Cheltenham, Glos.
Jones	Jill (nee Bury)	1952-1959	Beckenham, Kent
Joslin	Gillian	1970-1977	Beckenham, Kent
Joslin	Helen	1966-1973	Beckenham, Kent
Kew	Geraldine (nee Reardon)	1934-1940	Wells, Somerset
King	Joy (nee Clark)	1948-1953	Sidcup, Kent
Knowles	Anne	1954-1961	
Kubinec	Anna (nee Whiley)	'955-1962	
Lambert	Margaret	1946-1951	Longfield, Kent
Lambert	Janet	1949-1957	Longfield, Kent
Lane	Carole (nee Emus)	1957-1963	Centennial, Colorado
Lawrence	Tessa (nee Reardon)	1949-1952	Seer Green, Beaconsfield, Bucks
Leaver	Audrey (nee Forrester)	1924-1931	
Legg	Annette (nee Packer)	1958-1963	Banham, Norfolk
Lilley	Valerie (nee Evans)	1951-1957	Herne Bay, Kent
Lindsay	Glenda (nee Thornton)		Bristol
Loader	Valerie (nee Hill)	1950-1958	Sidcup, Kent
Lockton	Julie (nee McKnight)	1970-1977	Anerley, London
Makepeace	Alison (nee Davey)	1963-1970	Thornbury, Glos.
Marchant	Ruth (nee Jordan)	1944-1949	Beckenham, Kent
Marks	Louise (nee Solari)	1952-1958	
Marston	Shelagh (nee Scott)	1954-1961	Sheffield

SUBSCRIBERS

Martin	Marigold (nee Lee-Smith)	1941-1947	
May	Julie	1975-1982	Woolwich
McPhail-Smith	Sheena (nee Mobsby)	1964-1971	Newton Mearns, Glasgow
Montier	Patricia (nee Wixey)	1936-1942	Majorca
Moore	Margaret (nee Dungay)	1942-1947	Wilmslow, Cheshire
Moore	Kate	1994-2001	Beckenham, Kent
Moore	Victoria	1996-2003	Beckenham, Kent
Moore	Mary	1941-1948	Bromley, Kent
Moore-Martin	Gillian (nee Crewes)		
Moorhouse	Valerie (nee Coleman)	1946-1951	Beckenham, Kent
Morgan	Julie (nee Furlonger)	1970-1977	St. Paul's Cray, Kent
Morris	Shirley (nee Woolward)	1946-1951	
Nash	Sandra (nee Homer)	1950-1956	Spain
Nepstad	Lorraine (nee Lake)	1943-1950	Bromley, Kent
Newmarch	Mavis (nee Brown)	1956-1963	
Nicholson	Joy (nee Robinson)	1937-1942	Barley, Herts.
Parrott	Jean (nee Banks)	1943-1950	West Wickham, Kent
Parsons	Pat (nee Hodgkinson)	1957-1965	
Pauling	Jill (nee Henderson)	1954-1961	Cheltenham, Glos.
Paxton	Linda (nee Neal)	1952-1959	Whittlesey, Cambs.
Payne	Pat (nee Conolly)	1942-1947	Hayes, Kent
Pedgrift	Thelma (nee Flack)	1940-1947	Perthshire
Pogose	Jean (nee Kite)	1957-1964	West Wickham, Kent
Porrer	Brenda	1950-1957	Canterbury, Kent
Potier	Jean (nee Everett)	1946-1952	
Primavesi	Sarah (nee Dimmock)	1966-1973	
Privett	Laura (nee Clark)	1941-1946	Beckenham, Kent
Privett	Jennie	1974-1979	Beckenham, Kent
Purnell	Christine (nee Smith)		
Rand	Joan	1966-1976, Staff	1992-2002 Governor
Rees	Joan (nee Burns)	1941-1948	West Wickham, Kent
Riley	Helen (nee Mynett)	1955-1962	Clapham, London
Rippengal	Olive E. BD, AKC		Beckenham, Kent
Roberts	Pat (nee Finn)	1952-1959	
Rogers	Lydia	2003-2010	
Rogers	Sophie	2006-2013	
Rowswell	June (nee Horton)	1961-1968	Sidcup, Kent
Rudge	Beryl (nee Hortop)	1953-1958	Wokingham, Berks.
Rumm	Ann (nee Knight)	1947-1953	Orpington, Kent
Sanford	Gillian	1945-1952	Frinton-on-Sea, Essex
Sarjeant	Audrey (nee Handy)	1938-1946	West Wickham, Kent
Scaife	Norma (nee James)	1935-1940	Ontario, Canada
Scales	Sheila	1960-1967	

SUBSCRIBERS

Scales	Gillian (nee Grimsey)	1973-1978, Head	
Scott	Diana (nee Clements)	1943-1949	
Sharpe	Jessica	2007	
Sheldon	Valerie (nee Thornton)	1950-1956	
Shepheard	Gillian (nee Bennett)	1961-1968	Bromley, Kent
Sherwood	Catherine (nee Lunn)	1960-1967	Basingstoke, Hants.
Skidmore	Christine (nee Sime)	1964-1969	Wingrave, Bucks.
Skinner	Monica (nee Pooley)	1954-1961	Coulsdon, Surrey
Smith	Brenda (nee Thompson)	1942-1947	Beckenham, Kent
Smith	Muriel (nee Bailey)	1931-1936	Beckenham, Kent
Sparrow	Elizabeth (neeBertoya)	1973-1980	Chilbolton, Hants
Spicer	Marion	1957-1964	Bromley, Kent
Stanley	Jean (nee James)	1940-1947	
Stephen	Sheila (nee Muir)	1964-1971	Bridgend, S. Wales
Stevens	Margaret (nee Withers)	1955-1962	East Grinstead, Sussex
Stringfellow	Beryl (nee Ashley)	1945-1952	Nottingham
Sutton-Jones	Glenys (nee Creighton)	1945-1951	Weston-Super-Mare, Somerset
Taylor	Joan (nee Dean)	1934-1939	Nottingham
Thomas	Janet (nee Blaxill)	1953-1960	Shirley, Croydon
Thomas	Barbara (nee Austin)	1951-1958	Etchingham, E. Sussex
Tomlin	Janice (nee Wright)	1969-1974	
Upfield	Heather (nee Buckman)	1959-1966	Kilwinning, Ayrshire, Scotland
Vaines	Eileen (nee Smith)		
Vernier	Marguerite (nee Jaulmes)	1930-1937	Le Chambon-sur-Lignon, France
Vickery	Ann (nee Weir)	1952-1958	Brixham, S. Devon
Walker	Alison (nee Clarke)	1963-1970	North London
Waterworth	Judith (nee Clarke)	1969-1976	West Malling, Kent
Watling	Helen (nee Sears)	1950-1957	Longfield, Kent
Watmough	Chris	1975-2003	
Waugh	Ann (nee Harrow)	1945-1952	West Wickham, Kent
West	Carol (nee Robinson)	1970-1975	Bovingdon, Herts.
Whitaker	Clare	1973-1980	
White	Lorna	1944-1951	Wokingham, Berks.
Wiffin	Eileen	1944-1951	Chichester, Sussex
Williams	Betty (nee Smith)	1939-1942	Catford, London
Williamson	Eva (nee Dinneen)	1940-1948	Tonbridge, Kent
Williamson	Kathleen, Dr.	1961-1968	Chislehurst, Kent
Wood	Kathleen (nee Andrews)	1962-1969	Truro, Cornwall
Woods	B.Janet (nee Coling)	1948-1955	Petts Wood, Kent
Young	Marian (nee Barber)	1952-1959	Beckenham, Kent

Notes

Notes

Notes

Notes